Praise for
High Heat

"A blazing fastball of a story—compelling, relentless, riveting."
—KEN BURNS

"*High Heat* is a great idea brilliantly executed. Tim Wendel,
one of my favorite baseball writers, delivers this fastball with a
winning mix of science, biography, and mythology."
—DAVID MARANISS, author of *Clemente* and
When Pride Still Mattered

"In the wonderful *High Heat*, Wendel leverages
that tension—the fastball as both blessing and bane—
to mine a stunning amount of drama. . . . Wendel's writing is
also all fastballs. Sensitive and scrupulous, he never forgets that
for every [Nolan] Ryan and Sandy Koufax, lucky to have their
unearned gifts, there are flameouts like Steve Dalkowski. . . .
High Heat is 'a séance with the game's past,' an almost
literary fantasy in which all the great pitchers
throw side by side on the same diamond."
—*New York Times Book Review*

"Wendel draws you in right from the first pitch."
—*New York Post* ("Required Reading")

"[Wendel] explores the fastball's history and
powerful mystique, from the beginnings of baseball to
the present. . . . A delight for baseball fanatics."
—*Boston Globe*

"[A] highly entertaining exploration of the pitch
that has made so many careers (and destroyed so
many arms). Fascinating details emerge."
—*San Francisco Chronicle*

"*High Heat* hums when Wendel profiles the fastest
of the fastball pitchers, tracing the lineage of the pitch
from Amos Rusie in the 19th century to Walter Johnson in
the 1920s to Sandy Koufax in the 1960s and, finally, to
the Washington Nationals' 100-mile-an-hour
prospect Stephen Strasburg."
—*Los Angeles Times*

"[A] book of delightful digressions."
—*Washington Post*

"Like its subject, *High Heat* emits a disarming
hum . . . [It] takes a historical, statistical, and
mechanical look at baseball's most sacred skill . . .
At the end you may disagree with Wendel's choice
for the fastest ever. But the pages will go by
quicker than a David Price aspirin tablet."
—*Sports Illustrated*

"A sportswriter's search for the unknowable, and
why 105-mph Steve Dalkowski, the inspiration for *Bull
Durham*'s Nuke LaLoosh, never made the majors."
—*USA Today*

"Entertaining."
—*Newsday*

"In our era of moneyball and sabermetrics,
it's refreshing to read a book so vividly written that
we can easily envision the old-time players and scouts spit

tobacco juice to punctuate their opinions while disdaining mere radar readings. Wendel teaches us as much about the evolution of the values of our society as he does the development of the national pastime. . . . Highly recommended."
—*Library Journal*

"[Wendel] presents a satisfying search for the ultimate fastball pitcher, with a result that's just conclusive enough . . . while leaving plenty of room for baseball die-hards' second-favorite sport: debating other fans."
—*Publishers Weekly*

"Feel free to disagree with [Wendel's] conclusion, but be sure to enjoy the book. Far from just a statistical inquiry, it's packed with stories about baseball and some of its extraordinary players. . . . A fascinating book for a baseball fan."
—Associated Press

"Engrossing."
—*Booklist*

"Any book that sets out to name the top . . . fastball pitchers of all time is sure to provoke controversy and Tim Wendel accomplishes just that in his somewhat quirky, somewhat biased, freewheeling, and always entertaining book. . . . Wendel travels his own road, and he excels at bringing us along with him."
—*Spitball*

"Endlessly interesting . . . [Wendel's] brief profiles of each hard thrower resonate, because they explain what it's like to meet the high expectations established when an arm can throw a baseball at an astounding velocity."
—*Raleigh News & Observer*

"The joy of [Wendel's] quest, and of its telling,
lies in baseball's rich lore and legend. . . . As with
the game itself, the fun of the book is more in
taking part than in the outcome."
—*Roanoke Times*

"*High Heat* is more than just a cursory ranking of
baseball's fastest arms, it's a fun and fact-filled flip through
baseball's record books that brings to life the players we previously only knew from our baseball card collections."
—*ForeWord* magazine

"A journey through the past and present of
our national pastime, and a vivid reminder
of why we love the game."
—*Smoke* magazine

"Tim Wendel, one of baseball's leading contemporary
chroniclers, here dissects the fastball and those who would
throw it. . . . *High Heat* is a fascinating book written with pas-
sion and aplomb by someone who clearly loves the sport
nearly as much as he loves writing about it."
—*January* magazine

"Destined to be [a] hardball classic."
—*Washington Times*

High Heat

Also by Tim Wendel

Nonfiction

Going for the Gold
The New Face of Baseball
Far From Home
Buffalo, Home of the Braves

Fiction

Castro's Curveball
Red Rain

High Heat

The Secret History of the Fastball
and the Improbable Search
for the Fastest Pitcher of All Time

Tim Wendel

DA CAPO PRESS
A Member of the Perseus Books Group

Set in New Caledonia by the Perseus Books Group

Cataloging-in-Publication data for this book is available from the
Library of Congress.

First Da Capo Press edition 2010
First Da Capo Press paperback edition 2011
HC ISBN: 978-0-306-81848-6
PB ISBN: 978-0-306-81970-4
E-book ISBN: 978-0-306-81895-0

Published by Da Capo Press
A Member of the Perseus Books Group
www.dacapopress.com

Da Capo Press books are available at special discounts for bulk purchases
in the U.S. by corporations, institutions, and other organizations. For
more information, please contact the Special Markets Department at the
Perseus Books Group, 2300 Chestnut Street, Suite 200, Philadelphia, PA
19103, or call (800) 810-4145, ext. 5000, or e-mail
special.markets@perseusbooks.com.

10 9 8 7 6 5 4 3 2 1

For my children, Sarah and Christopher,
and my wife, Jacqueline.

In memory of Bill Glavin,
who helped show me the way.

Contents

Preface

On an autumn night, a few years ago, I got to talking baseball with Frank Howard. Even at the age of 72, Howard looked like he just strolled down from Mount Olympus. What the gods had in mind for a major-league slugger. Although the passing years have forced him to hunch a bit, at 6-foot-7, with his square jaw and broad shoulders, Howard still towered over the rest of us mere mortals that evening at the Presidents Club bar in the Nationals Park in Washington, D.C.

The occasion was a reception for major-league ballplayers who also served in World War II. Their ranks ranged from longtime New York Yankee Jerry Coleman to the hard-throwing Hall of Famer Bob Feller. There had been a momentary hitch as the bartenders couldn't locate any vermouth, thus ruling out such mixed drinks as manhattans and martinis. But after a bit of grumbling, the old ballplayers, who had been joined by 50 or so wounded warriors from Walter Reed Medical Hospital, shifted to beer or wine.

It was a night when legend and fable mingled, with the telling of one tall tale after another. Perhaps it was because Feller was in attendance, but I couldn't resist asking Howard who he thought was the fastest pitcher ever.

Of course, some consider that a loaded, even unfair question. Instead of trying to give a straight answer, some baseball experts and aficionados run and spin, emphasizing how difficult it is to compare players from different eras. How even in this era when every pitch is graded by scouts and clocked on radar guns, a comprehensive, reliable testing of high heat remains so problematic. And, indeed, most of those complaints are valid. But, to his credit, or perhaps because of the open bar, on this evening Howard was game.

"Now that's a story that takes a bit of telling, doesn't it?" he said, with a smile.

"But you must have an opinion on the subject, right?" I replied.

After all, Howard had once made his living launching a baseball as far as he could toward the distant horizon. He had come up in 1958 with the Dodgers and played 16 years in the majors, leading the American League in home runs in 1968 and 1970 with the Washington Senators. Here was a hitter who was nicknamed "Hondo" and "the Capitol Punisher" for his exploits.

"I was a fastball hitter. I loved hitting fastballs," he said in a voice that reverberated above the din of the bar conversation. "That's what I prided myself on doing. That's how I made my living. But if you add in that element of pure speed, I may still love the fastball, but maybe I'm not going to see it. That's what a great fastball can do— reduce you to nothing."

With that, he reluctantly took a sip of his white wine. With a moniker like Hondo, I half expected to be doing shots with him. But Howard was one of those disappointed by the lack of vermouth at the Nats' watering hole.

"There's a lot to be said for finesse pitchers," he continued. "There sure have been a lot of them down through the years. Guys like Jimmy Key and, lately, Jamie Moyer come to mind. I mean they're winners and they do the job. But so much of this game really comes down to a quality fastball and the ability to spot it. You got that, well, it's worth more than gold in this game.

"What did old Ted Williams say? That you have two-fifths of a second to make up your mind if the pitch is either a fastball or something softer? You have to decide that quick—be that certain. When a pitcher has a great fastball combined with maybe a quality breaking ball, your reaction time is about down to nil. Like I said, it humbles you. Before you know it, if you're a hitter, everything becomes a nightmare."

"So who'd you think was the fastest then, of all time?" I repeated.

The big man shrugged and took another sip of his drink.

"There's no pat answer to that kind of question," Howard replied. "It's one of those deep ones. One for the ages. Like you flip over one rock and it leads you to something else and then something else. Tonight, off the top of my head, I'd have to say one of the fellas we're honoring here this evening, Bobby Feller. I'd have to include my former teammate Sandy Koufax and, of course, Nolan Ryan. Tonight I'd put them in that order."

I nodded, contemplating what the old slugger had said.

"But then, in the next breath, other guys come to mind," Howard added. "There's Satchel Paige and Walter Johnson, the 'Big Train' himself. And sure as you and I are sitting here tonight, there's a bunch of modern-day guys you have to mention."

"Billy Wagner, Tim Lincecum, Joba Chamberlain, Jonathan Papelbon," I offered.

"And that kid down at Tampa Bay. The one who did so well in the playoffs."

"David Price?"

"That's right, Price. He looks plenty fast to me."

As Howard and I talked, I realized that baseball was different from other sports and acts of athletic prowess. In the national pastime, there is no direct correlation between physical size and the velocity of a quality fastball. For example, onetime Baltimore Orioles phenom Steve Dalkowski stood 5-foot-11, weighed maybe 170 pounds. In comparison, Feller was 6-foot, 185 pounds. Johnson, the "Big Train," was slightly taller and heavier, but Koufax was actually even taller in stature and Paige bigger than most. Yet, in the end, such dimensions hardly mattered. It was as if the Great Maker in the sky stood all the hopefuls who ever wanted to pitch in the major leagues shoulder to shoulder and only a rare few were bestowed with the ultimate blessing of pure, undeniable speed. Fewer still were able to wrestle this angel toward earth, to harness and truly embrace the gift from above. For many more the ability to throw hard, despite all their best efforts, remained nothing more than an untamed curse.

For those who can master the lessons of throwing high heat, history awaits. Not only do they become part of baseball lore, but their stories often extend into our national story, echoing through our collective consciousness. They become the icons kids throwing out on the Little League field want to be. Perhaps that's the ultimate allure and mystique of the fastball: The ones who can really bring it will always somehow speak to us.

"No, the question you're asking doesn't have a pat answer," Howard said. "To my mind, it's one of those riddles where the chase becomes what's important, if you catch my drift. You're going to have to hit the road some to really tease this out."

With that the slugger drained what was left in his glass and got to his feet. "It may not be easy to figure out," he said, "but it sure would be a talker, wouldn't it? Now if you'll excuse me."

"Good night," I said. "And thanks."

Across the room, a set of glass doors opened up onto the ballpark. For games, this was the portal for the affluent and well connected to stroll between their seats behind home plate and the bar and buffet here in the Presidents Club. Realizing that I might never have this opportunity again, I decided to check out the plushest seats in town.

Outside, the evening air held a hint of winter, and out beyond the outfield fence, the echoes of the nation's capital rose into the darkening sky. Howard was right: To determine the fastest pitcher ever, I was going to need to talk with the game's greats, try to chase down as many ghosts as I could find. The journey wouldn't be a straight line to the plate, but it promised to be a lot of fun.

The Windup

Walter Johnson
Photo courtesy of the National Baseball Hall of Fame Library, Cooperstown, NY

You can't hit what you can't see.

—FRANK "PING" BODIE

Slowness has never been an American characteristic.

—FRANKLIN ROOSEVELT

Bob Feller agreed to the stunt because he was as curious as everybody else. How fast could he really throw a baseball? Where did he possibly rank among baseball's fastest of the fast? That's what led him to the middle of a closed-off street running through Chicago's Lincoln Park that sunny morning in the summer of 1940. Standing there with a baseball in his right hand, waiting and then momentarily flinching as the Harley Davidson motorcycle with a city policeman roared closer to him.

Feller did as he had been instructed. As the Harley bore down at him, now going better than 80 miles per hour, Feller went into his windup. It wasn't a carbon copy of the distinctive high-leg-kick delivery that he exhibited on the mound. What he would normally perform in a big-league ballpark with a batter standing at the plate. How could it be? After all, Feller was in street clothes instead of a ballplayer's uniform. In wingtips instead of spikes and toe plate. Fresh from the Del Prado Hotel at 53rd and Hyde Park Avenue. Still, the Cleveland Indians' phenom was able to put plenty of zip on the ball. Just as importantly, the 21-year-old also threw the baseball accurately toward one of the two bull's-eye targets Major League Baseball's Office of the Commissioner had erected for the bizarre test.

"I was there because we all want to know, deep down," Feller says, "who was the fastest of all time."

That's what led me to fly nearly 70 years later to Cleveland, where the longtime Indians pitcher still makes his home. On the phone, a few days before, I'd offered to meet Feller wherever he wanted. But coffee and chitchat over the family kitchen table or at the Starbucks around the corner isn't exactly Rapid Robert's style. "At the ballpark—nine sharp," he said in a loud, brassy voice. As soon as I replied, "OK," he hung up. Feller sure left the impression that he doesn't tolerate any tardiness.

I enjoy going to Cleveland because it reminds me an awful lot of home. I grew up outside of Buffalo, New York, a three hours' drive away. Both cities hug Lake Erie and were once capitals of commerce, with the accent on shipping and heavy industry. Of course, such enterprises hit the skids long ago and the goal became how a city could reinvent itself. Playing off its link with the beginnings of rock and roll (local disc jockey Alan Freed coined the term "rock and roll"), Cleveland edged out Memphis as the permanent home to a museum and hall of fame. Cleveland's civic leaders pledged $65 million in public money to fund the construction. That financial package put the project over the top. As *Cleveland Plain Dealer* music critic Michael Norman later said, "It wasn't Alan Freed. It was $65 million. Cleveland wanted it here and put up the money." A pyramid-style shrine was erected to honor the Beatles, Chuck Berry, Bruce Springsteen, and other rockers along the harbor front, not far from where old Municipal Stadium once stood, the ballpark where Feller was a star. The Indians' new digs are also located downtown and, along with the Rock and Roll Museum, have fostered a renaissance in these parts.

In a way, the Rock and Roll Museum can be seen as a nod to our continued infatuation with speed. The average pop song is three to four minutes long. The MTV videos, which run in looped presentations at the museum in Cleveland, are minimovies created around a song. Of course, Feller has no interest in checking out the computerized "juke-box," containing virtually every song of every performer inductee, at the Rock and Roll museum. He's more of an easy-listening fan and always liked the Big Band sound. Still, Feller says he's happy that such civic landmarks bring visitors. "You need the out-of-towners," he says. "Without them, everything can get desperate in a hurry."

At 8:50 a.m., I'm ushered by a member of the Indians' public relations staff into a conference room at Jacobs Field. The room overlooks the emerald-green field several stories below. Feller is already there, waiting for me. He has a videotape of the motorcycle test and as we watch it for the first of several times, a small crowd of ballclub employees gathers to view the show.

"I guess it's our fascination with speed," Feller says, again cuing up the two-minute clip. "Who was the fastest pitcher of all time? The world will never know, may never agree, but it sure is fun to talk about, isn't it?"

That sunny day in Chicago was a generation before radar guns and such modern-day timing devices. So, Lew Fonseca, a player for 12 years in the major leagues, the American League batting champion in 1929, devised what will forever be remembered as the motorcycle test to clock Feller's legendary fastball. At the time Fonseca produced instructional baseball films. If he could capture Feller's speed on film, he believed he could precisely track and calibrate how fast the baseball was traveling. But to do so, Feller seemingly had to do the impossible: hit his bull's-eye target, about the size of a cantaloupe, from 60 feet, 6 inches away, just after the motorcycle roared past him.

The Harley motorcycle had a 10-foot head start on Feller's fastball and was doing 86 miles per hour when it flew by, just a few feet to the right of the Indians' ace. At that moment in U.S. history, Feller was just about the most famous ballplayer, certainly the most famous pitcher, in the land. Soon after he began pitching for Cleveland, at the age of 18, he was on the cover of *Time* magazine. Three seasons later, on this summer day in Chicago, Feller was arguably the best pitcher, the fastest fireballer, in the game. He was on the verge of leading the

American League in victories for the second time in three consecutive seasons and being the strikeout leader for the third time in four seasons. But in Europe and on the far rim of the Pacific, World War II was building, and too soon Feller, Joe DiMaggio, Hank Greenberg, Ted Williams, and the other stars of this era would leave the national pastime to enlist. Perhaps that's what makes the motorcycle test even more incongruous and precious when seen in the rearview mirror of today. Here's a window to a world before the Best Generation was tested by Pearl Harbor and Hitler. Feller's boyish face could be from any era. He smiles sheepishly as the cameras begin to roll. He knows he has the world on a string and has arrived at that station in life when participating in such a jerry-rigged experiment, the morning of a game in Chicago, somehow made complete sense.

"It was kind of a cute idea," Feller says. "I suppose I wanted to know as badly as everybody else how hard I could throw a baseball. Since I'd been a little guy, I'd heard people talking about how I was the next Lefty Grove or Walter Johnson.

"You look back at it now and ask yourself, 'What the heck were you doing?' But I knew I could throw the ball with the best of them. Deep down if somebody asks you to try and prove it, you step right up and give it a shot. No questions asked—you know what I mean?"

Seconds after the motorcycle flew past, Feller flung the regulation-size hardball. The ball quickly outraced man and machine, ahead by a good three feet when it split the paper bull's-eye target that was held upright by a wooden frame. Alongside Feller's target was another 10-foot-high target that the motorcycle sped toward. More importantly for the matters of science, Feller's speed ball hit the 12-inch-diameter dark bull's-eye in the center of the heavy paper.

"To this day I still don't know how I hit that target on the first try," Feller tells the growing audience at Jacobs Field. "It was the luckiest thing I've ever done."

"As lucky as pitching a no-hitter on Opening Day?" somebody sings out.

"Hey, don't be getting silly on me," Feller snaps back. "But afterward I told those guys doing this test, 'Give me another fifty chances and there's no way I can duplicate that.' I don't know if they believed me or thought I was just blowing smoke."

Seconds after Feller's offering broke the paper target, the motorcycle obliterated its target and Fonseca had satisfied enough variables to calculate the speed of the pitch. Soon afterward, MLB announced that Feller's fastball had been clocked going 104.5 miles per hour. Feller's throw gained 13 feet on the motorcycle over the 60 feet, 6 inches. So, with the motorcycle traveling at 86 milers per hour the calculation goes as follows: 86 divided by 60.5 equals 1.42. Now, add in the 13 feet plus 60.5. That equals 73.5. Multiply it by the previously calculated 1.42 and you have nearly 104.5 miles per hour.

That sounds pretty definitive and it certainly ranks Feller among the fastest pitchers ever in the game. But does that really make him the fastest of all time? Even Feller, a guy who isn't afraid to speak his mind or polish his accolades, isn't so sure. "I know it puts me in the ballpark," he says. "I know there's no arguing with that. But I'm also not foolish enough to think that's the end of the story."

Indeed, we're just getting started.

Two weeks before Christmas in 2008, I'm driving from Washington, D.C., just ahead of the worst ice storm to hit the Northeast in years. Climbing into the mountains north of Harrisburg, through the freeway roller-coaster ride leading into Wilkes-Barre and Scranton, the weather changes from freezing rain to sleet mixed with snow. The early-morning forecast back home in Washington called for a few inches of snow, which I'm somewhat prepared for. A shovel lies in the rear cargo compartment. But a wintry mix, of course, can be an entirely different story.

Exiting Interstate 88, between Binghamton and Albany, I drive as fast as I dare along Route 28 toward the Village of Cooperstown. The new world economy hasn't treated upstate New York very well. The Victorian homes of Oneonta and Milford could use a new coat of paint, and the once-proud region has too many traces of decay and downright poverty. At Hartwick Seminary, though, just south of town, the Cooperstown Dreams Park rises up from an old cow pasture. This is where kids' teams from across the country come during the summer months to play tournament ball. The complex is surrounded by ice cream stands, fast-food outlets, and miniature golf establishments. Of course, most are closed for the season, and on this afternoon all of them are being enveloped in a white glaze.

Entering Cooperstown proper, I turn right onto Main Street. My wipers are so coated with ice that they resemble giant popsicles being pulled across the streaky windshield. When I spy the National Baseball Hall of Fame and Museum, I turn left and slip-slide away downhill to the Lake Front Motel.

"You just made it," the desk clerk says as the door closes behind me. It's 2:45 in the afternoon. In the background, a TV hums with the latest weather update.

"What's the forecast?"

"Sleet and freezing rain until midnight," she says. "Then changing over to snow through the morning."

I check into my room but don't linger long. After changing into wool socks and more appropriate footwear, I'm outside, retracing my route on foot back up to Main Street and the Hall of Fame.

One reason I think so many books are written about baseball is that the reference staff at the Hall of Fame has no equal. Make the strangest request about the national pastime (Did Fred Lynn win the batting title his rookie year? The answer is no, but he did win the MVP), and they will try their best to accommodate you. The only catch is that best material usually requires a visit to Cooperstown.

Inside the main door, I hurry through the Hall of Fame Plaque Gallery. The room is T-shaped with the original five players inducted into the Hall in 1932—Babe Ruth, Ty Cobb, Honus Wagner, Christy Mathewson, and Walter Johnson—holding a place of honor on the far wall. After a nod in their direction, I turn up the ramp that leads to the Hall's theater and a bookstore. A door to the left of the bookstore's register opens into a room with a long wooden table and six chairs on either side. This is the main reference room for the Baseball Hall of Fame.

Sitting at one end of the table, awaiting my arrival, stands a plastic tub of files and books about many of the fastest pitchers who had ever hurled a baseball. After signing the proper release forms and donning the mandatory white gloves (all Hall materials must be handled with white gloves), I open the first file, one of three thick ones about Walter Johnson, aka "the Big Train."

Despite my good fortune in reaching Cooperstown ahead of the ice storm, my luck doesn't hold. A little after three in the afternoon, Tim Wiles, research director at the Hall, announces that the museum will be closing early due to the inclement December weather.

I reluctantly close the Walter Johnson file and return it to the plastic tub with the mounds of other material I haven't cracked yet. I've been at it less than a half hour.

"We'll reopen tomorrow morning at nine," Wiles says. "We'll make sure somebody is here to let you in."

Back outside, the sky has grown even darker, with the sleet indeed turning to snow. From the hotel parking lot, I gaze upon Otsego Lake, the Glimmerglass of James Fenimore Cooper's imagination. The far end remains shrouded in mist. Cooperstown has been called remote in terms of time and place. A perfect locale to really begin a séance with the game's past.

Long ago, the town embraced baseball and, as a result, Cooperstown has done better than most hamlets between Albany and Buffalo. The village latched onto baseball even if that meant putting up with droves of Little Leaguers and their parents from Memorial Day through Labor Day. Overall, it's been quite a gambit for Cooperstown, especially when one considers that its connection to baseball's roots remains tenuous at best. Myth has it that Abner Doubleday invented the national pastime here in 1839. Such theories proved to be as imaginative as Cooper's tales about Hawkeye and Chingachgook. But no matter. The village has found a way to ride out the worst financial blizzard since the Great Depression. It has baseball.

Cooperstown's small downtown area extends for a few blocks, from Fair Street to Chestnut. The redbrick Hall of Fame stands as a sentinel at one end, with easily half of the storefronts that roll out from there devoted to posters, T-shirts, jerseys, baseball bats, and books and photographs about the national pastime. Even the restaurants, the Triple Play Cafe and Short Stop Restaurant, have hitched their fortunes to baseball and the tourists that fill these sidewalks during the warmer months.

Winter, of course, remains another matter. Today the only ones out and about are the locals, shoveling away at crusty ice now topped with several inches of snow. I grew up in Lockport, New York, a place much like this one, a good 200 miles to the west. There I learned the proper etiquette of snow removal: When the white stuff flies, a person has a responsibility to soon clear the stretch of sidewalk in front of his or her home. That's part of being a good neighbor, dare we say a good citizen. It disgusts me when folks in warmer climes simply leave the snow and ice alone. As a neighbor in northern Virginia once told me, "Why bother? It'll melt soon enough."

Why bother? I could never wrap my mind around such a philosophy.

That evening, at Lake Front Motel, I fall asleep to the scrape of shovels and plows methodically clearing Cooperstown's small web of sidewalks and streets. The next morning, I find my car buried under four inches of ice, topped with several more inches of snow. I'm scheduled to leave late that afternoon, heading to Syracuse to pick up my daughter from college, and for a moment I begin the laborious task of digging out my Subaru station wagon. But when I can't pry open any of the doors after five minutes of trying, I adopt the approach of my neighbor back home in Virginia. It'll have to keep. I need to be back at the Hall of Fame.

True to Wiles's word, the baseball museum has opened its doors at nine o'clock sharp, even though Hall of Fame employees are about the only ones there. Back at the reference library, the plastic tub of files and books still awaits me. I pick up reading where I left off, trying to move through the vast amount of material as methodically as possible. Outside, more snow starts to fall.

The thick files are jammed with all kinds of stuff—newspaper clippings, letters, interviews, even old scouting reports. The trick seems to be to stay alert, always mindful of the next piece of paper. Crucial pages can be duplicated at one of the two copy machines in the reference room. But at 25 cents a page, I can't copy everything in sight.

As I slowly read through the files, starting with Walter Johnson and continuing on to Satchel Paige, I search for any kind of pattern or overarching narrative. A link between such talent and the beginnings of a story. After a few hours, no common thread found, I take a break and stroll throughout the lower floor of the museum. Of course, any good museum or exhibition hall takes history's abstractions and vagaries and transforms them into tales with bona fide heroes, even villains.

At the far end of the bronze-bust gallery stands the Hall of Fame's gift shop. There postcards of the enshrined players—actual photos of their busts—go for 50 cents apiece. Looking at the assortment in alphabetical order, I begin to pull down the fireballers, the fastest of the fast—Johnson, Paige, Bob Feller, Sandy Koufax, Bob Gibson, Don Drysdale, and Nolan Ryan. A proverbial Mount Rushmore of the pitchers who threw hard. But there are other, less-known names enshrined here at Cooperstown, too. Guys like Amos Rusie, Jim "Pud" Galvin, and Wilber "Bullet" Rogan.

Of course, there are others who were given the gift of high heat who never reached Cooperstown. "Sudden" Sam McDowell, Ryne Duran, Virgil "Fire" Trucks, Don Newcombe, Rex Barney, Herb Score, "Smoky" Joe Wood, and Steve Dalkowski are among the fireballers without a Hall of Fame postcard fashioned in their likeness.

As I take my short stack of postcards over to the cashier, I realize that whether or not they end up in Cooperstown, these pitchers belong to a select brotherhood. One that remains equal parts distinction and stigma. As soon as a kid begins to throw hard, he invariably hears the stories about whose footsteps he could follow in. More is expected of him, even though all he has to offer the world at the outset is speed, with little or no command. Throwing a baseball hard—really, really hard—remains a God-given gift. In the end, though, whether this gift will be remembered as a blessing or a curse depends upon the individual player and what luck, judgment, and good friends he finds along the way.

The Dalkowski file, for example, is plenty thick. That fact borders upon the remarkable when you realize that he never reached the majors and only went 46–80 in the minors. But many claim he was the fastest of all time. Only misfortune and the inability to throw his high heat for strikes kept him out of Cooperstown. Such is the allure, even the stubbornness, of baseball's most basic, yet important, pitch.

Perhaps we are enthralled with the fastball because after all these years, we're still struggling to truly comprehend it. Even though baseball has been around since the mid-1800s, few other things remain as constant and as mind-boggling as a little high heat. A quality fastball travels at least at 132 feet per second. How fast is that? How long does it take for such a quality pitch to travel from the pitching mound to home plate? According to the *Sporting News*, that's about as much time as it takes somebody to jerk his head from one side to another. Barely enough time to take a quick bite of a ballpark hot dog.

A few weeks later, I'm in New York City, on a commuter bus from Washington pulling into Penn Station. There to greet me is my friend Greg Downs, and we're soon aboard the B train, bound for Brooklyn and Green-Wood Cemetery. It seems that anybody who was anybody in New York has been laid to rest at Green-Wood through the ages. The ranks of the rich and famous include stained-glass artist Louis Comfort Tiffany, toymaker F. A. O. Schwarz, the influential newspaper owner and "Go West, Young Man" orator Horace Greeley, painter George Catlin, corrupt politician Boss Tweed, and composer and conductor Leonard Bernstein.

Green-Wood was one of the first "rural" cemeteries in this county, a concept imported from Europe. With its rolling hills and commanding vistas of the Manhattan skyline, it became a tourist attraction during the 19th century, drawing half a million visitors annually. "Green-Wood is as permanently associated with the fame of our city as the Fifth Avenue or the Central Park," the *New York Times* proclaimed in 1866.

Besides the Tiffanys and Tweeds of the world, the cemetery became the final resting place for many of baseball's early pioneers. They often played upon the Elysian Fields of Hoboken, New Jersey, on the other side of Manhattan.

"Green-Wood, the most prominent of all historic American cemeteries, was a well-preserved baseball time capsule," Peter Nash wrote in *Baseball Legends of Brooklyn's Green-Wood Cemetery*. "Arlington National Cemetery is home to our country's fallen military heroes, but nearly all of the important baseball heroes of the 19th century found their final rest amongst the half million or so men and women who now inhabit Green-Wood."

This group includes pioneer baseball scribe Henry Chadwick, Brooklyn Dodgers owner Charles Ebbets, and James Whyte Davis, who was buried, as requested, in his Knickerbocker uniform. According to Nash, the early memorials at Green-Wood served as models for later tributes to such Hall of Famers as Babe Ruth, Lou Gehrig, Joe DiMaggio, and Mickey Mantle at the old Yankee Stadium.

On this chilly morning in January, Greg and I are on foot, searching for the final resting place of James Creighton, the game's first true fireballer. Armed with a printout map from the computer kiosk at the cemetery's main entrance, we begin walking in a northeasterly direction between the headstones.

Back in the early days, baseball more resembled fast-pitch softball than what we witness today. Pitchers stood closer to home plate, and the ball was delivered underhand, like a bowler's delivery. In addition, the arm and wrist were kept stiff, a technique handed down from the game's early cousin, cricket. Creighton was the first hurler to push past such pedestrian guidelines, combining speed with control, and in doing so, he became the game's first superstar.

Born in New York City in 1841, Creighton grew up in Brooklyn. There he discovered the ever-evolving game of baseball. He began as an infielder for the Star BBC of Brooklyn in 1856 and got a chance to pitch in 1859. Instead of a soft toss to the batter, Creighton's low, swift delivery rose from the ground, often crossing the plate at the batter's shoulders. By the start of the 1860 season, Creighton was a star for the powerful Excelsior Club, and the debate was on about whether his newfangled delivery was legal or not. The *Brooklyn Eagle* dispatched a reporter to decide if his pitching was a jerk (something that was against the rules) or a "fair square pitch." The paper said it was the latter, and the path of baseball was set, the game forever changed. The verdict allowed speed and sometimes intimidation to seep into the game. Without Creighton, we would have had no Bob Gibson or Sandy Koufax a century later. Creighton's fast-paced pitching made the Excelsiors virtually unbeatable, and he was likely the game's first paid player. While the National Association of Base Ball Players prohibited actual salaries, it was rumored that Creighton was slipped money under the table.

Unlike many who followed him to the mound, Creighton was also a quality hitter and continued to star in the field. Many credit him with starting the game's first triple play.

"Not one player in 5,000 has the capacity to fill all positions ably and excel in each," Henry Chadwick once wrote, "the ability required being too great except for one like the admirable Creighton."

It was swinging a bat that led to Creighton's tragic demise, though. In October 1862, against the Unions of Morrisania—a ballclub from New York City—he lunged at a pitch. A loud pop was heard just before his bat struck the ball. Accounts differ on whether or not Creighton hit a double. What is known is that he shouted out to a teammate, "I must have snapped my belt."

But it wasn't his belt that was broken. Creighton soon passed out on the field. He was taken to his father's house on Henry Street in Brooklyn and died four days later, likely of a strangulated intestine. Some contend that he first suffered the injury a few days earlier and fatally aggravated it against the Unions. In any event, the game's first star was dead, only six months shy of his 22nd birthday.

In Creighton's memory, the Excelsior Club erected a granite obelisk, with bats, balls, and a scorebook carved into its ornate base. A marble stone baseball topped the impressive monument, and for years afterward players and fans made the pilgrimage to Creighton's resting place to pay their respects. And that's exactly what Greg and I have come to do today.

Angling away from Green-Wood's main entrance, hiking along Landscape Avenue, we planned to find Creighton's grave and still have time for lunch. After all, how hard can it be to find an obelisk with a stone baseball on top? But soon our plan goes awry. Although the computerized printout leads us to a lot in the cemetery's far corner, there are no Creighton headstones and certainly no granite spires with baseballs on top.

We fan out, walking through the tombstones, searching in all directions. While the January day remains mostly sunny, the wind has a cruel bite as it gusts in from New York harbor several blocks below us. We look and look, but don't see anything resembling a shrine to baseball. Soon, due to the cold, we're jogging through the graveyard with the crazed look that Eli Wallach has in the closing scenes of *The Good, the Bad and the Ugly*.

Digging through my backpack, I flip through the clippings the Hall of Fame supplied me with about Creighton. Without my gloves, my fingers soon grow cold in the wind. One of the older clips says that Creighton's obelisk stands upon the crest of Tulip Hill. I look around, seeing Tulip Avenue, Tulip Path, but no Tulip Hill.

A Green-Wood pickup truck comes roaring along the road and I flag it down.

"Where's Tulip Hill?" I shout.

The employee, a bona fide grave digger, climbs down from the cab, and together we study the map from the computer kiosk.

"That's Tulip Avenue," he says, pointing behind me.

"So is this Tulip Hill?"

"I don't know. Not for sure."

During the conversation, I've lost track of Greg. A tall, lanky guy, he finds basketball is more his game. He plays in weekly pickup games and teaches history at the City University of New York. I remember him saying something about actually bothering to read the inscriptions on the older monuments.

The Green-Wood grave digger and I begin to climb up what we hope is Tulip Hill. At the top, Greg is waiting for us.

"This is it, right?" he says.

Indeed, there's the name Creighton in block letters across the base, with the faint images of balls and bats still visible. But no stone baseball sits atop it.

"Things like that can fall off," the grave digger says. "Especially on the real old ones."

For a moment, the three of us gaze about, admiring the harbor off to the left and the famous Manhattan skyline beyond.

"I don't come back here much," the grave digger adds. "Not much business anymore."

"But if the stone ball did come off," Greg asks, "what would happen to it?"

"Most times, we bury things like that right next to the grave," he replies. "You don't want anybody taking them."

To make things official, I pull out the clips again and read aloud: "A monument was erected to Creighton upon the crest of Tulip Hill. Across the face of the column, surrounded by a pair of oak leaves cut in the granite, is a design embodying a pair of bats crossed, a cap, a baseball and a score book, surmounted across the top of a scroll with the world Excelsior carved upon it."

Greg is able to make out these images.

"And this must be Tulip Hill," the grave digger says.

We've found him—the game's original fireballer.

Exiting Green-Wood, we stop by the office and purchase Nash's book and pick up some more literature about the cemetery.

"Maybe we should have done this on the way in," I offer.

It would have been helpful because back on the bus to D.C., after lunch at Di Fara, Brooklyn's famed pizza kitchen, I read that the elements "totally disintegrated" the ball that once topped the monument to Creighton. Despite the monument being a shadow of what it once was, there's no denying the impact the man had on the game.

"One could argue that Creighton was as pivotal to the game's development as Babe Ruth," Tom Shieber at the Hall of Fame tells me.

Babe Ruth? The Sultan of Swat?

"Ruth was really the first to combine great power with a high average, right?" Shieber says. "Everyone knew that if you swung harder, you could hit more homers. But it was generally thought that this was poor form, as your batting average would drop and the gains of the homer would be outweighed by the losses in times reaching base. Ruth showed that he could hit homers and still hit for a high average. Others soon followed Ruth's lead, though not to the magnificent level of Ruth, of course."

OK, I'll buy that. But what puts Creighton in that kind of company?

"Others tried to follow Creighton's example as well, and initially, none could duplicate his speed and accuracy," Shieber explains. "Indeed, the result was a significant rule change. With pitchers trying to throw hard but not able to throw accurately, the governing body of baseball found that the game was slowing down with so many unhittable deliveries. Unhittable because they were not within reasonable reach of the batter. With Creighton imitators failing to duplicate his accuracy, the concept of a walk [bases on balls] was introduced in 1863, the season after Creighton's untimely death."

Whether you agree or not with Creighton being put in the same class with Ruth, there's little doubt that thanks to the Brooklyn star a quality fastball was here to stay. Following in Creighton's footsteps were George "the Charmer" Zettlein; Tommy Bond, who tossed an amazing 532 ⅔ innings in 1878; and Al Spalding, who reached the Hall of Fame in 1939 as one of the game's pioneers.

What further helped keep the fastball in play was a regular catcher. Most historians believe that Deacon White, who played more than 20 years of pro ball, was the first one to station himself behind home plate to take the throw.

Creighton may have fostered the call of balls and strikes, but the exact amount in play was like an early version of *The Price Is Right*. According to Bill James of the *Baseball Abstract*, the original number of balls required for a walk was nine. It was changed to eight in 1880, to seven in some leagues in 1881, to six in 1884, back to seven in 1886, to five in 1887, and finally to four in 1889.

Gone were the softball-like deliveries. Still, some curious restrictions remained. Until 1887, believe it or not, a rule was on the books that allowed the batter to actually call for a high or a low pitch. Sounds like tossing to your toddler at the playground, doesn't it? But the batter could demand that the pitch be high (waist to the shoulder) or low (waist to a foot or so above the ground). That was eliminated as the strike zone (starting at about the knees and up to the shoulders) became standard throughout the game.

Of course, rule changes can only go so far. Somebody has to come along and take things to the next level. That finally happened thanks to a series of pitchers people barely remember these days—Charlie Sweeney, Pud Galvin, and Amos Rusie. The latter two are enshrined at Cooperstown.

Sweeney was a right-hander who alternated between pitching and the outfield. He was a beneficiary of being permitted to use the full overhand delivery, and many consider him to have the best arm of the 1880s. His record of 19 strikeouts in a game stood (though tied a number of times) until Roger Clemens struck out 20 over a century later. But Sweeney was known as much for his carousing and for signing a lucrative contract with St. Louis of the Union Association as for his ability to throw bullets. Maybe even more than the great sluggers of the game, the fireballers really relished the good life. They remind me of the donkey boys in *Pinocchio*. Will they stay on the straight and narrow long enough to stop sprouting big ears and a tail? Can they slow down in life's fast lane long enough to put together a memorable career on the mound? More often than not the answer is a resounding no.

Somebody who did make the most of what physical talent he had was James "Pud" Galvin. One of the great things about baseball, at least before everybody started making so much money and got too prissy about such matters, was the plethora of swell nicknames. There was "Hustling" Hughie Jennings, "Buttermilk" Tommy Dowd, and George "Twinkletoes" Selkirk. One of my favorites was Sammy Byrd, often a defensive replacement for the Bambino himself, who was dubbed "Babe Ruth's legs." And perhaps the best one is Robert

"Death to Flying Things" Ferguson. (A so-so hitter in the game's early days, Ferguson gained his nickname for catching just about anything in sight.)

Galvin's nickname of "Pud" came about because his outstanding heater was said to turn batters to pudding. Born on Christmas Day 1856, Galvin grew up in the "Kerry Patch" section of St. Louis. Populated by Irish immigrants, the neighborhood was an early hotbed for baseball. Even though the professional game didn't reach St. Louis until 1873, there were plenty of quality amateur teams (the Empires and the Reds), and by the time he was a teenager, Galvin was considered the best prospect around. When the Reds became a professional outfit, they signed the right-hander, which was OK with Galvin, whose only other marketable skill was steamfitting.

For a guy who would one day reach the Hall of Fame, Galvin didn't look like much of an athlete. He stood 5-foot-8 and was close to 200 pounds. At first glance, the only feature that separated him from the pack was his handlebar mustache. But when Galvin took the mound he could bring the heat. In 1876, "the Little Steam Engine" (another of Galvin's nicknames) pitched two no-hitters for the home-town Reds. A year later, he was with the Alleghenies, an independent ballclub, and a season later found his way to Buffalo, which was then in the National League. There he fired two more no-hitters—in 1880 against Worcester and in 1884 against Detroit. One of his early gems is recognized as the first official perfect game in pro ball.

On the mound, Galvin made nearly every pitch an event.

"He turns the ball around in his hands six times," a writer of that period observed, "mops his forehead, pulls a kink out of the seat of his pants, pulls out his handkerchief and wipes his eyes, turns to the second baseman and asks what o'clock it is, pats both hands in the dust, wipes the dust off his trousers, licks the end of his fingers, tosses the ball over his left shoulder, absorbs a little more dust with his palms, tells the boys to look out, and pitches the ball."

Now that's pitching as performance art.

Despite being a bit of a drama queen, Galvin proved to be a work-horse. He finished his career with 5,941 ⅓ innings pitched, second only to the legendary Cy Young, who had a quality fastball himself. To get a good idea of how much the game has changed, consider the following statistics from the 1883 season: Galvin started 75 games for the Buffalo Bisons and completed an incredible 72 of them. He threw a league-leading 656 ⅓ innings in that season alone. Some teams today are lucky to get that many quality innings out of their entire starting staff. During his time with Buffalo alone, Galvin won 37, 20, 28, 28, 46, and another 46 games for a team that never finished better than third place. He pitched an incredible 639 complete games during his 14-year career.

Even though he followed in the footsteps of Candy Cummings, who popularized the curveball, Galvin believed in throwing fast and faster. Galvin further exploited the advantage of sheer speed by repeatedly picking runners off first base. Once he walked three men in an inning and then picked each one off first base in order.

"If I had Galvin to catch, no one would ever steal a base on me," Hall of Famer Buck Ewing once said. "That fellow keeps them glued to the bag. You notice that funny false motion of his that can't really be called a balk. He fooled me so badly one day that I never even attempted to get back to first base. And he certainly also has the best control of any pitcher in this league."

During the 1885 season, Galvin left Buffalo and joined Pittsburgh of the American Association. He remained in the city until a National League franchise was awarded the team two seasons later, and he won the first two games in the team's history. In his first four years in Pittsburgh, not counting the partial season of 1885, Galvin averaged nearly 26 victories a season. By 1890, though, his fastball was fading fast. Two years later, after splitting time between Pittsburgh and St. Louis, Galvin retired and opened a big-time saloon in Pittsburgh, which was so large that it had nine bartenders. Unfortunately for Galvin, the bartenders usually took home more money nightly than he did. It looked "as though he had found a sure road to prosperity," the *Pittsburgh Gazette* reported, "but Galvin was not a man of business."

The right-hander died penniless in a rooming house on the north side of Pittsburgh in 1902. He was only 45, and news of his death was overshadowed by the flooding of the Ohio River, which left thousands homeless.

The fastest of all time? It's hard to say. As Feller would say, Galvin was certainly in the ballpark. Few in modern times appreciate Galvin's accomplishments, and he wasn't elected to the Hall of Fame in Cooperstown until 1965. In reality, Galvin should be remembered as the fastball pitcher who bridged the gap from the underarm delivery of the game's beginnings to the conventional overhand method of today.

In a perfect world, Amos Rusie would have been recognized as one of the game's true pioneers, too, and inducted into Cooperstown while he was still alive to enjoy the honor. Instead, he was posthumously elected to the Hall of Fame in 1977—34 ½ years after he died. In a way, Rusie has become baseball's version of Forrest Gump: a guy who was always around the action, but whose own accomplishments are overshadowed by the events and history he helped put into motion.

No doubt about it, though, Rusie threw hard. Legend has it that as a boy he started going hunting without a gun. When his father asked where his rifle was, Rusie replied that he didn't need one.

When the hunting party came upon a jack rabbit, Rusie pulled a stone out of his pocket before his father or brother could fire. And with deadly accuracy, Rusie threw it, nailing the rabbit dead in the head.

"Where'd you learn to do that?" his father asked.

"Practicing,'" Rusie answered.

There are several versions of how Rusie came to play big-league baseball. In one, the Indianapolis Athletic Club had to replace a sick pitcher at the last minute. Rusie was summoned and did so well that the Indianapolis National League team picked him up. My favorite has one of the proprietors at the state fair hearing about Rusie's throwing prowess. The two of them worked up a scheme in which the barker would charge folks 25 cents apiece to have the honor of witnessing Rusie throw a ball through a wooden fence from about 20 yards away. It was a stunt that would become part of the game's lore. Steve Dalkowski, for example, once won a bet from a teammate by doing pretty much the same thing. Rusie was supposed to go easy every now and then, so that the ball didn't bust through the board right away. This was supposed to work up a bigger crowd. But he purportedly just couldn't contain himself and often proceeded to demolish the obstacle in a few minutes. Thankfully, one of those who caught the act was a scout for the Indianapolis ballclub. After inspecting the wooden fence, to make sure everything was on the up and up, he became convinced Rusie had the goods to make it in professional ball. The pitcher they soon called "the Hoosier Thunderbolt" was in uniform for the 1889 season.

At 6-foot-1 and 200 pounds, Rusie was reportedly "a perfect specimen of youthful vigor." Yet many of the same stories also mentioned how the fun-loving fireballer was easily tempted, which only added to his reputation and infamy as a fireballer.

Sam Crane, a major-league shortstop who became a sportswriter, said Rusie began "life with everything in his favor, [but he] went through his active pitching days as though on a continuous joy ride. He broke training when he felt like it and never looked upon life as a serious matter."

Just 17 years old when he joined Indianapolis in 1889, Rusie went 12–10 in his rookie year. During the off-season, the National League dropped Indianapolis and Rusie's rights fell to the New York Giants. His first season with them he lost a league-high 34 games, but he also won 29 and, more importantly, struck out 341. That would be the only losing season for Rusie in New York. Pitching every other or third day, he went 33–20 the following season and notched a no-hitter against Brooklyn.

Due in large part to Rusie's overpowering speed, the distance from the pitching mound to home plate was moved back five feet to its current 60 feet, 6 inches. While that helped batters against lesser pitchers, Rusie kept rolling along. In 1894, he posted a league-leading 36–13 record. Those who had the dubious honor of catching for him tried layers of sponge and even thin plates of lead inside their gloves to save their hands.

"Rusie was the fastest of them all," said Duke Farrell, one of those old catchers. "What a star he was and how few there are who will ever approach him. I have seen scores of pitchers come and go, and none of them inspired the terror in the batsman's heart that was put there by Rusie."

The fiery right-hander capped the 1893 season by pitching the Giants past Baltimore. (The modern World Series didn't begin until 1903.) The Orioles were a formidable lot with seven eventual members of the Hall of Fame, including "Wee" Willie Keeler, Hughie Jennings, and John McGraw.

"Yes, Rusie was the fastest of them all," said outfielder Jimmy Ryan, who played in the majors from 1883 to 1903, "the greatest in his way."

Cy Young was once asked to name the top fastball pitchers of all time and he replied, "Amos Rusie, Bob Feller, and me."

Lou Criger, who caught Cy Young, didn't even put his legendary battery mate in the final equation. For Criger, Rusie "was the greatest pitcher that ever stepped in the box and I never expected to see a better one."

The hard thrower soon became the toast of New York, with bartenders even concocting a cocktail called the Rusie. (Near as we can tell today, it was a cross between a daiquiri and a champagne fizz.) When he returned to town for the 1895 season, he was greeted by a marching band and thousands of adoring fans at the train station. Vaudeville teams worked up skits about Rusie's prowess, and Lillian Russell, the belle of Broadway, angled herself an introduction. Meanwhile, kids snapped up a pamphlet titled "Secrets of Amos Rusie: The World's Greatest Pitcher: How He Obtains His Incredible Speed on the Ball."

The only one who could seemingly derail Rusie was Rusie himself. And that's what he soon did. Team owner Andrew Freedman had instituted a curfew for the 1895 season. That season Rusie was roommates with shortstop William "Shorty" Fuller. One night in Baltimore, Rusie returned to the hotel before curfew but was told by the night clerk that Fuller was still out. And Fuller had the key. Rusie was scheduled to pitch the next day, so he took a key for another room.

The next day Freedman heard that Rusie hadn't been in his room and fined the star pitcher $100. Rusie didn't explain the situation in fear that he would get his roommate in trouble.

A few days later, Rusie reportedly thumbed his nose at Freedman from the mound during a game. That resulted in another $100 fine, which Rusie refused to pay.

"Those two fines amounted to $200," Rusie later told the *Indianapolis Star*. "When they sent me a contract for 1896, I refused to sign it unless the fines were restored to me. This Freedman refused to do, so I wouldn't sign and stayed out all year."

In essence, Rusie was one of the game's first holdouts. Several of the National League owners, notably Cincinnati's John Brush, became increasingly concerned about the pitcher's stance. Brush feared that it could lead to the dissolving of the game's precious reserve clause, which bound a player to the team that had him under contract. As a result, Brush led a campaign among the other owners to pony up $5,000, settling the case out of court.

Rusie's salary was a princely $6,250 for the 1897 season. Unfortunately, he still wasn't saving much of it. A soft touch, Rusie gave away a lion's share of his earnings to family, friends, and hangers-on, many often raising a Rusie cocktail to his health.

On the field, Rusie hurt his arm in midseason, trying to pick a runner off first base. Armed with only his curveball, he still won 20 games in 1898, only to suffer more self-inflicted wounds. Rusie sat out the 1899 and 1900 seasons due to marital problems. By then the Giants had had enough and traded his rights to Cincinnati for a 20-year-old pitcher named Christy Mathewson.

"The Giants without Rusie are like *Hamlet* without the Melancholy Dane," the *New York Press-Telegram* proclaimed after the deal.

Of course, Mathewson went on to be one of the game's best pitchers, part of the original class inducted into the Hall of Fame. But Mathewson was better known for his "fadeaway" pitch than a superb fastball—a precursor to today's screwball that broke down and in to a right-handed batter and down and away to a left-hander when thrown by a right-hander like Mathewson.

"A screwball—the pitch—got its name because it must be thrown in a way that is opposite of every pitch," Pat Jordan wrote in *Sports Illustrated Pitching: The Key to Excellence*, "because the ball spins in a way that is the reverse of a curveball; and, finally, because only a demented person would specialize in such a perverse pitch that is so hard to master and so damaging to a pitcher's arm."

Besides the demented factor, the fadeaway or screwball also isn't especially quick. Sloppy Thurston, one of the top fadeaway specialists before Mathewson, called it "a slow ball." ESPN.com's Rob Neyer likens the fadeaway or screwball, at least a slow one, to today's circle changeup. Considering the difficulty in learning it and the damage that could be done, the fadeaway seems downright un-American in a way. But thanks to Rusie, and others, signing a real fireballer had become akin to making a pact with the devil. The mighty fastball could certainly ring up a lot of batters, but sooner or later the ride always seemed to get too bumpy for everyone involved.

Rusie exited the game after the 1901 season with Cincinnati. During his career, he led the league in strikeouts five times. But his reputation as a loose cannon followed him into retirement. He squandered his success and became broke and jobless, until John McGraw, his former rival and now the manager of the Giants, eventually brought him back to New York as a ticket taker at the Polo Grounds.

"It's like climbing out of your grave," Rusie said, "and going to a dance."

Of course, the star of the Polo Grounds by then was Mathewson, the guy who Rusie had been traded for. "[He] was golden, tall, and handsome, kind and educated, our beau ideal, the first-all-American boy to emerge from the field of play," Frank Deford wrote in 2005. And the star pitcher Rusie now had to watch.

Control, not speed, was Matty's calling card. In an interview with *Baseball Magazine,* Mathewson detailed how in 1908 he walked only 42 batters in 390 ⅔ innings. Nicknamed "the Big Six," a reference to a train engine of the era, Mathewson played 16 years for the Giants, placing records for endurance (46 games started in 1904) as well as victories (37 in 1908). In the 1905 World Series he shut out the Philadelphia Athletics three times in five days.

As a result, proponents of the mighty fastball found themselves also looking for such a champion: a guy who could not only throw hard but be an exceptional citizen to boot. They finally found one in a gangly kid, who was pitching in what was left of the Wild, Wild West.

E xceptional pitching doesn't demand a fastball for the ages, a thunderbolt from Mount Olympus. But it's sure a lot more fun when that's part of the package, isn't it? That was the starring role seemingly preordained for Walter Johnson at the turn of the last century.

Born in Humboldt, Kansas, in 1887, Johnson had family that reportedly fought at Bull Run, Antietam, and Gettysburg during the Civil War. At first, the family earned a living by farming on the Great Plains, and years later Johnson would credit such an upbringing for his incredible physical strength and legendary endurance on the mound. During recess, one April morning at Crescent Valley School, he impressed the bigger boys with how hard and how far he could throw. As his biographer, Hank Thomas, later noted, this ability "was a gift, pure and simple." Much later in life, Johnson recalled that day when everything came together for him. "From the first time I held a ball, it settled in the palm of my right hand as though it belonged there," he said, "and when I threw it, ball, hand and wrist, arm and shoulder and back seemed to all work together."

When a drought hit eastern Kansas, the Johnson family was forced to move into town and, for a time, barely scraped by. Walter, 13 by then, struck up a friendship with an eighth-grade classmate and began playing catch with him in the street after school and on weekends. Humboldt wasn't home for long, though. Two of his mother's brothers had found work in the oil fields of southern California. Soon word drifted back about the boom times there and Johnson's father decided to pay a visit. He quickly found work, and by April 1902, Johnson and his four siblings were aboard a train heading for the West Coast.

The family settled in Olinda, a small town 20 miles southeast of Los Angeles. Their home, which had indoor plumbing, electricity, and gas heat, stood on Main Street and was owned by the Santa Fe Oil Company. Besides being a company man, Johnson's father was also a fan of the local ball team, the Oil Wells. He took his children to the games, and young Walter began to follow such national stars as Wee Willie Keeler, Honus Wagner, Ed Delahanty, and the prominent pitchers of the day, Cy Young and Christy Mathewson, in the newspapers. As for playing himself, Johnson didn't really get started until he was 16. He was too busy helping his father, who hauled supplies by horse and wagon for the Santa Fe Company from Olinda to Fullerton, about six miles away.

Johnson would later credit this delay, along with his many chores around the home, for his amazing durability. "By that time I had attained sufficient strength so I could not hurt myself," Johnson is quoted as saying in Thomas's award-winning biography.

When Johnson did begin organized ball, it was as a catcher. Despite playing with no mask or other protective equipment, Johnson soon gained a reputation for having a strong, accurate arm. Few dared to try and steal on him. It wasn't until 1904, after three other pitchers "had been clobbered," that Johnson was told to take the mound. Although he didn't enter the game until the fourth inning, Johnson struck out 12. His motion that day was much the same as it would be at the professional level. After a short windup, he delivered the ball to the plate with a smooth sidearm motion. It seemed as if he was almost casually flipping the ball toward home plate. In a way, that proved to be an optical illusion, belying how fast the ball was borne in upon the batter.

Even though legendary sportswriter Grantland Rice would later call the delivery "the finest motion in the game," it didn't stop managers and older players from trying to alter it. Real pitchers were supposed to throw overhand. Not sidearm, almost underhanded. To his credit, Johnson didn't pay much attention. Instead he began to throw rocks at empty cans in his spare time to sharpen his accuracy.

It wasn't long before the local team came calling. Johnson saw his first action for the Oil Wells on July 24, 1904. The local newspaper reported that he struck out six in three innings. Although Johnson pitched a few high school games, including an epic 0–0 tie with Santa Ana that lasted 15 innings, his primary team was the Oil Wells. He pitched and played right field and first base for them. In fact, he excelled in most aspects of the game except fielding. Still an awkward adolescent, Johnson often bungled bunts near the mound. There was no questioning his arm or the velocity of his fastball, however.

In the spring of 1906, Johnson traveled by train north to Tacoma, Washington. At the time, he seemed assured of a roster spot for the local team, the Tigers. But only days before Johnson arrived in Tacoma, one of the worst natural disasters in American history struck San Francisco. The earthquake and fire of April 18–20 impacted life up and down the West Coast. For several weeks, it appeared that the only way the Pacific Coast League would be able to play the new season was by merging with the Northwestern League. As a result, the Tacoma manager released Johnson. He figured better players would soon be coming his way. His parting advice to Johnson? Forget about pitching and focus on the outfield.

Disappointed, Johnson was on the verge of returning home, back to helping his father and pitching for his old team, the Oil Wells. That's when a former Olinda teammate wired him. Clair Head, once the Oil Wells' shortstop, was in someplace called Weiser, Idaho. The team there needed pitching. Was Johnson interested? You bet he was.

Located in southwest Idaho, near the border with Oregon, Weiser was a mining and farming community. For $75 a month, Johnson pitched for the local team, which played on the weekends in the six-team Southern Idaho League. The rest of the time he dug postholes for the Weiser Telephone Company. He was there until the following June, when Cliff Blankenship, a reluctant scout for the Washington Senators, signed him to a big-league contract.

"Looking back on it, playing in Weiser, Idaho, allowed Walter to kind of get his legs back under him again," Thomas tells me. "The situation in Tacoma hadn't been the best. He was looking for a place where he could just pitch, make his mark. But you have to think that with the fastball Walter had that somebody would have noticed, sooner or later. Anybody who saw him pitch in those days, who was intelligent enough to look past that sidearm business, soon recognized he had one of the best fastballs ever in the game."

I love how Thomas refers to Johnson simply as Walter. At first blush, it would seem to be a curious convention. But Thomas, who lives in Arlington, Virginia, is more than Johnson's biographer. He's also his grandson and was born in the same year that the legendary fireballer died.

When Thomas's grandfather arrived in the nation's capital to pitch for the hometown Senators, he was already being labeled as a phenom. At first, opponents and even his new teammates were dismissive of the 19-year-old's sidearm delivery. Such concerns disappeared when they stepped into the batter's box. The Senators' Jim Delahanty was said to be the first guy Johnson threw to in a team batting practice soon after arriving in D.C.

"The big raw rookie just took a short windup and let go with the ball. I never had a chance to take a swing," Delahanty later said. "It was in the catcher's hands before I knew it had left Johnson's. And, when he came back with another just like it, I just lay my bat down and talked to [manager] Joe Cantillon and said, 'I'm through.'"

Cantillon asked if Johnson truly had "a fast one."

"Has he got a fast one?" replied Delahanty. "No human being ever threw one as fast before."

That prompted the Senators' manager to ask if Johnson had a curve.

"I don't know and I don't care," Delahanty said. "What's more, I'm not going back to bat against that guy until I learn how good his control is. From now on, he can pitch for me but not to me."

In fact, the young phenom was also afraid of what would happen if he hit a batter, teammate or otherwise. Only a few, notably Ty Cobb, ever figured that out and used it to their advantage. To the rest of baseball, Johnson soon became known as a plainspoken kid from somewhere out west, who threw a fastball that nobody could touch.

His first big-league start was against the Detroit Tigers, and even though Johnson lost, 3–2, he certainly made an impression. "The first time I faced him, I watched him take that easy windup—and then something went past me that made me flinch," Cobb recounted in his autobiography. "I hardly saw the pitch, but I heard it. The thing just hissed with danger. Every one of us knew he'd met the most powerful arm ever turned loose in a ballpark."

J. Ed Grillo, covering the game for the *Washington Post*, wrote, "Walter Johnson, the Idaho phenom, who made his debut in fast company yesterday, showed conclusively that he is perhaps the most promising young pitcher who has broken into a major league in recent years. . . . He had terrific speed, and the hard-hitting Detroit batsmen found him about as troublesome as any pitcher they have gone against on this present trip."

The Senators were simply grateful to have something go their way for once. The ballclub had finished 55–95 the year before, second to last in the American League. "He's the best raw pitcher I've ever seen," Cantillon said after Johnson's debut. "Give him two years and he'll be a greater pitcher than Mathewson."

After going 5–9 his first big-league season, a dazzling stretch over Labor Day weekend the next season forever put Johnson on the map. The Senators were in New York to play the Yankees. The Yankees weren't the heavy-spending contenders that they are now. In fact, they were also-rans at the time, much like Washington. That didn't stop Cantillon from trying to play mind games with his young phenom.

At the team hotel, the manager showed Johnson a New York newspaper story that detailed the young pitcher's lack of success against the Yankees. No matter that Johnson hadn't pitched many games against New York. A bit fired up, Johnson went out and shut out the Yankees, 3–0.

The next day's paper read that Johnson had gotten lucky. That didn't sit well with the phenom and he asked Cantillon to pitch him again that day. Of course, this was well before pitch counts and pre-ordained days of rest. The Senators' manager liked how worked up his young starter was and let him have another go. This time Johnson won in another shutout, 6–0.

While that should have been the end of the story, the next day Johnson got talking with several of his veteran teammates in the hotel lobby. They teased that the newspaper writer still didn't think much of him. Johnson, not realizing that they were egging him on, asked Cantillon if he could pitch again against the Yankees in the doubleheader slated for Labor Day Monday. (Sunday was an off day.) Johnson started the first game and pitched his third shutout in four days.

After a disappointing third season, in which his fastball seemed to lose velocity, Johnson bounced back to lead the league for the first time in ERA (1.39) while posting a 33–12 record. From then on Johnson was a force to forever be reckoned with, leading the league in strikeouts 9 of 10 seasons, starting in 1910, and in victories 5 of 6 seasons, from 1913 to 1918. In addition, he pitched 56 shutout innings from April 10 to May 14, 1913, and three years later he pitched 369 ⅔ innings without allowing a home run.

Numbers in baseball give a degree creditability to what we've actually witnessed. Most fans know that the Triple Crown goes to the hitter who leads the league in batting average, home runs, and runs batted in in the same season. After the earned run average, or ERA, became an official statistic in 1912 in the National League and a year later in the American League, a similar high standard was available for pitchers.

"Earned run average can be analogous to batting average, since it is not affected too much by what teammates do," Leonard Koppett wrote in the *Sporting News.* "Won-lost percentage is like runs batted in, to the extent that it will reflect membership on a stronger team. And strikeouts are like home runs, in that they are an entirely individual feat."

In 1913, Johnson was the first to win pitching's equivalent of the Triple Crown, posting a 36–7 record, a minuscule 1.14 ERA, and 243 strikeouts.

Not only were the statistics there, but the personal testimonies and tall tales that began to surround Johnson were pretty amazing, too. The Cleveland Indians once loaded the bases on him with none out in the first inning. Johnson proceeded to strike out Tris Speaker, Chick Gandil, and Braggo Roth on ten pitches. Only Roth was able to even foul one off.

Another time the Detroit Tigers loaded the bases on Johnson thanks to three Senators errors.

"Don't worry, Big Fella," called out one of Johnson's infielders.

"I'm not worrying," he replied. "Just give me the ball and I'll get the next three guys."

Johnson did just that, striking out Cobb, Germany Schaefer, and Claude Rossman.

That he did all this with meager support borders upon the unbelievable. In the first five years Johnson was with the Senators, the ballclub never finished above seventh place. Still, the hard thrower managed to win 82 games.

With such accomplishments came the nicknames. He was called "the Big Swede," even though he had little Scandinavian ancestry, and "Barney," a play on Barney Oldfield, a top-notch auto driver of the time. But it was left to Grantland Rice to come up with the best moniker for the right-handed fireballer. He dubbed Johnson "the Big Train" after the fastest means of travel at the time.

B orn on November 3, 1918, in Van Meter, Iowa, Bob Feller heard many of the stories about the Big Train growing up. And the more he heard, the more Feller couldn't help thinking that the two of them had more in common than a blazing fastball. After all, they were both country boys, for the most part. Johnson grew up on the Kansas prairie, with the finishing touches in southern California. Feller was another hayseed—raised in a three-bedroom farmhouse with a trap door that led from the kitchen to the fruit cellar in case of tornadoes. Feller's father was a farmer, growing corn and wheat, and from early on the old man was sold on his son's ability to throw a baseball very, very fast. A belief that would spur Feller on to become one of the best teenage prodigies in sports history.

When young Bobby was 5 years old, he would fire a rubber ball back to his father with such velocity that Mr. Feller had to employ a couch pillow for protection. Errant throws also loosened the plaster on the living room wall. At the age of 10, Feller's father gave him his first baseball uniform. Even though it didn't have a number or name stitched on the back, it was made of flannel, just like the major-league models at the time, and it came with a matching hat and stirrups. By this time Feller already had a bat of his own and two gloves—a Rogers Hornsby model and a Ray Schalk catcher's mitt.

Most parents would have stopped there. But with his son already considered the best shortstop in the county, Bill Feller decided to take things to another level. He dug up part of the pastureland, put up a fence to keep out the livestock, and built bleachers and a scoreboard. He formed a local team called Oakview (named after the timber and a view of the Raccoon River less than a mile away). Games were played on Sundays during the summer, with admission being 25 cents—35 cents for doubleheaders. It was "a field of dreams" almost a half century before W. P. Kinsella penned his famous novel that was made into the movie starring Kevin Costner.

The Oakview ballclub had some of the best players in the area and competed against teams from nearby Des Moines and other Iowa towns. For the most part, the Oakview roster was made up of players in their late teens or early 20s. The lone exception was Feller, who was 13. Father and son were convinced, even then, that he had a good shot at playing major-league baseball.

"He and I were in it together," Feller remembers. "It wasn't like he was pushing me to do it. It wasn't like he was a stage mother or anything like that. I wanted to play ball and he did everything he could to help me. Later on, people made it sound like I was his puppet or something like that. Nothing could be further from the truth."

Unlike the pampered sports prodigies one sees today, Feller still had plenty of chores around the farm to do growing up. He says he practiced in "a block of time here and there and all of a sudden I had an incredibly strong arm for my age. This made it possible for me to be known as a young phenom throughout Iowa."

Feller fed the hogs, milked the cows, picked corn, pumped water, and toted bales of hay. The manual labor made his legs and arms strong, which years later he said was "exactly what a pitcher needs to be successful in the major leagues. This type of natural exercise was the best in the world, and the fact that my arm became strong was just a side benefit. The main reward was I knew I was helping my parents out and that meant the most to me.

"Later on, when I heard more about Walter Johnson and his story, I realized that this was something we had in common. Growing up the way we did made us strong on the mound."

A late winter wind buffets the redbrick building behind the backstop at Shirley Povich Field in Bethesda. Tarps cover home plate, as well as the pitching mound, and on harsh afternoons like this it's hard to imagine that spring and another baseball season are almost here. Up in the press box, though, the hot-stove conversation is crackling. Even in hibernation, the national pastime lends itself to not only what's on the horizon but what's gone down in the past. Such a nod to history has Bruce Adams explaining once again how his team got its nickname, the Big Train.

A decade ago, Adams's dream of placing a semipro team just around the corner from the Montgomery Shopping Mall, hard by Interstate 270, was almost reality. Most of the bases had been covered—erecting a lovely ballpark, ordering the uniforms, lining up the ballplayers. Yet somehow in the swirl of it all, the team's nickname had been left until the late innings.

So, Adams called a board meeting and told everyone to come with a list of monikers. To his surprise, the favorite soon became Johnson's best-known nickname, "the Big Train."

For those in the D.C. area, who went three-plus decades without a major-league team to call their own, who aren't quite sure who Walter Johnson was, Adams has a knee-jerk response. "Who was Walter Johnson?" he'll repeat, voice dripping with the same indignation that Tom Hanks's character, Jimmy Dugan, has in *A League of Their Own.* "He's only the greatest pitcher in baseball history and he lived right here, in Washington, in Montgomery County. If you're a baseball fan, you have to remember this gentleman."

Before Ali-Frazier, Riggs-King, Bird-Magic, there was Smoky Joe versus the Big Train. In September 1912, Johnson faced off against Smoky Joe Wood of the Red Sox at the new Fenway Park. It didn't matter that the first-place Red Sox were 16 games up on the Senators in the standings. What sold the place out was the opportunity to witness two of the best fireballers of all time go toe-to-toe.

The two pitchers couldn't have been more different in stature or delivery. Johnson was 6-foot-1 and 200 pounds, while Wood was 5-foot-11 and perhaps 165. Johnson easily threw the ball to the plate. His sidearm delivery belying how fast the ball arrived at the plate. In comparison, Wood had a pitching motion that bordered upon the violent as he put everything he had into the pitch. "I threw so hard I thought my arm would fly right off my body," Wood said.

Johnson feared for his rival's safety, too. "When I used to see Wood pitch, although I admired his speed and control, it made my shoulder ache to watch his delivery," he told *Baseball Magazine.* "That pitching with the arm alone, that wrenching of the muscles in the shoulder, would wear out my arm, I am sure, much quicker than the easy, swinging motion I always aim to use."

Johnson had won 16 consecutive games earlier in that season. Heading into their marquee matchup, Wood was on a 13-game winning streak, and the Boston faithful were convinced he was well on his way to shattering Johnson's mark. Between the streaks and the speed-versus-speed component, the showdown rapidly became a promoter's dream. And one that Senators manager Clark Griffith made sure came about by wiring the Red Sox management and personally challenging them to the contest. To add a little fuel, Griffith told the press that Wood's streak was meaningless unless he faced Johnson. The Red Sox took the bait and moved Wood up one day in the rotation to ensure that he would face Johnson at Fenway.

Incredibly, the game lived up to its hype. Johnson and Wood were on from the beginning, working out of jams in the early innings. It wasn't until the bottom of the sixth inning that the Red Sox broke the scoreless tie when Duffy Lewis drove home Tris Speaker. That slim lead held up until the ninth, when the Senators put a man on second base, thanks to a single and a sacrifice. It all came down to Wood against Washington catcher Eddie Ainsmith. Johnson's battery mate struck out swinging on a trio of Wood fastballs.

Even though Wood won, he would later call Johnson "the greatest pitcher who ever lived."

Smoky Joe would go on to tie Johnson's consecutive-victories record (he would miss out on his 17th in a row when a pop fly dropped safely, allowing the tying and winning runs). His gaudy 34–5 record that season included a no-hitter against St. Louis. He won another three games in the 1912 World Series as the Red Sox defeated the New York Giants and Christy Mathewson in eight games (4-3-1, as Game Two that year ended in a 6–6 tie when called for darkness). For a single season, there was nobody better, or more popular, in the game than Wood.

"The whole world did love me that day, it seemed like," Wood said years later. "It was my greatest season: 34 wins, 16 in a row and three more in the World Series. Then I hurt my hand and almost became a has-been."

For an Andy Warhol moment, the baseball world was as captivated by Wood's backstory as it was by his pitching prowess. Wood, like Johnson, grew up in the West. While Johnson came of age in the oil patches of southern California and was toughed up a bit by his time in Idaho, Wood grew up in southwest Colorado, a stone's throw from such places as Lizard Head Pass and Slumgullion Gulch.

"I see these western pictures on television and sometimes it just hits me," Wood told Lawrence Ritter in *The Glory of Their Times*. "I actually lived through all that in real life. Sort of hard to believe, isn't it?"

So was how he broke into professional ball. By the time Wood was a teenager, his family had moved closer to civilization—actually Ness City, Kansas, about 60 miles north of Dodge City. Wood became the star pitcher on the town team, playing against squads from Scott City, High Point, and Wakeeney. Toward the end of his 16th summer, the Bloomer Girls came to Ness City. They were a barnstorming outfit that toured the country, and several of their top players were guys instead of girls. Rogers Hornsby and Rube Waddell's brother were among those who donned wigs and the team's baggy Turkish-style trousers, especially when the promoter wanted to cover side bets with the locals.

The Bloomer Girls' manager was impressed by Wood's game and invited him to finish out the 1906 season with them. After getting over some initial confusion about the team's configuration, Wood agreed. He played out the last three weeks of the season for $35. For games, his name was Lucy Tolton. Things went well except for the time when his wig flew off at the end of his violent windup and Wood narrowly made it out of town ahead of an angry mob. Yet, as they say, what doesn't kill us can make us strong, and two seasons later Wood was pitching in the majors for the Red Sox.

As often is the case in the realm of high heat, though, the line between tragedy and triumph can be a fine one. The 1912 season was the pinnacle of Wood's pitching career. Within a few seasons after the Fenway showdown, his arm went dead, and Wood ended his 14-year career in the outfield.

"I have seen Joe Wood pitch some days when I thought that he was faster than I," Johnson later said, "and I believe that for two or three innings he has as much swiftness. But he could not hold it during the game. He has a jerky motion, and it is this motion that weakens him."

As Wood's career rapidly declined, Johnson kept rolling along. About the only fastball pitchers who came close to him in terms of velocity and longevity were Feller, Satchel Paige, and Nolan Ryan. As Wood was hampered by injuries, first a broken thumb and then a bum shoulder, Johnson led the league with a 36–7 mark in 1913 and was the American League's top game winner four of the following five seasons. Still, "the Big Train" sometimes struggled to win the so-called big games. Perhaps that reputation began with the epic showdown against Wood. It could have been perpetuated by his easygoing manner. For it is one thing to be regarded as a good guy, even a saint. It is quite another to be known as a big-game pitcher, no matter how fast you can throw a baseball. As Johnson's career wound down, he no longer led the league in victories, even though he continued to be the standard when it came to strikeouts.

In 1924, though, the planets in Johnson's baseball universe came into alignment. For the third time in his career he led the American League in victories, ERA, and strikeouts in the same season. More importantly, after 18 seasons in the majors, he finally reached the World Series, and much of the country was ready to cheer him on. Thanks to Western Union, 125 scoreboards for the games between the American League's Washington Senators and the National League's New York Giants were erected nationwide. Such star players as Cobb, George Sisler, and Babe Ruth were on hand to file special newspaper columns.

"Commercial radio, in its infancy in 1924, received a boost from the fledgling NBC network's live broadcast in Washington, New York and six other cities," Thomas wrote in *Walter Johnson: Baseball's Big Train*. "Crystal sets were the hottest-selling item at department stores, and hundreds of them were set up in government and business offices throughout Washington."

Of course, Johnson was the Senators' choice to pitch Game One. In the second inning, Giants slugger George Kelly lofted a deep fly ball to left-center field. Usually it would have been a routine play for

Senators outfielder Leon "Goose" Goslin. But he couldn't go back as far as normal due to a three-foot makeshift fence in front of the temporary bleachers. Despite Goslin's headlong dive into the crowd, the routine fly went for a home run and Johnson was quickly behind, 1–0.

The Giants upped their advantage to 2–0 in the top of the fourth inning. That's when the hometown Senators began to battle back. After shaving the lead to a run in the sixth inning, Washington rallied in the bottom of the ninth to tie the game at 2–2. With Johnson still on the mound, the contest barreled into extra innings. That's the way it remained until the Giants plated two runs in the top of the 12th inning.

The Senators refused to go silently in the bottom half, however. Rookie Mule Shirley, pinch-hitting for Johnson, reached second base after his pop-up was lost in the sun. A single promptly brought him home. With two down, the Senators had a man on third, with Goslin up. He lashed a hard ground ball to second base, which George "Highpockets" Kelly snared one-handed and flipped to first base. In a bang-bang play, Goslin was called out, the result being a heated argument between the umpire Bill Klem and several of the Senators. As Thomas later detailed, the squabble continued as President Calvin Coolidge filed past, headed for the exit. Despite striking out 12, Johnson had lost his World Series debut.

The Big Train was back on the mound for Game Five, with the series tied at two games apiece. On a chilly day in New York, Johnson started off well enough, holding the Giants scoreless through the first two frames. But New York took a 1–0 lead in the third. While the Senators tied it up in the next inning, the game soon unraveled for Johnson. The Giants picked up two runs in the bottom of the fifth inning and three more in the eighth.

"As the dying shadows of a chill October day crept down from Coogan's Bluff, Walter Johnson stood on the mound of the Polo Grounds taking his punishment without a murmur," wrote the Associated Press's Robert Small. "There was a spirit of a dying gladiator in the air. The stands were silent; the spectators were stunned."

It appeared that Johnson would only know disappointment in his first and perhaps his only World Series. He had started two games and lost both of them. Many wondered if he would ever have another chance. "A bright vision hung and held for just a moment over the Polo Grounds this afternoon—the vision of a tall, fresh-cheeked, fair-haired, brawny youth pitching with power, with blinding, dazzling speed," Damon Runyon wrote after Johnson's second loss. "It was just a mirage of other years. Now it has vanished. The youth is gone."

As the Senators boarded the train back to Washington and what appeared to be an anticlimactic Game Six and a likely New York World Series triumph, Thomas later detailed a pivotal conversation between Johnson and Clark Griffith. The Senators' owner was considered to be the only one who could raise the Big Train's spirits at such a low point.

"Don't think about it anymore, Walter," Griffith told Johnson. "You're a great pitcher. We all know it. Now tonight when we get home, don't stand around the box office buying seats for friends or shaking hands with people who feel sorry for you. Go home and get to bed early. We may need you."

More prophetic words were never spoken.

Somehow the Senators battled back to take Game Six, 2–1, behind Tom Zachary's complete game. That set up the epic Game Seven. The starting pitchers were Curly Ogden for Washington and Virgil Barnes for New York. But Senators manager Bucky Harris said he was ready to employ all available arms, in large part to keep Giants rookie Bill Terry off the base paths. After Harris went over his strategy with Griffith, the Senators' owner called Johnson at home. The Big Train was told to be ready for late-inning relief work. At first, Johnson's wife, Hazel, was ecstatic about the news. Then she realized that her husband could be a three-time loser in the World Series.

On a beautiful day in mid-October, the stands were filled to overflowing in the nation's capital. Posing for photographs before the opening pitch, President Coolidge told the opposing managers, "May the better team win."

Besides Johnson's inability to win with the nation watching, the 1924 World Series was also known for acrobatic catches or at least the attempts at such grabs. The Giants' Hack Wilson, perhaps trying to copy Goslin's Superman effort in Game One, soared toward the stands after Bucky Harris's home-run blast. But instead of clearing the fence, "Wilson's ample girth made full contact with the top of it," Thomas wrote.

To Grantland Rice, the collision sounded "like a barrel of crockery being pushed down the cellar stairs." You don't find sportswriting like that these days.

In the bottom of the eighth inning, the Senators scored two runs to tie the game at 3–3. Moments after the Washington rally, the sellout crowd began to chant Johnson's name. The hometown crowd was ready to see what magic the Big Train had left. But those up in the press box, especially the guest columnists, didn't like his chances. The belief was he was too exhausted, too old to do much good. Still, there was little doubt that he was coming into the ball game.

"[Harris] had at his disposal not merely the best pitcher on the team, or even the best in the league—he had The Greatest Pitcher in the History of Baseball to call upon," Thomas wrote in the biography of his grandfather. The capital letters are his.

Visibly nervous, Johnson walked out to pitch the top of the ninth inning. Even though some later remembered that his face was ashen, his warm-up throws were soon cracking Herold "Muddy" Ruel's catcher's mitt. As the warm-up continued, a buzz began to spread through the stands—the Big Train's fastball was back.

Or was it?

After Johnson got one out, Frankie Frisch scorched his offering into right-center field. Only a great throw by Earl McNeely held him to three bases. After a conference at the mound, the Senators decided to walk Ross Youngs, a left-handed hitter, bringing up RBI champion Kelly. Washington was playing the averages here, as the right-handed Kelly was only two for nine against Johnson. The gambit worked as Kelly went down on three fastballs. That made two outs, with Emil "Irish" Meusel coming up. Johnson got out of the inning when Meusel hit a grounder to third and 5-foot-8 Joe Judge stretched to snag the throw at first base.

Back and forth the teams went in extra innings, with the hometown crowd cheering wildly when the Senators were at bat and becoming quietly apprehensive when Johnson was on the mound. Through it all, Johnson pitched four innings of scoreless ball. "I'd settled down to believe, by then, that maybe this was my day," Johnson later said.

In the bottom of the 12th inning, Washington's glorious ending began innocently enough. With one out, Ruel, who was having a miserable series, appeared to pop up in foul territory. Giants catcher Hank Gowdy drifted back to make the catch, tossed off his mask, only to trip over it a few steps later. Given a second chance, Ruel doubled to left. That brought up Johnson. He hit the first pitch hard and when it was bobbled, he was safe at first.

Next up was Earl McNeely, and with men at first and second base he hit what appeared to be a tailor-made double play ball directly at third baseman Freddy Lindstrom. That would have been enough to end the inning.

For a moment, the ball appeared headed for Lindstrom's glove. On the last bounce, though, it seemed to hit a pebble or was levitated by the baseball gods themselves, perhaps a nod to Johnson. Whatever the reason, it bounded over Lindstrom's head and rolled into left field. Ruel rounded third and chugged for home, and the Senators and their longtime fireballer had at last won the championship.

As the fans poured onto the field, Johnson stood at second base, tears in his eyes.

Up in the press box, Christy Mathewson watched in disbelief. His body ravaged from being gassed during World War I, it would be the last World Series Mathewson would ever witness. "It was the greatest World Series game ever played, I'm sure," Mathewson said. "I'm inclined to think, indeed, that it was the most exciting game ever played under any circumstances."

Today, a monument of bronze and granite stands in tribute to the Big Train at Walter Johnson High School, located around the corner from Shirley Povich Field, where Bruce Adams's ballclub plays. The impressive slab, which shows Johnson pitching along with a list of accomplishments—games won (414), shutouts (113), strikeouts (3,497), and scoreless consecutive innings (56)—was unveiled at Griffith Stadium in 1947, less than a year after his death. President Truman presided at the event, where he called Johnson "the greatest ballplayer who ever lived."

Every year the student body celebrates Johnson's birthday (November 6, 1887) with sheet cake. When the high school team competes on the television show *It's Academic,* the squad often brings along a baseball talisman for good luck.

The Washington Nationals, the new professional team in town, were interested in moving Johnson's monument permanently to the new ballpark in southeast Washington. But the high school eventually turned down the request. Instead, the Nationals commissioned a statue of Johnson, along with ones of Frank Howard and Josh Gibson, which were unveiled outside before Opening Day 2009.

By retaining the monument, Principal Christopher Garran hopes that the memory of the Big Train will inspire future classes at Walter Johnson High. That they will even touch the slab for luck on the way to their games.

"We could have given it to the Nats, for the new ballpark," Garran says, "but it just didn't seem right in a way. After all, Walter Johnson is the person our school is named after. Once you learn a little about him, you realize what a hero the Big Train was."

B eing able to throw a baseball at speeds of 100 miles per hour or greater is certainly a gift. But during the careers of almost every fireballer—Johnson, Feller, Nolan Ryan, Steve Dalkowski—there comes a time when this gift will ultimately be remembered as a blessing or a curse. For Johnson, the moment was likely the 1924 World Series. For Feller, it came 14 years later, on the last day of the 1938 season.

The Indians hosted the Detroit Tigers in a doubleheader on October 2, a sunny day that held a hint of the long winter to follow. Hank Greenberg, the Tigers' All-Star first baseman, came into the game two home runs shy of Babe Ruth's 60 home runs in one season. At that point in history, it was baseball's most recognizable mark.

Many of the Indians vowed that Greenberg wouldn't break the Babe's record on their watch. Several of the veteran ballplayers, especially Hal Trosky, fondly remembered Ruth. Out of loyalty to the Babe, they didn't want to see Greenberg break the 60-home-run mark.

But there was also an undercurrent of prejudice, even religious zeal, that day in Cleveland. Greenberg was the first Jewish superstar in the national pastime. Across the Atlantic, Hitler was making religion a device for division and quickly gaining political power in Germany. Into this cauldron of escalating allegiances and pursuits of all-time individual records stepped Feller. He had been named to be the starting pitcher in the first game of the doubleheader. More than 27,000 fans attended the game to bid the Indians adieu for another season and to see if Greenberg could catch the Babe. Instead they were treated to a different record performance.

The Indians decided they would pitch to Greenberg. No intentional walks, even with men in scoring position. Going against Feller, the great Tigers first baseman, who was inducted into the Hall of Fame 18 years later, went 1-for-4. His lone hit in the first game was a double. He had better success in the second game with three hits, but they were all singles. He finished the day still with 58 home runs. The Babe's record would be safe until Roger Maris broke it in 1961.

In that first game, Greenberg was one of the few Tigers to have any success against Feller. The Indians' hurler would finish the 1938 season with 240 strikeouts and a modern major-league record 208 walks. But on this day, the elements of his game came together, becoming a template that would guide him to 20-plus victory seasons in the next three years, before World War II sent him overseas.

At the time, the major-league record for strikeouts in a nine-inning game was 17, set by another fireballer, Dizzy Dean. But early on against the Tigers, many in the crowd sensed that Feller's stuff, especially his fastball, had never been better.

"It was one of those days when everything feels perfect," Feller says, "your arm, your coordination, your concentration, everything. There was drama in the air because of Greenberg's attempt to break Ruth's record, and the excitement became even greater when my strikeouts started to add up."

After striking out rookie second baseman Ben McCoy in the first inning, Feller struck out the side in the second, third, and fourth innings. He picked up two more Ks in the fifth, two more in the sixth, and one each in the seventh and eighth, so by the time the ninth inning rolled around the crowd was on its feet, realizing that Feller was on a record pace.

That's when this 19-year-old phenom got Pete Fox for his 17th strikeout of the game. Feller's walk of Detroit catcher Birdie Tebbetts then brought up Chet Laabs. The odds were definitely working against Feller now. He had already struck out Laabs four times in the game. The next season Laabs would be traded to the St. Louis Browns, where he would lead the league in pinch hits. Just the type of batter the baseball gods will often befriend. The kind of future journeyman perfectly capable of derailing history.

But Feller quickly ran two fastballs past Laabs. When he first entered the big leagues, Feller was criticized for going away from his best pitch—that is, his fastball—with the game on the line. Early in his career, he had given up a game-winning home run to Joe DiMaggio when he went with a breaking pitch instead of his high heat. Afterward his father told him to stay with the fastball the next time he was in a tight situation.

So, on this day, with the hometown crowd behind him, Feller didn't make the same mistake again. He went with another fastball low at Laabs's knees. Home plate umpire Cal Hubbard decided it caught enough of the inside corner of the plate and called Laabs out on strikes. Feller had his 18-strikeout game and a career destined to one day land him in the Hall of Fame.

"I was lucky, too, because I threw in the American League," Feller tells the crowd in the conference room at Jacobs Field.

"I really believe that because the ball in the American League had blue seams. That's why I only use a pen with blue ink to this day. But I believe the American League model, with those blue stitches, was aerodynamically better for speed, for guys like me. Some of you may scoff at that, but I always believed it."

Whether it was the blue seams or his farm upbringing that so closely paralleled Johnson's, Feller retained his high-octane fastball. He returned from four years in the U.S. Navy in World War II, the longest tenure of any big-league superstar, to strike out 348 in 1946, one away from Rube Waddell's modern record. Yet the following season, his left leg came down awkwardly during that high leg kick of his at Philadelphia's Shibe Park, ironically on Friday the 13th. He injured a muscle in his back, and he claims his fastball was never the same. That didn't stop Feller from being a winner at the major-league level, though. From 1948 to 1956, he won 108 games and helped lead the Cleveland Indians to their last World Series championship in 1948.

"Three days before he pitched I would start thinking about Robert Feller, Bob Feller," Ted Williams once said. "I'd sit in my room thinking about him all the time. God, I loved it . . . Allie Reynolds of the Yankees was tough, and I might think about him for 24 hours before a game, but Robert Feller; I'd think about him for three days."

The only way the motorcycle test worked was by Feller hitting the cantaloupe-sized target with his first and only pitch. "I did it on the first try and you know something?" he tells the assembled crowd in Cleveland. "I'm as proud of that as anything I ever did in my career."

That includes three no-hitters and a dozen one-hitters.

At one level, the motorcycle test was inconsequential. There is no mention of it alongside his records in the Hall of Fame or *The Baseball Encyclopedia*. By now we've watched footage of the motorcycle test many times through, the room falling silent every time. Even though Bob DiBiasio, the ballclub's vice president for public relations, has seen the film many times before, he cannot resist watching it again.

"Now that's old school," he says. "You don't see a ball thrown like that anymore. It's remarkable."

Feller smiles and lets the film play through for a final time. Previously, he has stopped the tape here and rewound it, but now he lets it continue to roll. The motorcycle footage ends, sharp and ragged like the conclusion of a silent movie, to be suddenly replaced by the old comedy team of Abbott and Costello doing their famous routine "Who's on First?"

As the room breaks into laughter, Feller leans over and tells me that he often puts the two segments together. For decades, from the Little League annual dinners to his speaking engagements aboard cruise ships, he's rolled the two out as a twin bill, his own double-header.

"It makes sense, in an odd way," he says. "Me throwing against a motorcycle and then these two funnymen. I don't know which one I get a bigger chuckle out of these days."

The Pivot

Nolan Ryan

Photo courtesy of the National Baseball Hall of Fame Library, Cooperstown, NY

We come into this world head first and go out feet first;
in between, it is all a matter of balance.

—PAUL BOESE

The 2009 spring training season was the strangest in some time. Steroids were back in the news as the Yankees' Alex Rodriguez, arguably the best player in the game, admitted to performance-enhancing drugs after being outed in a *Sports Illustrated* cover story. In Florida and Arizona, where enthusiastic crowds gathered to watch their favorite major-league ballclubs get into shape, nobody was quite sure where the top players were. After a week or so with their regular-season teams, many of the best-known stars headed elsewhere to train with squads of their fellow countrymen in preparation for the second World Baseball Classic.

During the labor wars of the mid-1990s, an Olympic-style international tournament had been one of the few things that the owners and the players' union were able to agree upon. One could even argue that this infatuation to see the game's superstars competing under their nations' flags had played a major role in eventually leading baseball back from the abyss. What better way for a sport to get back on track than by producing another "must-see TV" sporting event?

Despite smiles all around, the WBC had plenty of problems. It was a far different animal than what I'd heard Paul Beeston, then representing the owners, and union boss Donald Fehr praise 15 years before. First off, the timing was all wrong. Crucial games, with national pride on the line were contested when the players weren't yet in midseason form. And to help prevent injury, pitchers were often limited to how many pitches they could throw—a rule that led to some curious pitching changes and perhaps helped foster such surprising outcomes as Italy defeating Canada (a squad that included Justin Morneau, Russell Martin, and Jason Bay), the Netherlands downing the Dominican Republic not once but twice, and Team Japan repeating as overall champs.

Through it all, Tampa Bay's David Price, a bona fide fireballer and one of the most promising young pitchers in the game, put in his work at the Rays' spring training complex in Port Charlotte, Florida. On potential alone, Price should have had a starting spot in the Rays' rotation locked up. After all, his fastball sometimes neared 100 miles per hour, and it wasn't unreasonable to expect him to gain even more velocity as he grew stronger and accustomed to the professional game. Only two years out of Vanderbilt University, where he had won college baseball's top honor, the Dick Howser Award, Price had sped through the Rays' farm system. In mid-August 2007, he signed a six-year deal with Tampa Bay, which included a $5.6-million signing bonus, reportedly the second largest in draft history to that point. (Justin Upton of the Arizona Diamondbacks received $6.1 million in 2005.) He had then gone 11–0 on the lower rungs of the Rays' farm system, turning heads every step of the way.

"He's amazing," three-time Cy Young winner Pedro Martinez, who ended up squaring off against Price during a rehab assignment in the minors, told the Associated Press. "That kid is very mature for his time in [the professional ranks], and very talented.

"At that age, I don't think I was like that. He seems far superior. . . . God bless him and keep him healthy."

In 2008, the Rays were one of the top stories in baseball. Rising from the cellar in the American League East, they reached the World Series, with Price a major reason for their postseason success.

He came out of the bullpen to win Game Two of the American League Championship Series against the Boston Red Sox and then came on in relief again in Game Seven to record his first career save, eliminating the defending champions. With that Price reached the World Series faster than any other top overall June draft selection, surpassing Atlanta's Chipper Jones and the Los Angeles Dodgers' Tim Belcher, who was drafted by the New York Yankees in 1984. In addition, he was only the third rookie pitcher to record a victory and a save in the same postseason series, joining Adam Wainwright (St. Louis, 2006) and Rawly Eastwick (Cincinnati, 1975).

With a new season set to unfold, the last glimpse many had of Price was of him celebrating on the mound, the fans at Tropicana Field ringing their cowbells after the last out against Boston. After such a marquee performance *ESPN: The Magazine* ranked Price, along with Matt Ryan in football and Ricky Rubio in basketball, as the top new faces in sports. But as spring training drew to a close in 2009, Price was having difficulty winning a spot on Tampa Bay's major-league roster.

It wasn't that he was pitching poorly. It was just that others were arguably pitching better. And there were also complications. Two of the Rays' other pitching prospects—Jeff Niemann and Jason Hammel—were out of options, meaning if they were designated to the minors another team could pick them up. Price didn't fall into that category. So despite all the success of the previous season, not to mention his meteoric rise to the majors, it appeared Price would be opening the season back with the Triple-A Durham Bulls for more seasoning.

"All I can do is throw well," Price told MLB.com after his initial spring training appearance. "There's a bunch of different stuff going on with that, so [I have to] just go out there and have fun."

Having fun can be difficult, however, when so much is on the line. Despite a maturity well beyond his 23 years, Price did let it slip how much he wanted to stick in the major leagues for good. Perhaps his patience was wearing thin after his success at the game's highest

level. Soon after arriving in camp, he told the *St. Petersburg Times,*
"I want them to not be able to look me in the eyes at the end of
spring training and tell me I'm going to Durham."

Yet, as the weeks passed under the Florida sun, that's precisely
where Price was headed to start the new season.

S ometimes, late in the afternoon, the home phone will ring and I'll
know it has to be Phil Pote. Parson Phil, as he's known to his
friends, has been a professional scout for more than 40 years. He's
the guy who discovered such big leaguers as Bobby Tolan, Willie
Crawford, and Bob Watson. Pote loves to talk baseball, especially
about pitchers who can throw hard.

"Where you heading next?" he asks. "Your grand tour of everything fastball?

"Looks like to Durham, North Carolina," I reply. "David Price
isn't going to make the big-league club."

"You had to except that."

"Why?"

"It will take him longer to pick up major-league time beginning
this season at Triple-A," Pote says. "That will help when it comes to
contracts and those types of things, which I don't know anything
about."

"But he's been throwing great. You have to agree, he's the next
great phenom."

"Hey, partner, all young pitchers struggle," Pote says. "Unless
they're Fernando Valenzuela. And you and I both know those kinds
of arms come along once in a blue moon."

Pote's right. Circumstance had placed David Price at a crossroads
all too familiar to fireballers dating back almost to the game's origins.
No matter how great the gift, the potential that's seemingly bestowed
from above, everybody seems to struggle at some point. Walter Johnson, "the Big Train" himself, had to pay his dues on local ballclubs in
southern California and was met with indifference in Tacoma, Washington, before coming of age in the frontier town of Weiser, Idaho—

2,500 miles from the team that finally signed him, the Washington Senators.

The sheer ability to throw a baseball with great velocity often makes things appear easy early on, especially to those looking on from the sidelines. Perhaps this is what drives the ultratalented hurlers in our midst to such distraction. Everyone expects them too soon to win almost every outing, just because they can throw hard. But rarely does anything of genuine consequence and achievement happen without a little torment and perhaps a bit of heartache along the way. In every pitcher's journey, there are obstacles to overcome. How they respond, and what they learn about themselves and the world in front of them, is often the tale. In the big leagues, it takes much more than being able to throw hard.

As the Rays broke camp, ready to defend the American League pennant, the 6-foot-6 Price, easily their most promising and arguably their best-known pitcher, was already 592 miles away, as the crow flies, in Durham, North Carolina. The Rays' management had decided the phenom needed more seasoning.

"When we came into camp, we came in with an open mind, knowing full well that there were certain developmental issues that we wanted him to focus on and also the workload," Andrew Friedman, the Rays' executive vice president of baseball operations, told the Associated Press. "We had a lot of conversations about ways to get creative. And we went through it for the last two or three weeks at length and ultimately decided that—all things considered—this was the right move for David and in turn the organization."

Price had gone 2–0 with a 1.08 ERA in three appearances in spring training. Even though he kept his composure when meeting with the media after the decision, there was little doubt he felt he belonged with the big-league ballclub. "You come in here because you can play," Price says. "And this team likes you, and they want to get more looks at you. You get sent down, that's disappointing."

Many of the top fireballers who have preceded Price have gone through similar ordeals. The best not only survived; they rose to the occasion and often became icons of the game. As for the rest? They never came close.

A t first it can seem so easy. Just throw the ball to the catcher's mitt and the sheer velocity, often coupled with great movement, makes the whole world sit up and take notice. But soon enough something more is asked of a fireballer. He's urged to develop other pitches to complement his high heat. As Hall of Fame slugger Eddie Mathews once said, a good hitter "can time a jet coming through that strike zone if you see it often enough." And for many in the game, that's as good as gospel.

To compound matters, coaches and managers often tell a hard-throwing prospect to take something off the fastball. How it's better to gain an ounce of precious control. But what if you believed, deep in your soul, that you can win without such measures? That all this talk of compromise and strategy didn't add up in some basic way? That it might take away from your talent—what got you here in the first place? At such a crossroads, a serious question is asked of any-body trying to bring a gift, something radical of purpose, into the world: Which voice do you choose to believe in? The experts' or your own? Perhaps that's how many become so lost so soon. A fear builds up inside that's often at odds with the lessons being taught. Perhaps that's how it was with one of the most enigmatic of fastball pitchers, Steve Dalkowski.

At first glance, the left-hander from New Britain, Connecticut, didn't look like much of an athlete. He stood 5-foot-11 and weighed maybe 170 pounds. But once he strode onto an athletic field, Dalkowski soon became the only show in town. On the football field, he was the quarterback of the New Britain Hurricanes' 1956 state champions, breaking the school's passing records and twice earning an honorable mention on the state's all-star teams. Still, it was on the diamond that the legend of Steve Dalkowski grew to unprecedented proportions.

New Britain's nickname is the "Hardware City." Stanley Works, Corbin Locks, and North & Judd all called it home. Dalkowski's father worked in the town's electric-tool plant and played shortstop in an industrial league. He trained his son to play the outfield, but once Steve Jr. got a chance to pitch there was no looking back.

For old man Dalkowski, the stations of life flowed between the plant, home, and the local tavern. He, like many of his working-class buddies, drank hard on the weekends and by the time Steve Jr. reached high school he was already following in his father's footsteps. Word had it that Steve Jr. liked his beer and regularly hung out with older guys who could get it for him. Still, in high school, Dalkowski kept his nose clean. He never missed practice and was in good shape. It wasn't until well after his high school graduation that reports trickled out, from Pat Jordan and others, that he had been pulled over at least once during his schoolboy days for drunk driving.

All of that was on the far periphery during those glory days in New Britain. Despite his slender stature, Dalkowski had big hands, gangly limbs, and a nasty whipping motion to his delivery. Even though he didn't receive much instruction from his Little League coaches, the buzz around town was the kid could throw. By eighth grade, his father didn't dare play catch with him anymore. Junior's fastball was too hot to handle. In fact, it was fast and getting faster, and the general consensus soon became to leave well enough alone. The kid had the gift and soon nobody could remember a pitcher from their part of the world throwing as hard as Dalkowski.

The left-hander made his first high school start in the spring of 1955, his sophomore year. He gave up seven hits against Bristol, a respectable showing. Those seven hits would be the most Dalkowski would give up until the final game of his high school career against Hartford Bulkeley—when he made his second appearance on the mound in three days.

Early in his junior year, in a game the local newspaper billed as "the great battle of southpaws," Dalkowski lost a 1–0 decision to Hartford Public's Pete Sala. Sala was impressive, striking out 17. But

Dalkowski, in a losing effort, fanned 20. After he struck out 20 more in his next start, New Britain had itself a new local hero.

Crowds of 700 or more began to look on at Walnut Hill Park, the ballclub's home field. The crowds continued to swell after Dalkowski fanned 20 batters for the third consecutive game, this time against Hillhouse of New Haven. But Hurricanes fans also suffered from "nervous indigestion," according to local newspaper accounts, as Dalkowski also walked 13 that day. Soon his pitching line read like a misprint. Hits were inconsequential to nonexistent. Strikeouts and walks were sky-high—two stats that for Dalkowski would become forever linked.

After Dalkowski finished his junior year by fanning "only 13," he headed directly to the American Legion season. It was there that the issue of control became a major concern. In his first game that summer, Dalkowski allowed only one hit. But he walked eight and had five wild pitches. When he could put the ball over the plate, though, nobody could lay a bat on it.

In his second start for the Eddy Glover Post team, Dalkowski struck out 26. In the 8–0 victory, he gave up only one hit. Four days later, he was even better—pitching a no-hitter against Bristol. He struck out 21 and walked only five.

The following week, against league-leading Southington, it appeared that Dalkowski would lose despite giving up no hits. Thanks to walks and wild pitches, Southington held a 1–0 lead going into the final inning. But after a teammate singled, Dalkowski came to bat and gave the opposition a taste of its own medicine. He worked a walk and eventually came around to score the winning run. Dalkowski had now pitched back-to-back victories, and both were no-hitters. He fell just short of recording three consecutive no-hitters when he lost the next game, 1–0, allowing a lone hit.

"It was easy then," Dalkowski remembers. "It was like just handing the catcher the ball. If I didn't strike out 18 a game, it was a bad day."

Back in the 1950s, high school sports weren't that far removed from Bob Feller's era. Spring and summer were for baseball, winter for basketball, and in the autumn football was the game. Athletes, no matter how much they excelled in a particular sport, rarely focused on it year-round. So, it wasn't that far-fetched when Dalkowski was named to the National High School All-America team in football, too. Still, he knew his future was in baseball. Just before his senior season, he told a local reporter that he planned to attend Seattle University, but only if he didn't sign a major-league contract.

On April 16, 1957, New Britain was scheduled to open a new season at Walnut Hill Park against East Hartford. Of course, coach Billy Huber wanted to go with his ace, Dalkowski. But in the days leading up to the game, Dalkowski was reportedly "below par," suffering from a cold.

"He hasn't been feeling well," Huber told the *New Britain Herald*, "but I'm fairly certain he'll be pitching this afternoon."

For a pitcher who was under the weather, Dalkowski served notice that his senior year would be one to remember. Remarkably, he delivered a no-hitter against East Hartford, striking out 20. Along the third-base line, fans stood several rows deep. Afterward, in newspaper accounts, park officials were chided for not having enough bleachers set up to accommodate everybody.

Among those attending his games were scouts from a dozen or more major-league teams. They included some of the best in the business—Fred Maguire of the Red Sox, Bill Enos of the Athletics, and Frank "Beauty" McGowan of the Orioles.

A handsome man with silver-gray hair, McGowan was known for being a fashion plate and a fine judge of baseball talent. After playing for three teams as an outfielder in the majors, he had become a key man in the Orioles' scouting department. The ballclub was known for doing its homework and during its heyday signing such major-league stars as shortstop Mark Belanger, catcher Andy Etchebarren, infielder Davey Johnson, and pitchers Dave McNally, Darold Knowles, and Jim Palmer. Still, the Orioles weren't opposed to rolling the dice on this hard-throwing, yet unassuming prospect.

Even in pitching a no-hitter on Opening Day, Dalkowski exhibited traits that would eventually test the best professional coaches and instructors. Even though Dalkowski had the game well in hand (there were only three putouts by Hurricanes outfielders), he did get the local crowd buzzing in the middle innings by throwing a ball 10 feet over a batter's head. "But to fans who have followed his high school career closely, the promising major league prospect showed more polish," the *Herald* read the next morning. "For one thing he did not seem to be striving to 'blow down' every batter."

A week later, against Weaver High School, before another large crowd at Walnut Hill, Dalkowski recorded his second consecutive no-hitter. What he had done the previous summer in American Legion play was indeed a harbinger for the high school campaign. He had plenty of speed. Now could he only harness it?

"The whole town's talking about the Dalkowski boy, and it's easy to understand," read the lead sports story in the *Herald*. "In pulling his Johnny Vander Meer act before the largest crowd to see a high school baseball game here in years, Steve had all kinds of control trouble and issued 11 walks, hit a batsman and uncorked a wild pitch."

During the game, *New Britain Herald* sports columnist John Wentworth remembered talking with an old-timer behind home plate when Dalkowski "cut loose with a torrid fastball," which eluded catcher Bob Barrows and hit up against the wire-mesh screen behind home plate.

"Looks to me," the old-timer told Wentworth, "as though the boy needs to be tamed down just a might. He's got a live pitch though, hasn't he?"

Due to wild pitches and walks, the game, which started at 3:30 p.m., didn't end until 6:45. Still, observers said that Dalkowski didn't appear fatigued and was throwing just as hard to the final batter as he did to the first.

Any chance of a third consecutive no-hitter soon ended in the next game against New London. In the third inning, after walking a man, Dalkowski gave up a home run to deep left-center field. In the return match against New London, though, he gained a measure of revenge. Before 800 fans and scouts now representing every major-league team, he struck out a state-record 24 batters in a 5–0 shutout victory. In giving up four hits, Dalkowski threw 123 pitches. Of course, today, in the age of pitch counts, no major-league prospect would be allowed to throw anywhere close to that many pitches.

In his senior year, the Hurricanes finished with a 9–5 record, good for second place in the Capital District Conference. Dalkowski's high school career included two no-hitters, four one-hitters, and six two-hitters. In three seasons, he struck out 311 and walked 181.

"The walk figure is clearly indicative of Dalkowski's need to better his control," wrote Ken Saunders, another local columnist, "but this may come as he gets more experience in fast company."

For good or ill, fast company was certainly on the horizon for Dalkowski. The night of his high school graduation, when he became officially eligible to sign a big-league contract, every ballclub except the Cleveland Indians had a scout visit his home. Dalkowski decided to go with McGowan and the Orioles, due in large part to the amount of money the team offered him under the table. Back in 1957, major-league teams were prohibited from officially offering a prospect more than $4,000. Of course, the Orioles offered that, plus a new Pontiac car and at least $12,000 more under the table. Years later, Dalkowski claimed that amount was $40,000.

"When I signed Steve in 1957, he was a shy, introverted kid with absolutely no confidence," McGowan later told pitcher-turned-writer Pat Jordan. "Even in high school he walked everybody. But we gave him a $4,000 bonus, the limit at the time, because [Orioles pitching coach] Harry Brecheen said he had the best arm he ever saw. Everyone knew it was a gamble, but we all thought it was worth it."

Of course, the Rays have far more invested in David Price these days. About $8 million. With so much on the line, plenty of folks were keeping an eye on him at the start of the 2009 season, and few were as knowledgeable or as experienced as pitching coordinator Dick Bosman. An 11-year journeyman in the majors, Bosman once threw a no-hitter against Oakland and posted the American League's best ERA in 1969. But he never threw anything that came close to Price's stuff.

"When guys have good arms," he says, "you generally sit up and take notice because of the way the ball comes out their hand. By that I mean that it has life. The ball sizzles a little bit. It's not only fast, but it moves. David's ball has all those things."

By spring 2009, Bosman had seen the promising left-hander pitch as much as anybody in the Rays' organization. During the season, Bosman travels between the Rays' four full-season minor-league teams and three short-season ballclubs. He first witnessed Price in action almost two years before—back when the phenom arrived in the Rays' minor-league system. His immediate reaction? "He was mature beyond his years."

Unlike most pitching prospects, Price could already throw a two-seam and a four-seam fastball. The two-seamer will tail or run away from right-handed hitters, while the four-seamer will bear in upon a batter's hands. Not only had Price mastered both variations of the fastball; he had a good idea of when to throw them, too.

But what really got Bosman's attention was Price's delivery. In baseball terms, it was "clean," meaning it had few cricks or contortions as he threw the ball to the plate. Bosman, who often watches the Golf Channel in his hotel room after another long day at the diamond, compares the motion with Tiger Woods's golf swing. Both are efficient and able to be easily fine-tuned because they're "relatively simple in nature."

That said, Price had plenty of obstacles to overcome. Not only was there plenty of competition to make the Rays' staff coming out of spring training, but there was concern about how many innings Price could realistically pitch this season at the big-league level. The previous two years he had thrown about 120 innings. A regular spot in Tampa Bay's starting rotation would see that workload approach 200 innings. "That increase for anybody," Bosman says, pausing for the right words, "is something you'd rather not do."

Although Bosman says Price "went through the [Rays'] minor league like Sherman through Atlanta," a list of things to work on awaited the young phenom as the new season began. They ranged from gaining better control of his slider to knowing the correct situation to throw his changeup. Despite Price having one of the best fastballs to come along in some time, Bosman wasn't interested in working on an increase in Price's velocity. In fact, the more he saw the young phenom pitch, the more he became convinced that Price's stuff moved best in the mid-90s, not when he approached 100 miles per hour on the radar gun.

"There's something to learn and something to accomplish at every level, especially spring training," Bosman says. "David did a great job in the big leagues last year, but we all know that the pitcher has the advantage the first time around. When you're honking it up there at 96, 97 miles per hour and doing it from the left side, that's a pretty good advantage the first time around.

"But if you're going to go out there and face a lineup three or four times a game, you're going to need more than a fastball to do that. I don't care how hard you throw. Hitters can tune it up a little bit and they're going to get to you. You need other weapons. You need to know exactly what you're doing out there. That's something that hasn't changed since forever in this game."

One of the things I love about baseball is that so many great players come from such mythical-sounding small towns straight out of Americana. Bob Feller was from Van Meter, Iowa; Lefty Grove from Lonaconing, Maryland; and Walter Johnson from Humboldt, Kansas. It reminds me of the scene from *The Natural* where the train stops in the middle of nowhere and a young buck, somehow played by Robert Redford, steps out of the shadows and shuts down the big-time slugger. It seems as if the next great arm is out there amid the rows of corn, as elusive as the ghosts in *Field of Dreams*, ready to stride to the mound, if only we can find him . . . and sign him to a long-term deal.

Nolan Ryan was another fireballer who seemingly came out of nowhere. He was born in Refugio, Texas, and his family moved to nearby Alvin, Texas, when he was six weeks old. Located almost midway between Houston and Galveston, Alvin has become more suburban outpost than small town since Ryan's upbringing in the years after World War II. Even Ryan, its most famous favorite son, admits that the weather in Alvin can often be lousy and the place can be thick with mosquitoes and humidity during the summer. Rain and hurricanes can plague it during the winter months. But for Ryan no place was better suited for his development as a person as well as a big-league pitcher.

"I never found a place where I wanted to live more than Alvin," Ryan wrote in his autobiography, *Throwing Heat*. "I guess if I were a member of the Chamber of Commerce, I'd have trouble selling the place. . . . [But] for me it's where my roots are, where I've always been. It's home."

Alvin had a population of about 5,000 when Ryan was growing up there. The town would close up tight by 10:00 p.m., and Ryan later compared it to the backdrop of *The Last Picture Show*—the kind of place where it's early to bed, early to rise, and everybody knows everybody else's business.

Ryan's father, Lynn Nolan Ryan, worked in the oil industry. Other dads grew rice or raised cattle, and pretty much all the moms stayed at home. The Ryan homestead was a four-bedroom on Dezo Drive, where Ryan was the youngest of six children. When it was time for his two older sisters to head off to college, the family was in need of extra cash, so Ryan's father got a second job delivering the morning paper, the *Houston Post*. Much more is made now of how to raise a bona fide sports superstar. Of course, Woods was swinging a golf club right out of diapers. Up in Canada, kids begin to skate as soon as they can walk, with their parents daydreaming about their offspring being the next Bobby Orr or Wayne Gretzky. But Ryan's father never pushed sports. Sure, he and the other dads in town helped lay out the first ball fields in Alvin, one of which now sports Nolan's name. But things had a more serious purpose back then. When that second job, folding and delivering the *Houston Post* papers at 2:00 a.m., needed to be done, it was decided that young Nolan should tag along. At an abandoned Sinclair service station in town, Ryan folded papers from two to three in the morning and then headed back home to grab a few more hours of sleep before school.

"I got quite an education," he said in his autobiography. "Oh, there'd be an occasional drunk staggering by from out of the pool hall down the street. . . . And I'd see skunks crawl out of the drainage system to eat the popcorn that people dropped coming out of the movie."

Beginning in second grade, Ryan rolled papers until he was 14 and was old enough to drive and have a route of his own. The family distributed the paper until Ryan was out of high school. Later on, some would claim that Ryan's longevity and strength throwing a baseball came from flipping those papers out the window of his 1952 Chevy in the early-morning hours. Unfortunately, that myth was disproved when Ryan later revealed that he used his left hand, not his pitching arm, to peg those papers. That said, Ryan did reveal in his autobiography that he was able to roll and tie 50 newspapers in five minutes. That kind of exercise had to result in strong wrists and fingers.

"When I was in ninth grade, they had the President's Physical Fitness tests. It was really a joke because it had little to do with physical fitness," Ryan recalls. "You ran 40 yards, did X number of push-ups, sit-ups, and one of the deals was softball toss. So we go out to the football field, with no warm-up, no nothing. It was here it is, just throw it. I threw it 309 feet. I'll never forget that number."

He adds, "As a kid, I could always throw the ball farther than anybody else. But my velocity was no different than the top four or five kids in Little League. I was not a standout in Little League.

"Then I hit my last growth spurt as a sophomore in high school. That was the first year in high school back then. I went to baseball practice right after the basketball season ended. All of a sudden, it was like I had a different arm."

Growing up Ryan played baseball and basketball, but in talking with him, you almost get the sense that sports in his family were a definite afterthought. They certainly weren't regarded as a ticket to stardom, even when he began to throw with much greater velocity. Ryan, like Steve Dalkowski and others, began turning heads by his sophomore year in high school. Perhaps that's one factor that remains the same through the years—if you aren't making waves by early high school, a college scholarship or a big-league contract probably isn't in the offing. Certainly there are exceptions. Billy Wagner and Kevin Brown are two pitchers who gained speed in their fastball later on. But such cases are unusual. By the time Ryan was 16, it was acknowledged that he was the fastest pitcher in and around Alvin. He couldn't get the ball over the plate half the time, but the speed was apparent to anybody who was really watching.

Incredibly, not many were. Unlike Dalkowski, whose high school games had dozens of big-league scouts in attendance, Ryan had basically one guy in his corner back then—John "Red" Murff. In March of 1963, Murff was working for the lowly New York Mets. He had left the Houston Colt 45s and was pretty far down the baseball totem pole. After pitching in 26 games in the mid-'50s for the Milwaukee Braves, he had become a bird dog: a guy who beat the bushes for talent and tried to convince the higher-ups that what he found had some merit.

Murff's Saturday morning had begun in Galveston and he had about an hour to kill before another game that evening in the Houston area. There was a high school tournament going on in Alvin and Murff decided to stop by. There was only one other scout in attendance, Mickey Sullivan from the Philadelphia Phillies. Murff can't remember the name of the team Alvin High was playing—it was either Clear Lake or Clear Creek—but he'll never forget the tall, lanky right-hander he saw on the mound that day for Alvin.

"You almost hear that ball explode," Murff later recalled.

Other than the fastball, the kid didn't have much. The first batter he faced hit a double to right-center field off an awful hanging curve. Still, that fastball was something. In it, Murff saw glimmers of the gift, something that cannot be taught.

He asked Sullivan who the kid was.

"Nolan Ryan," Sullivan replied. "He doesn't have too much, does he?"

Murff bit his tongue and agreed with Sullivan. Yes, indeed, the kid had a lousy breaking ball.

A few weeks later, Murff found himself at Colt Stadium in Houston for several major-league games between the home team and the visiting Cincinnati Reds. The 45s' Turk Farrell and the Reds' Jim

Maloney were both hard throwers, with fastballs supposedly in the mid-90s. But as Murff watched them work, he realized the skinny kid he'd seen back in Alvin may have been even faster. From then on there was no arguing the scout off this point, and certainly there were many in the Mets' organization who tried to do just that. For Red Murff, Nolan Ryan had the goods, and he was going to do his best not only to sign the kid, but also to protect him.

As Ryan's sophomore year came to an end, Murff paid a visit to Alvin High School. He told Jim Watson, the baseball coach, that he had 1 of the 10 best arms in the country on his team. On his third guess, Watson finally realized that Murff was talking about Ryan.

Murff convinced Watson to keep the kid away from the weight room in the off-season. He was afraid that if Ryan bulked up, the velocity on his fastball would suffer. In addition, Murff asked Watson not to send in the school's scores to the Houston papers.

"What's the point of that?" Watson asked.

That kind of attention would hurt Ryan's concentration, Murff told him. Of course, keeping the scores from being called in to the big city newspaper was also a ploy that would help Murff keep the young prospect under wraps. While Watson agreed to keep Ryan away from the weight room and the scores strictly hush-hush, he couldn't quite fathom what Murff saw in the lanky young pitcher.

"Nolan didn't have any idea where the ball was going, but he didn't exactly have to thread the needle back then," Watson said years later. "Those kids were so scared, they'd swing at anything just to get out of there. Once he broke a player's wrist, and once a kid just refused to come up and hit against him. He'd average fifteen, sixteen strikeouts sometimes in those seven-inning games.

"In Texas, back in the '60s, football was king. We only played baseball because the state made us. The major leagues to us in Alvin were a million miles away."

Ryan saw how wide that chasm was when he went to a game in Houston and saw Sandy Koufax pitch. He came away amazed by how fast the Dodgers left-hander was. How sharp that curveball was. The idea that he could do the same thing someday seemed downright ridiculous. But through it all, Red Murff believed. He assigned Robert "Red" Gaskell, who lived in Texas City and had some extra time on his hands, to attend every one of Ryan's games. He was to report back to Murff about the games Murff couldn't see in person. And more importantly, he needed to alert Murff if any other scouts came around. Scouts for other organizations did occasionally pass through town, but none showed any genuine interest in Ryan.

"Back then, I was 6-2 and weighed 150," Ryan says. "But Red Murff did his homework. He talked to my dad, who was a big man, and learned about my family history. He knew I'd fill out, but the rest of them didn't think so. Red thought outside the box and stuck up for me."

As for that promising speed? Why didn't that make for more believers?

"There were no radar guns—I didn't know how fast I was. I was so wild," Ryan says. "I was just a kid with a great arm. I didn't know what I had. No one did—only Red Murff."

Ryan remained below the radar well into his senior year at Alvin. That's when Bing Devine, the Mets' assistant to the team president, made a special trip to south Texas to see him pitch. The timing couldn't have been worse for an audition. Watson's club had lost back-to-back 1–0 games, and as a consequence the coach first had his ballplayers run wind sprints and then forced them to face Ryan, wild as ever, in a team batting practice. It wasn't until this day of penance and contrition was winding to a close that Murff got in touch with Watson. Devine would be in town tomorrow, he told the coach, and Ryan had to pitch.

At first, Watson told Murff there was no way. Between the wind sprints and the extra pitching session, Ryan was spent. Couldn't they do it another time? But Devine was only going to be in town one day. Ryan just had to go, Watson said. And the high school coach reluctantly agreed.

Ryan's outing the next day was one of the worst of his high school career.

"Well, Ryan pitched and he was bad," Devine later told Harvey Frommer. "He just had a miserable day. We didn't have radar guns in those days, so we relied on the scout's eye and his personal analysis of how hard a pitcher threw. The way I checked to see if a pitcher threw hard was to see if the opposing hitters made contact at all, if they even hit foul balls.

"If the hitters at that level of play made contact, then you realized that the pitcher wasn't as fast as he appeared. Not only was Ryan wild that day, but the other team hit the ball. The team made considerable contact."

Afterward Ryan was disconsolate, thinking he had blown his big chance. He had only pitched into the third inning and left the game trailing 7–0.

Devine departed with Murff, heading back to Houston and the airport. Murff remembers the traffic was terrible and both men were in a foul mood. Finally, the scout asked Devine, "What do we do now? You gonna knock me out of the box?"

"You've been seeing this fellow for three years in high school. You know what he can do," Devine replied. "Obviously I won't be able to corroborate your great report when we sit at a meeting up there in New York City and set up our list of draft choices. But I won't fight it. I'll just say that Red Murff says Ryan is better than I saw him, and he undoubtedly is."

In the weeks that followed, the Mets went a step further. They sent Murff around the country to see five of the other top arms coming out of high school. Just to make sure that old Red wasn't sipping too much of the Kool-Aid. But even after his tour, Murff maintained that none of the other pitchers he had seen compared to one Nolan Ryan. The kid from Alvin, Texas, remained on the team draft board, and the Mets ended up taking him in the 12th round, the 295th player taken overall. That's a long way off from the maximum bonus money allowed, more illicit cash under the table, and perhaps a new Pontiac, blue with a racing stripe, thrown in to boot.

While Ryan was initially disappointed at how far he had fallen in the draft, Murff told him it was OK. At least the young phenom was in the game now.

If Steve Dalkowski's contract signing resembled an auction, Ryan's occurred with a curious tension. Despite his being a low draft pick, the Mets put together a $30,000 package, with incentives. As part of the negotiations, the Ryan family had allowed a local sportswriter, Steve Vernon, to sit in. He was supposed to be a fly on the wall, staying silent on the big signing day. But when Ryan hesitated to sign the contract, it was Vernon who finally blurted out, "What's the matter with you, boy? You crazy? Sign!"

With that Ryan finally put pen to paper, and his professional career was under way.

S teve Dalkowski was scared to death when he left his home in New Britain, Connecticut, at the age of 18. On the train trip down to Kingsport, Tennessee, where he had been assigned in the Orioles' minor-league system, he stared out the window, watching the landscape fade from small-town New England, roaring past the big cities of the Northeast Corridor—New York, Philadelphia, Washington. There were two things he couldn't get out of his mind. One was the color of the very land itself. As he went further south, it became reddish-brown, almost the color of dried blood. This red-dirt clay was so unlike where he had grown up. The other thing that rattled around in his head was that if he was so good, could throw so hard, why were the Orioles sending him so far away from Baltimore, where the big-league team played?

Of course, Dalkowski was a long way from being ready to play in the major leagues. But consider how much has changed since Dalkowski and so many other young prospects were signed a generation ago. Today the latest phenom is routinely coddled and pampered to the point that it riles the old-timers.

"It's a world apart from what we went through," says Jerry Coleman, who was a second baseman in the majors from 1949 to 1957 and later became the radio voice of the San Diego Padres. "After a while, they finally figured out that the well of talent wasn't bottomless. That you better be careful with the arms you sign and develop what you have."

Indeed, the concept now extends throughout most organizations in baseball. Visit the academies in Venezuela or the Dominican Republic, and the players' dorms or barracks often resemble the chain hotels. The kind that a lucky prospect could call home in Great Falls, Montana, or Modesto, California. Lessons in English are often mandatory, and some recruits can even gain their high school diploma while training for baseball. In Dalkowski's era, it was much more sink or swim. A Darwinian situation where the players had a lot of down time and little guidance.

His rookie year, at Kingsport, Tennessee, Dalkowski learned how to chew tobacco, struck out 19 batters in a game he lost, and led the league with 39 wild pitches. Seeing that Kingsport was a dry town, he caught rides across the state line to get his beer. It was also in Kingsport that the legend of his wildness gained a new chapter.

One night an opposing hitter was crowding the plate and a Dalkowski fastball sailed up and in, striking him on the side of the head. Legend has it that the pitch tore off part of the batter's ear. Filmmaker Tom Chiappetta, who has spent a dozen years putting together a documentary about Dalkowski, doesn't believe that the story is true.

"The guy he hit was named Bob Beavers and he played for the Bluefield Dodgers," Chiappetta says. "From what I understand Mr. Beavers's ear may have been nicked, but it was still pretty much intact."

Beavers went to the hospital with a concussion, however, and soon retired from baseball. John-William Greenbaum, a student at Indiana University who has done extensive research on Dalkowski's career, says the errant pitch caught Beavers "just above the right ear," splitting the cartilage. "There was a lot of blood," Greenbaum says. "From what I'm told there was a pretty serious scar. But if it took anything off, it was a very small amount of flesh."

After the beaning, Dalkowski was so distraught that when he returned to the clubhouse he threw his glove out the window. Later, he visited Beavers at the hospital and told him how sorry he was.

"From that point on, Steve became frightened of killing somebody with a pitch he threw," Chiappetta says. "I'm sure it changed him just enough, so he had difficulty moving forward as a professional ballplayer from that point forward."

Dalkowski went 1–8 in his rookie year of professional ball, with 121 strikeouts, 129 walks, and an ERA of 8.13.

During the 2008 season, the Yankees eventually fell out of contention in large part because their young pitchers didn't come through. Ian Kennedy, Phil Hughes, and Joba Chamberlain were either injured or struggled under all the attention that comes with being in the Big Apple. Of course, Chamberlain is considered the kind of prospect who could one day blossom into the next Bob Feller or Nolan Ryan. He throws in the upper-90s, and with his cap pulled down low—a look of indifference at times bordering upon genuine dislike upon his face. Chamberlain's the kind of pitcher batters begin to have nightmares about. But for Chamberlain, the 2008 season was more of a disappointment than a star turn.

Chamberlain was moved from the bullpen, where he had experienced success as the setup man for Yankees closer Mariano Rivera, to the starting rotation in large part because there were so many openings there. With the exception of right-hander Mike Mussina, the New York rotation was a patchwork job at best. In 2009, as Chamberlain struggled in his new role and eventually returned to the bullpen, I found myself thinking about Ryan. In many ways, Chamberlain's experience echoed what "the Express" went through.

"Playing in New York, Boston, big markets like that, demands a different mind-set," Yankees catcher Jorge Posada says. "You have to be careful. You can get sidetracked so easily."

In fact, Posada and Rivera, two guys who have been a pitcher-catcher battery since the minors, still take it upon themselves to talk shop the day after any of Rivera's relief appearances.

"You'd think because we've known each other for so long," Rivera says, "that we wouldn't need to do that. But it's still a requirement."

"If not, if we don't talk pitches, what we just did, how Mo's arm is feeling," Posada added, "the next thing you know you're out there, in front of another full house, trying to communicate at this high level. Without those regular meetings, talking honestly even after a bad outing, the big successes don't happen as much."

After talking with Posada and Rivera, I found myself wondering why we prepare prospects from outside our borders better than we do the kids signed closer to home. In my travels to the Dominican Republic especially, which is now the biggest exporter of raw baseball talent to the U.S. major leagues, I'm often surprised how little is left to chance.

Between the major-league and Japanese professional teams, there are 30 or so baseball academies now in the Dominican Republic. Most are modeled, in large part, on Days Inns or Holiday Inns. The effect can be jarring. Dirt roads in the jungle dead-end at vast complexes with emerald-green fields and residence hotels that would be at home off any U.S. interstate. The equipment and playing surfaces surpass most situations found in the U.S. inner cities. In addition, prospects from the Dominican Republic and Venezuela are usually required to hit the books, taking English lessons several hours a day. One could argue that the formal education they receive at the baseball academies exceeds what's available in the regular schools down the road.

"Even if baseball never works out for them," says Junior Noboa, a former big-league ballplayer now operating an academy in the Dominican Republic, "I'd argue that they're better off because of the time they spent here."

Compare that with the philosophy that was prevalent during Dalkowski's, even Ryan's time. After signing with the Mets, Ryan took his first airplane flight to Marion, Virginia, in the rookie Appalachian League. In the summer of 1965, he pitched in 13 games, going 3–6. He struck out 115 in 78 innings. For Ryan, like Dalkowski, control became a constant issue. Ryan walked 56 and hit eight batters. After spending the winter with the Mets' instructional league in St. Petersburg, Florida, he was promoted to Class A ball in Greenville, South Carolina. There his control was as lousy as ever. In fact, in one game a pitch sailed on him and plunked a woman leaning against the screen behind home plate. The errant throw broke her forearm. The woman was a season ticket holder and asked for a new perch a row farther back in the stands.

She wasn't the only one afraid of Ryan's wildness. In going 17–2 that season, Ryan recalled that the "hitters helped me out by swinging at a lot of bad pitches. As far as learning to pitch, I made little progress."

That didn't stop the Mets from promoting their phenom, a kid who was being compared to Koufax in terms of sheer velocity, to their Class AA team in Williamsport, Pennsylvania. There he struck out 35 batters in 19 innings. But Ryan also sent his catcher to the sidelines with a concussion after another wild one got away. A game against Pawtucket typified how much potential Ryan had and, unfortunately, how far he still had to go. Twice Pawtucket base runners stole home en route to a 2–1 victory over Williamsport, a game in which Ryan struck out 21 and somehow still lost.

The parent club didn't seem overly concerned by such inconsistency, though. On September 1, the date prospects are routinely called up from the minors for the last month of the regular season at the big-league level, Ryan flew to New York to join the Mets. He was only 19 years old. He had spent all of 14 months in the minor leagues. He was regarded as a thrower rather than a pitcher. But none of that really seemed to matter to those in charge. Ryan had the gift of epic speed. All the rest—throwing his fastball for strikes, finding complementary pitches, learning how to challenge major-league hitters—would have to work itself out along the way. If not, Ryan would return to Alvin and another kid pitcher would take his roster spot.

In 1966, there were several constants in the game. One was that the Mets, Ryan's new team, were a pretty lousy bunch. Not a single position player batted above .300. Few of the pitchers came close to having a winning record.

The other story line was the weird symmetry that often comes into play with baseball. Ryan's first year in the majors was the last time around the block for Sandy Koufax, the legendary southpaw with the Los Angeles Dodgers. It was Koufax who once said that "every pitcher's best pitch is the fastball. It's the fastball that makes the other pitches effective. While they are looking for the breaking pitch, the fastball is by them." In 1966, the legendary left-hander led the National League in victories (27), ERA (1.73), games started

(41), and complete games (27). He was less than a year removed from his epic perfect game, which is detailed in Jane Leavy's *Sandy Koufax: A Lefty's Legacy*. Due to arthritis in his pitching arm, the 1966 season would be his last.

Of course, Ryan had followed Koufax's career since seeing him pitch in Houston several years before. In his autobiography, Ryan noted how Koufax "went out in a blaze" that final year. In hindsight, the plot makes perfect sense: one hero stepping away and a new one coming onstage. But Ryan's rookie year, he was a long way from such heights. It would have been like a young politician looking up at Mount Rushmore and daring to believe that his face would one day be chiseled alongside those of Washington, Jefferson, Lincoln, and Teddy Roosevelt.

Ryan's first big-league appearance came in relief on September 11, 1966, against the Atlanta Braves. He served up a home run to Joe Torre and got his first strikeout (Pat Jarvis, another rookie pitcher). Afterward, Hank Aaron said Ryan had one of the best fastballs he had ever seen. While such praise may have flattered some rookies, Ryan found himself troubled by Aaron's comments. After all, it was one of his fastballs that Torre had smacked well over the outfield fence.

Ryan's first major-league start was a Texas homecoming in Houston, at the Astrodome. It was a disaster, with the 19-year-old lucky to last one inning. As his first full season of professional baseball came to a close, Ryan realized that he still had a long way to go.

"It dawned on me that I'd been force-fed to the Mets and that I would have to channel my abilities—be not just a thrower but a pitcher," he later wrote in his autobiography. "I really needed guidance, somebody to work with me not only on the physical approach to pitching, but also on the mental game.

"I was just out there stumbling about. If I hadn't had the ability and the determination to work to develop myself, I would've been just another one of those kids that comes along with a great arm. And two years after they sign with a major-league team they just fade out into the sunset and people ask, 'Whatever happened to that kid?' I was determined that something like that would not happen to me. I spent a lot of time observing, picking up whatever insights I could get into the art of pitching."

But such insights came few and far between on the Mets. Whitey Herzog, the team's director of player development, considered Ryan to be "a lazy Texan. He always seemed to be sleeping on the bench when I was talking."

Ryan came down with a sore arm while working out with Jacksonville in the Florida State League. Due to the injury and time spent in the U.S. Army Reserve (his unit at one point was scheduled to go to Vietnam), he didn't pitch at the major-league level in 1967. That year's highlight was marrying Ruth Holdorff, his high school sweetheart, at the Methodist church back in Alvin.

By 1968, Ryan was back in New York, and he and his bride tried to make a go of it. They started at a motel near Shea Stadium and then moved into apartment complexes in Elmhurst and later in Brooklyn. Ruth Ryan once tried to explore the city but got stuck on a crowded expressway in the rain, driving a car without working windshield wipers.

At the ballpark, Ryan kept searching for somebody to help him, especially with his control problems. He found a confidant in Tom Seaver, who had been promoted to the parent club the year before. Seaver became a good friend—the guy who first told Ryan about Walter Johnson and the Big Train's all-time strikeout record, which Ryan would eventually break.

What drove Ryan to distraction was that he threw harder than any of the other young pitchers the Mets were bringing on board— Seaver, Jerry Koosman, and Tug McGraw. But he wasn't enjoying nearly as much success. Bothered by blisters, especially on the middle finger of his pitching hand, he appeared in only 21 games in 1968, posting a 6–9 record.

"I was so frustrated that I nearly quit several times," he says. "I was ready to go back to Texas, probably go back to school. Mentally and emotionally, I wasn't into what I had to do to be a pitcher. So, I nearly quit."

Let's pause a moment and allow that comment to hang in the air like a bad breaking ball. One of the best pitchers of all time, a guy who would one day make the Hall of Fame on the first ballot, came close to walking away from the game forever. Why? Because he couldn't do right by what he had been given.

"Looking back on it, I've come to believe that if you're blessed with the ability to throw hard, you have to consider all the factors," Ryan adds. "It's a gift that you did nothing to earn. It was given to you and what you do with it is up to you. Once I realized that I said, 'Hey, this is a blessing and I'm going to take advantage of it and be the best I can for as long as I can.' Only after I decided that did I decide to stay."

Despite the frustration, there were glimmers of what could be. Ryan struck out the side on nine pitches for the first time in his career in April of that year. After that the New York media couldn't help comparing him with Koufax, Bob Feller, or the game's then current star hurler, Bob Gibson.

In a season that baseball pundits refer to as "the Year of the Pitcher," nobody was better than Gibson. The fierce right-hander for the St. Louis Cardinals posted a league-leading 13 shutouts and the third-best ERA (1.12) since the 1890s. Tommy John recalls that Gibson was so good, his stuff so nasty, that he seemed "capable of pitching a shutout every time out" in 1968.

In fact, that wasn't too far from the truth. Baseball researcher Bill Deane chronicled a stretch in the middle of that season in which Gibson threw 99 innings (June 6 through July 30) and gave up two runs. As Deane later told ESPN.com, both of those were almost flukes. One came on a borderline wild pitch, while the other was the result of a bloop double that fell inches fair.

"I went to the mound once after he'd put a couple of men on base," Dal Maxvill, the Cardinals' shortstop and a .217 hitter, later told ESPN.com. "I started to say something to him, like, 'Things are fine.' He looked me right in the eye and said, 'Get out of here. The only thing you know about pitching is that it's hard to hit.'"

Known for pitching inside, Gibson regularly intimidated batters in winning 15 consecutive games that season. His crowning achievement was striking out a record 17 Detroit Tigers in the opening game of the World Series, an accomplishment now immortalized on YouTube. Gibson allowed only one run in the first two games he pitched in the 1968 Fall Classic, setting up the Cardinals to repeat as champions. (St. Louis had defeated Boston's "Impossible Dream" team in seven games the year before.) But Jim Northrup's two-run triple, which was uncharacteristically misplayed by Cardinals center-fielder Curt Flood, made Detroit a winner in the deciding Game Seven. Still, Gibson finished with 35 strikeouts, a single-Series record.

That year Gibson won the Cy Young and Most Valuable Player awards. In the American League, the Tigers' Denny McLain did the same thing after becoming the first pitcher since 1934 to win 30 games in a season. Gibson and McLain had plenty of company for pitching honors. In total, 17 pitchers had ERAs of 2.50 or lower, with the Dodgers' Don Drysdale pitching 58 ⅔ consecutive shutout innings and the Giants' Gaylord Perry and the Cardinals' Ray Washburn tossing back-to-back no-hitters.

Such quality pitching was too much for the lords of baseball. They wanted runs and higher scores. So after the 1968 season, they shrank the strike zone. It had been from the batter's shoulders to his knees. Now it was from the armpits to the top of the knees, and the way some umpires began to call the game it was destined to shrink even further. In addition, the mound was lowered five inches. Carl Yastrzemski would later say that this last adjustment favored sinkerball pitchers and put the power pitchers, those who threw a hard fastball and curveball, at a real disadvantage.

"I know for a fact that pitchers love throwing on a high mound more than they do a lower one," legendary pitching coach Leo Mazzone wrote in his *Tales from the Mound*. "They lowered the mound in '69 because of the domination of pitching, because of Bob Gibson and Don Drysdale. Now I think you have to have an equalizer of some sort on the other side. It's favored the offense over the last few years."

Although Ryan won his first game at the major-league level in 1968, that was little more than a footnote in "the Year of the Pitcher." By 1969, Ryan was mostly pitching out of the bullpen. Seaver and Koosman were the staff aces as the Mets came from 9 ½ games back to overtake the Chicago Cubs and capture the National League East Division and later the pennant. New York mostly did it with pitching, putting up 16 shutouts. Ryan chipped in with six victories, none of them a shutout. In the year of the "Amazin' Mets," New York could do little wrong. The Mets even won a game in mid-September when Steve Carlton struck out a record 19 batters.

Ryan came out of the bullpen to win a game in the National League Championship Series against the Braves. Some in the media expected that would earn him a start in the World Series against the heavily favored Baltimore Orioles. But Ryan didn't see any action until Game Three at Shea Stadium. The Mets were ahead 4–0 when starter Gary Gentry loaded the bases with two out in the seventh inning. That's when manager Gil Hodges signaled for Ryan.

Anxious to get the ball over and not walk in a run, Ryan threw a fastball to the Orioles' Paul Blair. As soon as the ball left Blair's bat, Ryan knew it was trouble. It was deep, heading for the fence in right-center field. But Mets outfielder Tommie Agee somehow tracked the ball down, sliding onto one knee to make the grab.

"It was an amazing catch, a catch that sent a charge through all the fans at Shea," Ryan later said. "I felt like applauding, too. Agee had gotten me off the hook, and I [had] gotten away with a bad pitch."

After that bit of luck, Ryan pitched into the ninth inning, when he loaded the bases with two out. Even though the Mets still led 5–0, Hodges nearly took Ryan out. Knowing he was on a short leash, Ryan threw two fastballs by Blair again and then struck out the Orioles' outfielder with an unexpected curveball. Ryan got the save and the Mets went on to upset Baltimore for the title.

"This will be an important spring for Nolan," Hodges told reporters in spring training. "He's now on the threshold of becoming not only a good pitcher but a great one."

Yet the Mets weren't as patient as their manager. In 1970, Ryan was as frustratingly inconsistent as ever. He went 7–11 that year and 10–14 the following one as he was also required to travel to four different military bases to satisfy his U.S. Army Reserve obligations. In fact, Ryan was becoming so disillusioned with baseball in general that he again talked seriously with Ruth about quitting the game, returning to Alvin, and going into a new line of work.

After the 1971 season, Ryan returned home to Alvin. His first child, Reid, had just been born. In his autobiography, Ryan remembered that he was heading out the door to class at Alvin Junior College when the phone rang. It was the Mets with news that he had been traded to the California Angels in the American League along with outfielder Leroy Stanton and prospects Don Rose and Francisco Estrada for infielder Jim Fregosi. Fregosi had batted .233, with five home runs and 33 RBI in 107 games the year before.

In the subsequent newspapers stories, Hodges told the press he had approved the trade. His patience had run out as well. The Mets' manager added that Ryan, among all the young pitchers on his team, was the one he would miss the least.

The Stride

Bob Feller

Photo courtesy of the National Baseball Hall of Fame Library, Cooperstown, NY

I got brains. But you got talent. Your god damn left arm is worth
a million dollars a year. All my limbs put together are worth
seven cents a pound—and that's for science and dog meat.

—CRASH DAVIS, *BULL DURHAM*

Atop Hollywood producer once told me that the trick to making a memorable movie, a real blockbuster, is to have "two or three scenes people still remember days after they walk out of the theater."

"Give me those," he said, "and I can do the rest. I'll fill in the backstory and figure out the best places to shoot it, get a star or two on board. But if I don't have those two or three big scenes, it's tough to really make it work."

Maybe that's why there are so many lousy movies out there these days. Too often the so-called big scenes are ginned up with digital effects and Dolby surround-sound and offer little in terms of character or story. When we stumble upon a movie that offers a healthy slice of both, it often sticks with us far longer than anybody expected.

That's what runs through my mind as I enter the front lobby of the new Durham Bulls ballpark. I'm in town to catch up with left-hander David Price, who was sent down to Triple-A after spring training to work on his slider and changeup. What was repeated by everyone in the Tampa Bay Rays' organization was that Price possessed one of the top fastballs in the game but needed to work on his overall consistency.

Down on the field, the Bulls are caught up in team photo day and Price is posing with his minor-league teammates. Even though the imposing left-hander is expected to rejoin the parent club sometime this season, action photos of him adorn the cover of the Bulls' 2009 media guide. With some time to kill, I head for the team gift store. If in doubt, squander the time by buying trinkets, right? It's there I'm greeted by a poster of Kevin Costner, aka Crash Davis himself.

Costner has starred in his share of baseball movies: *For Love of the Game* and *Field of Dreams*. But the one flick that fans and players both agree Hollywood got right, that had more than its share of boffo scenes that would make any producer sleep like a baby at night, was *Bull Durham*. Filmed at the old Durham ballpark in 1987, its memorable moments include the scene where the team gathers on the mound to talk wedding gifts rather than game strategy. Or the quick tutorial about sports clichés aboard the team bus. Or when the wild fireballer beans the Bulls mascot on purpose.

The film's big moments often revolve around how the game is a curse to some and a gift to only a select—dare we say, undeserving—few. In *Bull Durham,* Crash Davis portrays baseball's version of Shakespeare's everyman. The guy who knows as much about baseball as anybody under the sun but will never make the majors for longer than a cup of coffee. His foil is the hard-throwing pitcher Ebby Calvin "Nuke" LaLoosh. Played by Tim Robbins, the young fireballer doesn't have a clue about the game or life in general. Yet he has an arm capable of throwing lightning bolts. To heighten the plot line, both ballplayers are determined to win the affections of the lovely Susan Sarandon.

The movie poster in the Bulls' souvenir shop details Crash's philosophy of life: "I believe that Lee Harvey Oswald acted alone. I believe that there outta be a constitutional amendment outlawing Astroturf and the designated hitter. I believe in the 'sweet spot,' voting every election, soft core pornography, chocolate chip cookies, opening your presents on Christmas morning rather than Christmas Eve, and I believe in low, slow, deep, soft, wet kisses that last for seven days." Perhaps more than any one scene, it's Crash, himself, that's so memorable. But I think the reason why so many love the movie, and identify with Crash, has more to do with an acknowledgment that life, at some basic level, isn't fair. If it were, the more deserving Crash would be the one bestowed with the stupendous fastball instead of the often clueless Nuke.

Bull Durham was written and directed by Ron Shelton. He drove to minor-league ballparks throughout the South, determining where to film. He kept coming back to the old stadium in Durham, which still stands on the north side of town.

"I loved that it was located among abandoned tobacco warehouses and on the edge of an abandoned downtown and in the middle of a residential neighborhood where people could walk," he once told the Associated Press. "In the '80s, minor-league baseball wasn't happening. Now, of course, it's huge business. I thought that it had a feel of the kind of baseball I loved—small-town, intimate, the players could talk to the fans and back and forth."

Shelton had spent several seasons playing in the Baltimore Orioles' minor-league system, beginning to play professional ball about the time Steve Dalkowski was falling out of the game. During that time Shelton heard the stories about a real-life Nuke, the unfortunate pitcher who never found a catcher like Crash Davis to steer him straight.

"It was a groundskeeper in Stockton who first told me about Steve Dalkowski, the fastest pitcher of all time," Shelton wrote years later in the *Los Angeles Times*. "'Dalko once threw the ball through the wood boards of the right field fence,' he said. The groundskeeper studied the broken boards, maintained like a shrine, and the Dalkowski stories started flowing. In minor-league ballparks all over the country, they still talk about the hardest thrower of them all."

Those tall tales included Dalkowski being so wild one night that his pitch hit the announcer's booth. Dalkowski scholar John-William Greenbaum tells me that this story "is patently false." But that didn't keep Shelton from including it in his movie. An incident where a Dalkowski pitch hit a poor fan standing in line for a hotdog became Nuke plunking the Durham Bulls mascot at Crash's urging. Perhaps the ultimate tribute by Shelton to Dalkowski was Nuke's statistical line: 170 innings pitched, 262 strikeouts and 262 walks. In real life, Dalkowski did just that for the Stockton Ports in 1960.

A s the 2009 season got under way, many in the baseball world had heard of David Price. Most wondered why he was in Triple-A Durham instead of Tampa Bay, pitching for the big-league ballclub. Such talk only grew louder when the Rays stumbled out of the gate, going 8–14 in the first month of the new season. Still, the team stuck to its plan of building up Price's innings in the minors. The powers that be had deemed he needed to work on his control and pitch repertoire.

"Just because things aren't going the way we thought they would right now, doesn't mean you blow everything up and start all over," Rays manager Joe Maddon says. "We tend to not do that."

Indeed, the Rays stayed amazingly even-keel even though they play in the American League East, arguably the toughest division in baseball. One in which the Toronto Blue Jays and Boston Red Sox were off to good starts in 2009 and the New York Yankees reveled in the hubbub of moving into their new majestic $1.5-billion ballpark. Down in Durham, Price did his best to focus on the challenge at hand.

"I know what I need to do," he says. "I cannot control when I get called up. So, you make the best of it, you know. You tell yourself to just keep working, getting better."

As Price spoke, he gazed out on the field, watching the grounds crew water down the mound and drag the infield one last time. The PA system carried the local sports talk show until the topic turned to steroids and Alex Rodriguez's return to the big leagues. Then somebody changed the station to classic rock. The gates were due to open soon, with a crowd of 6,000-plus expected. That's a decent attendance figure for a weekday night in the minors. But, of course, it's a far cry from the big leagues.

During the games, when he's not pitching, Price says that his mind can wander. He'll sneak trips into the clubhouse, where the MLB Network, the new 24-hour channel broadcasting all things baseball, is often on. Tonight the Rays are in Fenway Park, playing the Red Sox. Price knows as well as anybody that several members of Tampa Bay's rotation—Andrew Sonnanstine, James Shields, and Jeff Niemann—have struggled at times, and that if they continue to do so he could be just the guy to bolster the pitching staff. He surfs the Net daily. He knows what they're saying in Tampa—how he could be the answer to a lot of problems with the big-league ballclub.

Despite such technology constantly allowing him to be in the loop, always at the ready, on this evening in Durham the major leagues seem well over the horizon. Price agrees that perhaps he got a bit spoiled during his star turn with the Rays last fall. Of course, before that he burned through the minor leagues, going 12–1 at three levels in the Rays' minor-league system. He got used to doing things fast, being a young man in a hurry. The concept of slowing down, refining his changeup and slider, well, it can get a little old at times.

"In the majors, you never have to get up for a game," Price says. "It's always just there, whether you're pitching or not. When you come to the park up in the majors, it's so much different. Hours before the game, there are already 20,000 fans there, the place is filling up. Being down here is just different. It's just different. That's about the only way I can explain it. I cannot wait to get back up [to Tampa]."

Any time Price takes the mound, a dozen or more scouts from rival teams monitor his every move. It's a kind of joke, really. The Rays aren't looking to trade their young phenom. But the curiosity about how good this kid could be extends well beyond the Tampa organization. So, the scouts have been there to witness when he's lost focus every now and then. They saw how his fastball rarely got out of the low 90s during a loss at Norfolk. How a left-handed hitter was somehow able to turn on one of the southpaw's offerings and drove it out of the ballpark. After a month at Durham, Price's record was a rather pedestrian 1–3, with a 3.92 ERA. Although the left-hander was averaging a strikeout an inning, at least one scout wasn't all that impressed. "The kid's got to toughen up," he says. "That's what this level of baseball is all about. It all comes down to how much you want it."

Of course, that's what Crash is trying to get across to Nuke. Shelton later acknowledged that when he wrote about LaLoosh he was channeling the real-life Steve Dalkowski. Trying to wrap his mind around the question of whether the gift of such an arm "was an act of grace or just a cruel trick."

Dalkowski's fastball rose markedly from the time it left his hand until the moment it crossed home plate. So much so that the more savvy catchers who caught him, beginning in high school and on throughout his roller-coaster ride in the Orioles' farm system, often told him to aim below the batter's knees, or even at home plate itself. It was the only way to keep the heat from riding too high in the strike zone.

"Even then I often had to jump to catch it," says Len Pare, one of Dalkowski's high school catchers. "That fastball? I've never seen another one like it. He'd let it go and it would just rise and rise."

What made the pitch even more amazing was that Dalkowski didn't have anything close to a classic windup. No high leg kick like Bob Feller or Satchel Paige, for example. Instead Dalkowski almost short-armed the ball with an abbreviated delivery, which only kept opposing batters all the more off-balance and shocked at what was too soon coming at them.

"His right leg rises a few inches off the ground. His left arm pulls back then flicks out from the side of his body like an attacking cobra," Pat Jordan wrote in *The Suitors of Spring*. "There's a sharp crack as his wrist snaps the ball toward the plate. Then silence. The ball does not rip through the air like most fastballs, but seems to just reappear silently in the catcher's glove as if it had somehow decomposed and then recomposed itself without anyone having followed its progress."

For a pitch that seemed to disappear and then reappear, Dalkowski's fastball was as light as a feather to snare. This comes from the guys who caught him. Cal Ripken Sr. claimed he could catch Dalkowski bare-handed, at least when he was sure what was coming. Getting the pitch near the plate, though, was often another story. For a fastball that could often be easily corralled by a catcher's mitt, it caused mayhem when it sailed out of control.

"Ripken always said, 'If the ball left his hand belt high, you just turn and run for the screen.' It was going to sail, in other words," Steve Barber told John Eisenberg of the *Baltimore Sun*. "And if it left his hand looking like it was going to hit the ground, it was going to come in as a strike. But all his balls were so light, that was the amazing thing."

Boog Powell added, "They'd get him to hold the ball across the seams, you know, to keep the ball down. If you throw a cross-seamer with the seams, it'll sink. They had him doing that and everything else, but it was still taking off. It was something to see."

In 1958, Dalkowski began the season in the minors, at Knoxville, Tennessee. Soon he had the fans there ducking for cover, too, when three of his fastballs tore through the wire-mesh screen behind home plate.

"[The last one] went through the screen and hit a hotdog vendor in the butt and knocked him down," Dalkowski says. "Boy, was he mad."

One Knoxville dad told the fireballer he was no longer going to bring his young son to games Dalkowski started. He felt the left-hander set a poor example about how baseball was supposed to be played.

Of course, a lot of coaches at the minor-league level had bright ideas about how to harness Dalkowski's heater. One afternoon, before a night game, manager George Staller set up a square wooden target over the bullpen plate near right field and gave Dalkowski a bucket of balls. He was told to keep throwing until all the balls were inside the target.

"I shattered the bastard," Dalkowski says. "Broke it in half. And it wasn't just plywood, either. They had a boy there who was supposed to bring the balls back and he ran away."

When Dalkowski returned to the ballpark for that night's game, a crowd of ballplayers was gathered around a heap of splinters and chunks of wood—what was left of Staller's target.

Dalkowski played for three teams in the Orioles' system that season—Knoxville, Wilson (North Carolina), and Aberdeen (South Dakota). Each step was a demotion, and he didn't have a winning record at any of them. His ERA ranged from 7.93 to 12.21 to 6.39. In addition, at every stop his walk totals surpassed his strike out totals.

Early on, Billy DeMars, a former big-league shortstop who often managed the phenom, noticed that Dalkowski's plant foot often stayed on the pitching rubber well after he had released. Could this be the key to the phenom's wild streak? DeMars sincerely thought so. He believed he had found the Rosetta Stone. "Essentially he had no follow-through," DeMars later told the *(New York) Daily News.* "It was unbelievable when you think about it. This kid was throwing 100 miles per hour with his arm alone.

"I told him, 'Stevie, I'm gonna yell from the bench to let it go every time you don't follow through.' We would work on it and in the next start he walked only five batters and struck out 20. They took our pictures together in the local paper and I got quoted as saying he was the fastest pitcher I'd ever seen. I think that's how 'the fastest ever' legend got started."

Indeed, as the 1959 season got under way, Dalkowski showed promise of coming around. He pitched a no-hit, no-run game for Aberdeen, in which he tied a Northern League record with 21 strikeouts. But as soon as Dalkowski began to show signs of harnessing the gift, things fell apart. In the next game after the no-hitter, he walked the first eight batters he faced. His wild streak lasted for the next four games.

During those early years, he constantly crossed up the poor souls who had to catch him. One time it was Cal Ripken Sr., father of the Ironman. Ripken was definitely looking for something else when Dalkowski's rising fastball took off. The ball flew past Ripken's glove and hit the umpire flush in the face mask. The protective headgear shattered and the poor ump was carted off to the hospital.

"I've umpired for Koufax, Gibson, Drysdale, Maloney, Seaver, Marichal, and Gooden, and they could all bring it, but nobody could bring it like he could," umpire Doug Harvey once said of

Dalkowski. "In one season, he broke my bar mask, split my shin guards, split the plastic trim on my chest protector and knocked me back 18 feet."

Compounding the lack of any semblance of control was the company Dalkowski began to keep. Even though management warned him to steer clear of teammate Bo Belinsky, the two pitchers became fast friends. Soon they were both reassigned to Pensacola in the Alabama-Florida League. Not a good move. Belinsky was a ladies' man (he would go on to date actress Mamie Van Doren), who didn't keep regular hours.

"Bo wasn't really as bad as everyone thought," Barber told Jordan. "He was very conscientious about getting eight hours of sleep a night. He just didn't get the eight when they wanted him to."

Somehow the Orioles allowed Dalkowski and Belinsky to drive from Aberdeen, South Dakota, to their new assignment in Pensacola with a stop in Baltimore along the way. The leg to Baltimore alone took nearly a week, with the two wild-living pitchers spending several days in Chicago, hitting the strip clubs. Things went from bad to worse in Florida because that's when the pair hooked up with Barber, another hard-throwing pitcher who loved the good times.

"Bo and me were roommates in Pensacola," Dalkowski explained to Jordan. "He was going out with a girl at the time. One day, he went on a road trip with the team—I stayed behind with a cold and there was this knock on the door. It was the sheriff and the girl's mother, looking for Bo. He never came back from the road trip.

"You know what I always wonder? Bo made the big leagues and he didn't throw hard. How come? It blows my mind sometimes."

Indeed, Belinsky did make the majors, a journeyman at best. He played for five teams in eight years after breaking in with the Angels in 1962. By then Dalkowski was down to his last strike.

In 1960, Dalkowski was featured in *Time* magazine, which called him the fastest, wildest pitcher the game had ever seen. At 21, he was already a legend—often for all the wrong reasons. The Orioles tried to enforce a curfew on him to help curb his drunkenness, and his manager in Stockton, the long-suffering Billy DeMars, even took him to a psychiatrist that practiced hypnotism. None of it worked. Dalkowski set a league record for walks at Stockton (262 in 170 innings). His wildness continued the next season at Kennewick, Washington (196 walks in 103 innings). In one minor-league game, he struck out 24, walked 18, hit four batters, and lost 8–4. In another memorable contest, he finished with a one-hitter, striking out 15, but he also walked 17 and lost 9–8.

Throughout it all, the occasional guy who connected with one of his fastballs never forgot it. In a Stockton-Reno game, Dalkowski was on the verge of recording his league record 20th strikeout. At the plate was a rookie, Bobby Cox, who would go on to be the Atlanta Braves manager. Cox had struck out in his previous four at bats, and Dalkowski soon had two strikes on him. But somehow Cox connected with the next pitch, driving it out of the ballpark for a game-winning, grand-slam homer. "It's something I'll never forget," Cox says. "Hitting one off the likes of him."

B efore a night game in mid-May, at the Durham Bulls Athletic Park, David Price and I are talking in the home dugout. Almost sheepishly he admits he has never heard of Steve Dalkowski—this old fireballer I'm so excited about. Price feigns interest when I tell him about that rising fastball, how Dalko was the real-life basis for Nuke LaLoosh in *Bull Durham*. But when I begin to talk about how Dalkowski fell in with the wrong crowd, allowing his gift to be corrupted by others, I begin to sound like another jaded adult.

Triple-A baseball remains the game's best version of purgatory. Rosters are populated by two types of players: ones ascending to the sport's highest level, the major leagues, and those on their way down, probably forever. In April 2009, the Bulls' roster included Adam Kennedy, who was once a cog on the St. Louis Cardinals and Los Angeles Angels of Anaheim. Unlike topflight prospects like Price, Kennedy was fighting for another chance at the major leagues. (He soon got one after being traded to Oakland.) Target almost anybody on either team tonight, and the stakes are the same as they are in the movie: Can a guy make the last step and reach the promised land of the major leagues? Sometimes who does and who doesn't can be pretty unfair. Just ask Crash Davis.

The Bulls moved into this new ballpark before the 1995 season. The new digs sit alongside Durham's state-of-the-art performing arts center and headquarters for one of the Triangle area's television stations. Out in left field lies "the Blue Monster," a knockoff of the left field wall in Boston's Fenway Park. Atop it stands a billboard of an angry bull, standing upon a field of green grass. "Hit the Bull, Win a Steak," says the inscription. "Hit the Grass, Win a Salad." On this night, nobody comes close to either culinary offering.

Of course, the billboard is another nod to yesteryear. One like it stood in the old ballpark, where such major-league stars as Joe Morgan and Chipper Jones played. That can be a great thing about baseball. The way the past, present, even the future can be rolled into one night's experience, complete with Cracker Jack and cotton candy. Until steroids knocked the whole rig into the ditch, one could string Babe Ruth, Roger Maris, Mark McGwire, and Barry Bonds together into the same sentence, and most fans would know you were talking about the game's single-season home-run record, at one point the most cherished mark in sports. But for the guys playing Triple-A ball, history doesn't mean much, and maybe that's how it should be.

When he was growing up, David Price's first home didn't have a basketball hoop. So, by the age of three, he had dreamed up his own solitary game. With a plastic ball and bat, the youngest of three boys would hit the ball up onto the roof, often clear over the house, and then tear around to the other side to catch it. The game kept him happy for hours at a time.

"I've never seen a little kid be able to do that," recalls Debbie Price, David's mother. "He could throw that little ball up with one hand and get both hands on the bat in time to smack it up in the air at that age. We were living in a one-story ranch home back then, so we're not talking about a huge place. Still, Dave could hit that ball so hard that it would carry quite a bit. He'd run around to the other side; I remember he had to unlatch the gate to get from one side to the other side, too. Then he'd hit it back over again. The ball was one of those solid plastic ones and the bat was one of those thick red ones you'll still see in the stores.

"Our older two sons, who were both good athletes, wouldn't have been able to hit that ball until they were seven or eight years old. Here was Dave doing it by the age of three, so we knew this kid had something special here."

Even though his stepbrother, Jackie, had won a football scholarship to Kentucky State and Price's middle brother, Damon, was a basketball star in high school, David's first love was baseball.

"We always had all kinds of balls around the house," Debbie Price says, "but it was always that baseball that David gravitated toward. Typically, we'd be cleaning house on Saturdays and trying to catch up on some things. I remember having to set the timer in the kitchen and tell Dave, 'OK, I've got to clean house for 15 minutes. When the timer goes off, we can go outside and I'll throw you the baseball.' When he was little all he wanted to do was throw and hit that baseball. When that timer went off, he was coming around that corner, looking for me, ready to go outside. We did that all Saturday.

"I played catch with him until he was age 11. By then I wouldn't throw with him anymore because he threw too hard. He was 13 when my husband stopped catching with him. He was always able to throw it a whole lot harder than you'd think a kid his age could."

By the age of eight, Price was pitching to kids four years older than him. The buzz was the Price kid could bring the heat. "Since I was small, I always throw hard, harder than the other kids," he says. "I guess it was always there. It's funny, I didn't really notice it that much, but other people sure did."

Ironically, as Price made his way up the ranks, starring at Vanderbilt University, baseball became irrelevant to the African American community. In 2007, according to the University of Central Florida's Institute for Diversity and Ethics in Sports, the percentage of black players at the major-league level fell to 8.2 percent, an all-time low.

To understand how far baseball has come and how far the game still has to go at the grassroots level, especially among today's kids, the game's next generation, I accept an invitation from Phil Pote to tour inner-city Los Angeles. Pote was a pitcher and outfielder for the Los Angeles State College of Applied Arts and Sciences, now California State University at Los Angeles, in the mid-1950s. After his playing days were over, he coached at several of the Los Angeles high schools. Pote went on to become a scout for the Seattle Mariners, beating the bushes for talent in a pickup with a camper shell that occasionally blew off as he barreled down the southern California freeways.

A generation ago, Los Angeles was home to such future major leaguers as Ozzie Smith, Eddie Murray, Reggie Smith, Darryl Strawberry, and Eric Davis. A single high school, Fremont High, produced 23 major leaguers. Today, though, few scouts and fewer college coaches travel the hard streets of Los Angeles to seek out ballplayers at such high schools as Locke, Crenshaw, Centennial, Fremont, and Dorsey.

"You'll still go there," Pote says as we turn onto the freeway bound for Crenshaw High School. (I can't help glancing back at the camper shell to make sure it's still secure.) "But it's not a priority like it once was. In the old days, you didn't dare not go."

Crenshaw's open-air campus bustles with activity this morning. Nearly 3,000 kids attend this school, and Darryl Strawberry still ranks as one of Crenshaw's most famous sports celebrities. In many ways, Strawberry's star-crossed career symbolizes the promise and heartbreak of L.A. ball. If a pittance of the fame or fortune that he garnered as a member of two world champions, the Mets and the Yankees, had come home to roost, Crenshaw and inner-city baseball would be the better for it.

"But it's almost unfair to hold Darryl to such comparisons, especially now," says Willie West, the former coach of Crenshaw's prestigious basketball team. "With all the troubles Darryl has had, he's having a tough enough time taking care of himself, let alone trying to help us out."

No doubt West was referring to Strawberry once owing almost $4.5 million in back taxes, alimony, and other debts. In recent years,

Strawberry has attended the occasional football game at Crenshaw, signing autographs in the stands. During the 1994 labor meltdown, he and Eric Davis, who were teammates on a Connie Mack team in inner-city L.A., worked out at their old high schools. Still, to many kids, the ballplayers are little more than riddles. The names might be familiar, but any real recognition has long since faded.

"The vast majority have no idea what they did, how good they were," says Ken Maxey, Crenshaw High's ex-assistant athletic director. "Part of that may be the players. I suppose it's easy to blame them. But I think the whole problem goes deeper than that."

John Young, who started several youth baseball programs in South Central L.A. during the late 1970s, says the game "lost a generation of players."

"Anybody who scouted this area could see that," he adds. "The gangs had taken over the parks. Kids in this city weren't getting a chance to play. The schools that used to turn out such great talent weren't generating much of anything."

A short drive from Crenshaw lies Los Angeles's "Field of Dreams." The state-of-the-art field cost nearly $500,000 to build and hosts games almost every afternoon and night. When Pote was a kid, this stretch of land was empty fields and sandlots. Kids rode their bikes across the open space and nicknamed the area "Devil's Dip." Today, gazing out the van window, Pote surveys what has become the epicenter for baseball's revival in L.A. "It was worth the wait," he says.

If baseball intends to keep young people as part of its fan base, it must embrace its roots, especially in the inner city. "That remains our biggest challenge," says former National League President Leonard Coleman, who is actively involved in Reviving Baseball in Inner Cities (RBI), a Major League Baseball–sponsored program. "I look at cities, and I say we have to take baseball in those communities to the next level. We have to for this game to continue to grow."

Price agrees and wonders if the game may have turned some kind of corner in the 2008 World Series. Months after the Philadelphia Phillies defeated the Tampa Bay Rays in the Fall Classic, a study revealed black participation in major-league baseball had increased to 10.2 percent.

"Right now in the African American community, baseball isn't deemed very cool," Price says. "Certainly that's the case compared with basketball and football. That's why the World Series was great. I mean not just for me on a personal level, but for what it did for the game in the African American community. You had Ryan Howard, Jimmy Rollins, Carl Crawford, B. J. Upton—there was just a ton of guys out there. That's good for the game and showing fans. Many of the superstars on both teams were African American and that's great for how this game has to grow."

Price made two appearances in the 2008 World Series, pitching in relief in Games Two and Five. Certainly it wasn't as heady as getting the final four outs to clinch the American League pennant (three of those outs came on strikeouts), but he was there, a part of it all. Those are the moments that he still thinks about, admittedly a bit too much, on evenings like this at Triple-A Durham.

In spring training, Price focused on winning a place in the Rays' starting rotation and was disappointed when that didn't pan out. Now, almost six weeks later, he wonders if he made a mistake. Perhaps he should have said he was willing to move to the bullpen and taken the same direction as Jonathan Papelbon of the Red Sox, who advocated to be the team's closer when many in the front office still saw his future in the rotation. "I could have been a good starting pitcher," Papelbon explains. "But I can make the Hall of Fame as a closer."

Price nods when he hears that statement. "I'm very blessed and I know that. God has given me a gift he doesn't give to a whole lot of people, especially from the left side," he says, smiling. "As for what's best right now, I don't know. In spring training, I was focused on making the rotation, being a starter. Now I'd go back even if it meant coming out of the bullpen. I just want to get back up there."

Sometimes a change in scenery can mean everything in the world to a pitcher. Such was the case with Nolan Ryan. Moments after he was traded from the New York Mets to California, Angels general manager Harry Dalton called him on the phone. "You're the main part of my first trade and I want it to be a good one," Ryan remembers Dalton telling him. "You can be a big star with California, and we're going to give you every chance to be one. Here you will get a chance to pitch."

After struggling to land a regular turn in the Mets' rotation, that was sweet music to Ryan's ears. So, in 1972, he headed west, to the Angels' spring training camp in Holtville, California. Although the ballclub was excited to have him on board, somebody forgot to tell coach Jimmie Reese to go easy on the newcomer.

Reese ordered Ryan to take infield practice and started peppering ground balls at him. This went on for a good 20 minutes, with Reese hitting them to Ryan's left and right, until the pitcher was ready to keel over. "One more ground ball would have done it," Ryan remembers. "I was about spent."

That's when pitching coach Tom Morgan called Ryan over to pitch batting practice. Although Ryan had barely escaped with his dignity, Reese's impromptu workout had made an impression. Ryan decided he needed to be in better shape, a commitment that continued throughout the remainder of his 27-year big-league career. In addition, he and Reese became fast friends, with Ryan regularly taking infield practice with the enthusiastic coach always ready to swing the fungo bat.

"There was no quit in that guy," Reese said years later. "I could tell from the minute Nolan walked in the door, he was willing to do what it took to be a big winner in this game."

In short order, Ryan had gotten Dalton's commitment from the front office and a primer in fitness from Reese. But arguably what helped to really turn his career around was his work with catcher Jeff Torborg.

I've often found catchers to be among the most intelligent guys in the game. Joe Torre, Cal Ripken Sr., and Mike Scioscia come immediately to mind. Years ago, when I was an editor with *Baseball Weekly*, I profiled all-star catcher Tony Pena as he caught three categories of pitchers—a rookie (Mike Gardiner), a journeyman (Greg Harris), and a superstar (Roger Clemens)—on consecutive nights against the White Sox on Chicago's South Side. How Pena effectively assumed different personas, moving from a teacher in dealing with the rookie, to a drill sergeant with the journeyman, to a confidant with the staff ace, remains one of the best tutorials in business management I've ever seen.

In Torborg, Ryan found a guy who had caught Don Drysdale and Sandy Koufax in the Dodgers' organization. At their initial workouts in Holtsville, Torborg told Ryan that he was rushing his delivery.

"I've always worked hard to get the ball up there," Ryan replied. "I thought that was what helped account for my speed."

"No, Nolan," Torborg said. "When you rush your motion and you stride out too soon, your arm can't catch up and the ball gets released too soon. That's why you're wild. You're not wild side to side but wild high."

So began almost daily sessions with Ryan throwing to Torborg that the Hall of Fame pitcher would later describe as "learning to pitch all over again."

Those early days with the Angels were almost derailed by a players' strike. Torborg was the team's player representative and gathered the team, as best he could, for workouts at a playground down the road from Anaheim Stadium. That would be the first place his teammates really got a look at Ryan's live arm and, more importantly, where the refinement of his pitching motion progressed.

"When Nolan came to the Angels, he was already a legend," Torborg says. "At least his arm, how hard he could throw, was. Whether he'd ever be a winning pitcher was the question.

"He was shy but he had this physical presence, and there was no doubting what a great arm he had. But Nolan hadn't had much success with the Mets and you could tell that was bothering him. Thinking back on it, I suppose I was a bit spoiled after catching stars like Sandy Koufax, Don Drysdale, and Bill Singer earlier in my career. Right away, though, I saw that Nolan had as good an arm as any of them. The problem was his mechanics weren't there. Not yet anyway."

One of the first adjustments, and perhaps the pivotal one, that the Angels made with Ryan's delivery had to do with his lead leg and foot. This was the left one he raised in the air as he went into his motion. Torborg noticed that as Ryan tried to throw harder, the left foot came up and then too far back in the windup phase. Instead of staying square to home plate, the left leg moved past the pitching rubber toward center field. That caused Ryan to lose balance and, as a result, control.

"Ideally, you like to see a pitcher bring that lead leg back no farther than the pitching rubber," Torborg says. "Of course, every pitcher is different. But when Nolan brought that leg back past the rubber, it caused the top half of his body to open up. His control went downhill fast as he flew open in the rest of his delivery. So that's the first thing we started to work on.

"After that we began to experiment. How best to stay balanced throughout the delivery, how high the leg kick should be. You'll notice that later in his career Nolan had a higher leg kick. That's how he was able to maintain that great velocity later in his career. But all of those adjustments started back in the spring of '72."

When the two-week strike ended, pitching coach Tom Morgan was back in the mix, and the Angels officially began spring training at Palm Springs. As the exhibition schedule got under way, though, Ryan continued to struggle in game situations. Off the field, Ryan was about broke, thanks to the work stoppage. He had to borrow from a bank back home in Alvin, using his 1971 tax returns as collateral. For a time, he and Ruth lived out of a camper-trailer at the local KOA campground. Through it all, Ryan couldn't help thinking that perhaps he "wasn't cut out for the baseball line of work."

In the Angels' camp, the coaching sessions picked up steam. Now when Ryan went into his motion, Morgan began to stand a few feet in front of him and slightly off to the pitcher's left side.

"I'd never seen a coach do anything like that before," Torborg says, "but it was a brilliant move. If Nolan swung too far to the left in his follow-through, he'd literally run into Tom. With Tom standing there, Nolan had to stay square to the plate and stride straight toward the plate with that left leg. This is all small stuff and it can be exhausting to work on day after day. But Nolan was up for it. He was hungry to do whatever it took to make him a better pitcher."

Ryan adds, "That's the moment when things began to really make sense to me. Tom slowed down my delivery and then he'd stand there, just off to my left side as I threw. It was a small thing maybe, but as a result it kept my elbow up. That maintained my velocity and also helped my control.

"What it allowed me to do was to get the feeling for finishing [the delivery] in the right way. Once that happened, it soon started to make sense. All that frustration I had began to disappear. For the first time I started to believe I could do this."

As the regular season began, Ryan won his first outing, a 2–0 victory over Minnesota. By mid-May, however, his record had sunk to 2–4, and Ryan appeared to be headed back to the bullpen. That's when Morgan told manager Del Rice that he believed Ryan was about to turn the corner and that it would be best to keep him in the rotation. While the coach was probably blowing smoke, the suggestion bought Ryan a bit more time. The pitching clinics went on, with Torborg, Morgan, Art Kusnyer (the Angels' other catcher), and coach John Roseboro (a former big-league catcher) now involved.

"It was exhausting work, mechanical work, boring at times, but those days turned around my career," Ryan later wrote in *Throwing Heat*. "To accomplish anything in life you need faith and you sometimes need help. I was getting the help from those guys on the Angels, and I will always be in debt to them for caring for a young, wild-armed pitcher. I got faith from the help they gave me, and then it all started to pay off."

Ryan shut out the White Sox and a few games later three-hit the Tigers over seven innings in a close loss. He followed that up with a two-hitter against the Athletics, and by mid-season he had won 10 games. A regular man in California's rotation, he was pitching every fourth day and seemed to feed off the routine. On July 9, Ryan enjoyed the best game of his career, striking out 16 against Boston. Eight of the strikeouts came in a row, which set an American League record.

Thanks to another movie, *Von Ryan's Express*, Nolan Ryan gained a nickname—"the Express." Old-timers began to compare his fastball with those of the legends. Oakland manager Dick Williams, who had faced Sandy Koufax in intrasquad games when both were with the Dodgers, claimed Ryan was faster. "[Ryan] threw a heavy ball," Williams is quoted as saying in Ryan's autobiography. "Even his change of pace, at 85 miles per hour, was faster than most other pitchers' fastballs."

Ryan was named to the All-Star Game in 1972 and ended up leading the American League with nine shutouts and 329 strikeouts, the fourth-best total ever in the modern era (post-1900). Despite his also leading the league in walks and wild pitches, the Angels nearly doubled his salary to $54,000 for the next season.

In 1973, his second season with the Angels, Ryan quickly served notice that those sideline sessions would lead to an even bigger payoff. On May 15, against the Royals in Kansas City, he took a no-hitter into the eighth inning. An over-the-shoulder grab by shortstop Rudi Meoli kept the Royals hitless. In the ninth, it came down to Ryan against Kansas City's centerfielder, Amos Otis.

His last time up, Otis had sharply grounded out on a curveball. As a result, Ryan decided "all I'd give him this time was heat."

Otis swung and missed at the first fastball. But the second time around, he tattooed a long fly to right field. Ryan remembers the drive being "catchable." Torborg, who was back behind the plate, wasn't so sure.

"After Amos hit it," Torborg says, "I remember thinking to myself, 'What a shame. We came within one pitch of a no-hitter.'"

Yet outfielder Ken Berry, a late-inning defensive replacement, ran down Otis's ball at the warning track. Ryan had the first no-hitter of his career. As his teammates mobbed him on the mound, Torborg—who knew something about no-hit contests, having caught Sandy Koufax's perfect game—kept repeating, "That was beautiful."

A few months later, on July 15, Ryan took the mound in Detroit. Torborg was sidelined with a broken finger, and Ryan decided to call his own pitches. In fact, that would be standard operating procedure for much of the rest of the season, even when Torborg returned to the lineup.

"We devised signals in which he'd touch his cap certain ways and my signals were to help relay the signals to the infield," Torborg says. "Of course, the danger of that is that if [the catcher] doesn't pick up exactly what he's going to throw, he could kill the guy behind the plate with that fastball of his."

For this contest in Detroit, the only ones in danger were the Tigers' hitters. On the way in from the bullpen, Ryan felt so good about his stuff that he told Morgan that if he ever was going to pitch another no-hitter it would be now.

Art Kusnyer, the Angels' other catcher, mishandled Ryan's first pitch—a sharp breaking curve. When umpire Ron Luciano called it a ball, Ryan made a mental note to go with his fastball, which had plenty of pop that day.

As Ryan began to set down the Tigers in order, Detroit manager Billy Martin started to needle him. But much as he had with Luciano behind the plate, Ryan shrugged off such distractions and "just zoned in on what I had to do."

And did he ever. Ryan struck out 16 batters in the first seven innings. In the top of the eighth, the Angels batted around, breaking up a close game. Even though the big inning assured Ryan of the victory, the long time on the bench seemed to take something off his fastball. Still, he held the Tigers hitless into the ninth inning.

With one out, Gates Brown scorched a line drive. But once again shortstop Meoli was there to snare it. Detroit's hope of breaking up the no-no rested with Norm Cash. As he stepped into the batter's box, Ryan noticed that Cash wasn't exactly holding a bat in his hands. The Angels' pitcher gestured to Luciano to check it out. Upon closer inspection, the bat was determined to be a leg ripped off the snack table in the Tigers' clubhouse.

Cash, ever the wily veteran, argued with the umpire that he should be permitted to use it. The debate lasted several minutes and perhaps would have broken the concentration of another pitcher. But Ryan was sure of himself now. Several of the most flamboyant figures in the game were center stage on this day—Luciano, Martin, the showboating Tigers hitters—and none were able to get under his skin.

With the debate over, and Cash forced to swing a conventional bat, Ryan got him to pop out on a 1–2 fastball.

Some pitchers only dream of throwing a no-hitter, and Ryan had done it twice in the same season. If you believe Torborg, that amount could have been easily doubled.

"What people don't remember is that Nolan could have had two more no-hitters that season," Torborg says. "He came close against the Yankees, that's for sure. In that game, Thurman Munson hit a pop-up in the first inning that fell between our infielders because nobody called for it. The scorer called it a hit. New York didn't come close to getting another hit the rest of the day.

"The other near miss came against the Orioles. It was late in the game and Mark Belanger was up for Baltimore. Earl Weaver had him bunting on the first pitch and Belanger took it for a strike. Weaver took the bunt sign off and Belanger was lucky enough to tag the next pitch for a base hit.

"When you think about it somebody like Bob Feller had three no-hitters for a career. Nolan nearly surpassed that total in one season."

E ven though David Price isn't pitching tonight in Durham, half a dozen scouts sit in the rows behind home plate, setting up their radar guns in empty cup holders. When neither of the starting pitchers, right-hander Jack Cassel for Columbus and left-hander James Houser for the hometown Bulls, register anything faster than 90 miles per hour on the gun, they begin to talk more among themselves. Still, every pitch is dutifully recorded and filed away for reports that are sent almost daily to the parent club.

Batters are timed running to first base. An outfielder is critiqued on how well he pegs the ball to the cutoff man. But as far as pitchers are concerned, any scout worth his salt has a sweet spot for sheer velocity. So often that's the basis for quality pitching, either in the starting rotation or out of the bullpen.

In recent years, several big-league teams have turned around their fortunes by finding a pitcher or two who can throw really hard. The Detroit Tigers reached the Fall Classic in 2006 thanks in large part to Justin Verlander. Of course, the Red Sox repeated as champs in 2007—this time with Jonathan Papelbon as their closer.

"Overall, velocity among pitchers everywhere you look has been going down on average," says Rob Ducey, a scout for the Toronto Blue Jays. "That's why everybody's got an eye out for a pitcher who can bring it. Find that guy and it can mean all the difference to a team's season. A guy with a great fastball can flip things in your favor almost overnight."

To hear scouts talk, there has never been enough high heat to go around. In the 1980s, for example, the quality fireballers could often be counted on one hand—Ryan, Mario Soto, and Rich "Goose" Gossage.

"There's no question in my mind there are fewer hard throwers today than there used to be," Pete Rose complained to *Inside Sports*'s David Whitford in 1983. "We used to go to Houston and face Jim Ray, Don Wilson, Larry Dierker and Turk Farrell. Los Angeles had [Sandy] Koufax and [Don] Drysdale. San Francisco had Bobby Bolin, Gaylord Perry and [Juan] Marichal."

The list of fireballers for that era was made even shorter when J. R. Richard collapsed while playing catch before a game in the Astrodome on July 30, 1980. Richard, the first National League right-hander to strike out 300 batters in a season (303 in 1978), was rushed to the hospital. There doctors worked for 18 hours to finally remove a clot from the junction of two arteries in his neck.

"J.R. was the fastest pitcher I ever saw," says Ralph Avila, a Cuban-born scout who helped establish the Los Angeles Dodgers' baseball academy in the Dominican Republic. "He and Nolan Ryan were a step above the rest, in my opinion, and J.R. may have been a bit faster than Nolan."

Such was the state of baseball—there was a definitive power shortage in the pitching department—until Mark Langston, John Wetteland, Robb Nen, and Mark Wohlers came along in the 1990s.

In a sport that has become so scientific, the fastball remains mysterious, downright mystical. Even though professional franchises search the globe for talent, often spending millions in developing prospects, finding an authentic fireballer who can pitch at the major-league level remains elusive. "You can't teach a good fastball," says Troy Percival, who once averaged better than a strikeout an inning when he could really bring it. "You can teach a good curveball, you can teach a changeup, but you can't teach arm speed. It's a God-given ability."

As a result, anybody who has a good fastball tends to become coveted, because even in flush times there are often few such hurlers around. So no matter who's pitching, regardless of how long a track record he may have, the scouts invariably pause after almost every pitch and check the reading on their radar guns.

As a scientific concept, radar was discovered by German Heinrich Hertz in 1886. If his homeland had done a better job of developing "radio detection and ranging," or radar for short, the course of World War II might have gone much differently. Decades later, it was left to British scientists Henry Boot and John Randall to develop the "resonant cavity magnetron." This allowed radio waves to be sent out by a high-frequency transmitter. The waves would hit a distant object and bounce back to the transmitter. From there, such variables as the distance and speed of the object could be calculated.

On the eve of World War II, several countries had fledgling radar systems. In fact, there was a radar station near Pearl Harbor in Hawaii, but the technology was so new that it was dismissed on the fateful day of December 7, 1941. But as the conflict escalated, the race was on to refine radar into a defensive network against approaching aircraft. Nobody did a faster, better job than Great Britain. Radar has been credited with helping to save England during the Battle of Britain. *Newsweek* magazine reported that in August 1940, the Nazis lost 15 percent of their planes over England. In the air battle of September 15, 1940—one of the turning points of World War II—185 planes of their original 500 were destroyed. The Germans changed tactics and began to attack at night. But thanks to radar-directed night fighters and antiaircraft batteries, the new ploy failed as well.

After the war, radar moved into everyday life, notably at airports and on the highways. Law enforcement employed it to corral speeders, and that was the link that brought radar to baseball. In 1974, Michigan State baseball coach Danny Litwhiler was reading the student newspaper. One of the local headlines reading "Be Careful! Don't Speed on Campus!" was accompanied by a photo of a campus policeman pointing a modern radar gun at would-be speeders. Litwhiler immediately wondered: Could a radar gun clock a baseball thrown by one of his pitchers?

Before taking over the Spartans' program, Litwhiler had played 11 years in the majors and had a .281 lifetime average. In 1942, he became the first major-league outfielder to play every inning of every game in a season without committing an error. His glove from that season found a home in the National Baseball Hall of Fame and Museum in Cooperstown. Now another piece of equipment that Litwhiler would use would find its way there, too. He convinced the campus police to come down to the baseball stadium. Radar guns back then were far from portable. The device was powered by the automobile cigarette lighter, so Litwhiler had the police car drive out onto the field, parking it near the pitcher's mound. He had one of his young hurlers throw, and the radar gun began to pick up readings ranging from the mid-70s to the high-80s. Litwhiler contacted the company that made the radar gun, but it didn't see much potential in marketing the device to baseball. So instead, Litwhiler called the inventor, John Paulson, directly and was able to convince him to make a handheld model with a battery.

That spring Litwhiler took the portable radar gun to spring training, and Baltimore Orioles' Manager Earl Weaver "went crazy about it," he remembers. Weaver had already coached several of the fastest of the fast, including the enigmatic Steve Dalkowski and future Hall of Famer Jim Palmer. After the ballclub wouldn't authorize the $1,200 to buy one of the first radar guns, Weaver decided to take the amount out of his own pocket.

"I'd save that much in bonus money by not signing some guy who couldn't throw hard," Weaver explains. "This thing measures speed factually, without trusting to guesswork."

But if the technology was perfect, much of the debate over who was the fastest of the fast would have ended with the rise of the radar gun. By the mid-1970s, three major-league clubs were using the gun, and today almost every scout has a portable device of his own. But there is a major difference between the various manufactures. Scouts say the JUGS gun, which Litwhiler helped popularize, measures the speed of the ball soon after it leaves the pitcher's hand. The Decatur RAGUN, which soon followed in development, is said to measure the speed of the ball closer to the batter and home plate. So the JUGS gun was soon known as the "fast gun" and the RAGUN as the "slow gun." Routinely, there was a four-mile-per-hour difference between the two.

These days, most scouts use the Stalker Sport. Even though the gun is a high-powered, more consistent version of those earlier models, many believe grading baseball talent will always be a crapshoot. "I'll look around sometimes after a quality pitch and everybody will have slightly different readings," Ducey says. "Part of this whole game is still about trusting your gut, too. Realizing what you're really seeing."

Such was the case with injured catcher Cliff Blankenship. In the spring of 1907, he was sent west by Washington Senators manager Joe Cantillon. Even though Blankenship was reluctant to make such a long trip, Cantillon was insistent. He had been receiving letters extolling a young right-hander playing semipro ball in Weiser, Idaho. "This boy throws so fast you can't see 'em," read one missive, "and he knows where he is throwing the ball because if he didn't there would be dead bodies strewn all over Idaho."

Blankenship's road trip began in Wichita, where he signed a promising outfielder, Clyde Milan, for $1,250. The Senators' manager had seen Milan play the spring before on a barnstorming tour, and Blankenship confirmed that the kid had talent. (In fact, Milan would go on to be one of the best outfielders in Senators history.) After signing Milan, Blankenship was eager to return home. But Cantillon told him to first check out the young pitcher in Idaho.

Blankenship wrote a friend, as later detailed in Hank Thomas's biography, that he had "to look over some palooka who they say is striking out everybody. Probably isn't worth a dime, and I'm on a wild-goose chase for Cantillon."

When Blankenship saw Walter Johnson for the first time, however, he immediately knew that the 19-year-old was the real deal. Of course, he made his determination well before the days of the radar gun. Johnson lost the game that day, 1–0 in 12 innings, as his infielders booted a pair of grounders for the lone run. Afterward, Blankenship flashed a $100 bill, telling Johnson it was an immediate signing bonus and promising a contract that would pay the prospect $350 a month.

At first glance, Johnson had hick written all over him. He was 6-foot-1, 200 pounds, with dangling arms and, as Shirley Povich later noted, "a behind-the-plow gait." Yet when it came to negotiations, Johnson proved as adept as he was on the pitching mound. He told Blankenship that he wanted expenses to travel to Washington. Blankenship agreed. But the scout was taken aback when the kid insisted that the Senators also guarantee his train ticket home, in case things didn't work out in the nation's capital.

What Blankenship didn't know was that several other major-league clubs had been scouting Johnson as well. The Pittsburgh Pirates missed out when they wouldn't pony up for the $9 train ticket that would have brought Johnson to the team's training site in Hot Springs, Arkansas.

After some dickering, Blankenship agreed to the travel round-trip expenses and Johnson was soon en route to Washington. "Fastest pitcher since Amos Rusie," Blankenship wired Cantillon.

Anxious to take the heat off his struggling ballclub, Cantillon told the press. The story the next day in the *Washington Star,* June 29, 1907, reported that the Senators' manager "has added a great baseball phenom to his pitching staff. The young man's name is Walter Johnson."

The story went on to say that "Blankenship is very enthusiastic, but fails to state whether the great phenom is right- or left-handed."

Since the Big Train's heyday, every method imaginable has been tried to measure the sheer speed of a pitched baseball. Even

Johnson, the gold standard back in his era, was roped into demonstrating how hard he could throw.

In the closing days of the 1912 season, with the New York Giants and Boston Red Sox facing off in the World Series, *Baseball Magazine* convinced Johnson and Brooklyn's Nap Rucker, who was said to be the fastest pitcher in the National League, to travel to Bridgeport, Connecticut. There, at the Remington Arms Company's bullet-testing range, "a pitched ball was accurately measured for the first time in history," the magazine proclaimed.

The range comprised a tunnel that was shoulder height and used to calculate the speed of bullets fired from a standing position. The speed was calculated by how fast a projectile—in this case a regulation Spalding National League baseball—broke one of the myriad of copper wires at the front of the chute and then smacked into a steel plate at the rear of the shooting gallery.

"The distance from the muzzle to the plate is accurately measured," the magazine explained, "and a comparison of the time elapsing between the breaking of the copper wire and the strike of the bullet against the plate readily gives the velocity of the bullet in number of feet per second."

"It may have made sense on paper," Hank Thomas, Walter Johnson's grandson, reminds me. "But they forgot that Walter didn't throw over the top. He threw sidearm and had difficulty getting the ball to go straight through that plate with the copper wires."

Baseball Magazine reported that "after some effort and with a consequent loss of speed" Johnson was finally able to muster a reading. His best throw was clocked at 127 feet per second (86.6 miles per hour). The best Rucker could do was 113 feet per second or about 76 miles per hour.

As Thomas outlines in his biography of his grandfather, such numbers require some perspective. The best we can do is to compare them to another series of tests done two decades later. In June 1933, Lefty Gomez of the New York Yankees and Van Lingle Mungo of the Brooklyn Dodgers headed up to West Point and were tested with similar equipment. The top pitches were less than impressive, as Mungo hit 77.4 miles per hour and Gomez 75.7 miles per hour.

In 1946, Washington Senators owner Clark Griffith borrowed a cumbersome photoelectric cell from the U.S. Army post in Aberdeen in order to test the speed of the fastest pitcher of that day—the Cleveland Indians' Bob Feller. The device was used in the military to determine the speed of projectiles. "The military used that thing to test everything from bullets to shells," Feller tells me. "It was a helluva lot more accurate than what you see used in some ballparks today."

Well, maybe. In any event, Griffith heavily advertised the event and reportedly had a walk-up gate of 20,000. Unfortunately, he forgot to run the scheme by Feller.

"He never contacted me at all," Feller wrote in his autobiography. "I was on the rubbing table in the clubhouse, getting ready to warm up. Our trainer was stretching my pitching arm and legs when Mr. Griffith came in. He told me it was about time to get out there and start throwing smoke. I told him as soon as he paid me for it I would."

The Indians' ace didn't agree to the stunt until Griffith agreed to pay him $700. ("I mean I had to get something out of the deal, too," Feller recalls.) At that point, there wasn't a faster or better pitcher in the game. The wildness that had hampered Feller earlier in his career was gone and he was on his way to winning 26 games and striking out 348.

The photoelectric cell, a cumbersome cratelike framework that the ball had to be delivered through, was set up atop home plate. Before the game, Feller warmed up for about 10 minutes and then threw about five pitches through the contraption to a catcher, who squatted on the other side of the device. More than 30,000 fans sat in near silence that evening, awaiting the announcements of the specific speed levels. Feller claims that the device was able to calculate the highest average speed, as well as the velocity of the ball as it reached the framework over home plate. He says his best average speed was 107.9 miles per hour and the highest clocking at home plate topped out at 98.6 miles per hour. "That was also my body temperature when I calmed down after my showdown with Mr. Griffith," Feller says.

Steve Dalkowski was another pitcher tested by the Aberdeen equipment. He was told to throw the ball through a metal box, roughly the width of home plate, in which a laser was being beamed. Sounds simple enough, right? But as with most things surrounding the career of the unpredictable left-hander, things didn't go according to plan. Even though the mechanism and physics were similar to those in Feller's test, Dalkowski had to throw off a flat surface. At least Feller had been able to throw off a mound at Griffith Stadium. In addition, Dalkowski had pitched the night before his Aberdeen test, which some claim took 5 to 10 miles per hour off his best heat. Despite it all, Dalkowski was game to try. The season was 1958, when Dalkowski fanned 17 and walked 16, throwing 283 pitches, in a single game. At Aberdeen, it took him 40 minutes to throw anything close enough to the sensors to even get a reading. The device clocked him at 93.5 miles per hour at the target, 5 miles per hour slower than Feller. At that point, everybody decided to call it a day. "That was a crazy, crazy time," Dalkowski recalls. "It made no sense. Like so many things that happened, it seemed like things were stacked against me."

In 1960, Sandy Koufax was one of a half dozen pitchers to be timed by a high-speed camera in a test by *This Week* magazine. Koufax was joined by his hard-throwing Dodgers teammate Don Drysdale, as well as Herb Score of the Cleveland Indians, Steve Barber of the Baltimore Orioles, and Bob Turley and Ryne Duren of the New York Yankees. Unfortunately, the test took place in spring training and was the only time Koufax was clocked.

"You would have thought they would have waited a couple of months until we were in peak condition," Drysdale told *Street & Smith's Baseball* magazine. "We were told there was going to be a test of some sort but it was not big deal. We didn't ever set up for it and it was actually done without us knowing when."

Barber led the pack with an offering of 95.5 miles hour, followed by Drysdale (95.3), Koufax (93.2), Duren (91.1), Score (91.0), and Turley (90.7).

In 1974, the California Angels tried to be more precise by using the best scientific equipment of the time to test their fireballer,

Nolan Ryan. Four Rockwell International scientists rigged up an infrared radar device from the press box. Fans were invited to guess to the nearest one-tenth of a mile per hour how fast Ryan could throw. Entries were sent care of Ryan Express at the Angels, with the grand prize being a trip for two to the American League Championship Series that season.

The event was hyped on CBS Sports, and by the time the day came around—a September 7 game versus the Chicago White Sox—Ryan had had enough of the hoopla. "I didn't like it," he said afterward. "It takes too much away from your concentration."

The infrared device only tracked strikes, and Ryan voiced his concern that "a lot of balls outside the strike zone have more velocity." A pitched ball needed to pass through an infrared beam 17 inches wide and 2 inches high to record a reading.

Tom Egan, Ryan's catcher that day, added that he had seen the Express in better form. "He didn't have his real stuff," Egan told the Associated Press. "All that activity took away his concentration. I don't know why there is all that fuss anyhow. Everybody knows he's the fastest that ever lived."

For the record, Ryan's best clocking by infrared was 100.9 miles per hour. His teammates and members of the Angels press corps later claimed that he could easily throw 5 miles per hour faster on a better day. In fact, he may have done just that.

Rockwell International acknowledged that Ryan was actually clocked approximately 45 feet after the ball left his hand, rather than at home plate. The rule of thumb tends to be that a pitched ball loses up to 10 miles per hour by the time it reaches the plate. So, in this case, "that means that on a modern gun, Ryan was at best throwing 105.9 miles per hour," says John-William Greenbaum, who besides knowing a lot about Steve Dalkowski is an expert on testing devices, too. "On the bright side, it makes Ryan the fastest right-hander of all time, since his pitch was still probably traveling faster than Joel Zumaya's best offering."

Of course, almost every ballpark in the game, from the minors to the major leagues, clocks pitches today. The results are regularly flashed on the scoreboard. You would think that advances in technology would have made clocking speed more definitive by now, but some argue radar guns have only made things more confusing.

"They help you get the answer," Pat Gillick once told *Baseball America*. "But they're not the answer themselves."

"I don't put much faith in what they're using to guess speed today," adds Andy Etchebarren, a former catcher with the Baltimore Orioles and a coach with the Southern Maryland Blue Crabs during the 2008 season. "Take a guy like Steve Dalkowski. He would have hit 107–108 [miles per hour] on the radar guns they used today. I have no doubt about that. You see guys hitting 94, 95 on the gun now that wouldn't have been considered fast at all back in my day. Us old-timers joke about it."

If anything, heightened technology—namely, the radar gun—has made it possible for everyone to be an expert. Fans can play big-league scout by jotting down the timings via the scoreboard. Such pitch-by-pitch tabulation led *The Bill James Handbook* to credit Seattle's Felix Hernandez with the fastest *average* fastball in the American League in 2008 (94.6 miles per hour) and Colorado's Ubaldo Jimenez in the National League (94.9 miles per hour), with San Francisco's Tim Lincecum right behind them.

"You know what the radar gun is for? The fans," says Red Sox closer Jonathan Papelbon. "I personally don't even think we should have them in the ballpark because it's a tool that benefits only the hitter, not a pitcher at all."

Such sentiment didn't stop the tabulators from adding another category—pitches 100-plus in velocity. Before he was hurt, Detroit's Zumaya accomplished that feat 30 times in one season; the New York Mets' Billy Wagner 18 times.

"And in the end, all those numbers leave you nowhere," says Phil Pote. "It's too much information. Plus, you cannot compare it with Walter Johnson or Bob Feller or Lefty Grove. Once we didn't have enough scientific readings, now we have too many."

Midway through the 2009 season, Zumaya had the fans at Comerica Park in Detroit cheering after the stadium radar clocked his fastball at 102–104 miles per hour. In comparison, his changeup was 85 miles per hour that day, and to everyone's amazement Zumaya opted for this "third best pitch" with the game against the visiting Cubs on the line.

"I mean, that's what I've been working on," the Tigers' reliever explained after Chicago's Micah Hoffpauir hit the changeup for a two-run homer.

Detroit manager Jim Leyland said the selection was "not a good choice." He wondered if the buzz from the crowd caused Zumaya to commit one of baseball's cardinal sins: thinking too much.

"It might be exciting for the guy in section 129, seat 6," Leyland said of the public radar reports, "but it's not worth a hoot to me."

Pote, another old-school guy, couldn't agree more. "I started my scouting career without a radar gun and I'll end without one," he says. "I guess I'm a curmudgeon because I still trust my eyes. Is the fastball good enough that batters cannot catch up with it? If so, I'm a believer no matter what some gun may say."

Howie Haak, a legendary scout pivotal in bringing Tony Pena, Manny Sanguillen, Jose DeLeon, and Roberto Clemente to the Pittsburgh Pirates, used his eyes and a trick of the trade to gauge how hard a player could throw. While sitting down, Haak would raise his forearm to shoulder level as a prospect was about to throw. Haak's arm would be bent at the elbow, the joint often on the arm rest. When the player let fly, Haak would allow his forearm to drop toward his lap. The closer the forearm was to Haak's legs when the ball hit the catcher's mitt, the faster the prospect could really bring it.

Nobody ever became as famous for wielding a radar gun as Mike Brito. For years he was a fixture, standing 20 feet or so behind home plate (usually the optimal place to get the best reading) at Dodger Stadium. He got to be such an omnipresent figure that people watching at home on TV wondered who he was.

What many don't realize is that Brito was the one who convinced the Dodgers to sign left-hander Fernando Valenzuela, who arguably had the best screwball since Christy Mathewson. In fact, when Valenzuela struggled to stay focused during his banner rookie year, he moved in with Brito and his family.

When I attend ball games, no matter what level, I hang with the scouts. Most press boxes are too sterile and removed from the hubbub down on the field. Kind of like watching a ball game in a multiplex movie theater. Plus, I enjoy how upbeat most scouts can be. They realize that every game is a chance to be surprised by, to even stand in awe of, what somebody they maybe never even heard of can do.

"Every time I'm at a game and seeing a good player, if it's tomorrow or last week, it always fires me up," the Nationals' Mike Rizzo once told the *Washington Post*. "It's in my blood."

Being a scout allows one to be passionate about the game. Pote has even penned poems about the profession and the search for the fastest pitcher of all time:

Everyone's dream, a second chance, is our story
Will he at long last get but a touch of fame and glory
And will we catch a glimpse of his greatness to be, back then
Being left to wonder at all that mighta been.

That's the closing stanza to one entitled "The Ultimate Fastball and What Might Have Been."

Being a scout also means sticking by one's assessment of talent, even when everybody else disagrees with you. Perhaps Nolan Ryan doesn't get signed without somebody like Red Murff in his corner. Before Tommy Lasorda managed the Los Angeles Dodgers, he toiled for that organization as a scout. He was the one sent to Fresno in 1965 to evaluate a 20-year-old Tom Seaver.

"This boy showed a good fastball with good life," Lasorda wrote in the report he filed with the team. "[He] has good command . . . plenty of desire to pitch and wants to beat you."

In all likelihood, a talent like Seaver would have reached the majors without Lasorda's glowing review. When Lasorda was a scout, though, the position was still considered a step toward managerial stardom—a way to make your mark. Today scouting is regarded by some organizations as a dead-end position. Despite the brief recognition of a half dozen scouts in the late 1990s (Haak, Joe Cambria, Cy Slapnicka, Wish Eagan, and Bobby Mattick), scouts aren't eligible for induction into the Hall of Fame in Cooperstown. Through it all, the best scouts still refuse to back down when they believe a player has ability. Such was the case with Don Welke and Jim Abbott.

Born without a right hand, the left-hander became an inspiration to millions. His father, Mike, dreamed up the deft way Abbott transferred the baseball glove from his right wrist to his left throwing hand to catch the ball. He began the technique during solitary games of catch when he was four years old, throwing a rubberized ball against the brick wall of his family's townhouse. From such beginnings, Abbott went on to pitch around the world and recorded a no-hitter for the New York Yankees in 1993. His deeds included an Olympic gold medal, and the Sullivan and Tony Conigliaro awards, as well as being the first American pitcher to win in Cuba in 25 years. He threw in the mid-90s, and his cut fastball—a cross between a fastball and a slider—sawed off many bats and induced tons of ground balls. Before such stardom, though, somebody had to believe.

Welke, who was in charge of the Midwest for the Toronto Blue Jays' organization, first saw Abbott pitching during his senior year at Flint (Michigan) Central High School. The veteran scout can still rattle off the date like it was a loved one's birthday—May 5, 1985.

In Abbott, Welke saw a tremendous competitor. The last ballplayer that he had scouted that belonged in Abbott's class was Kirk Gibson. After that first game, Welke wrote a glowing scouting report: "six-foot-four . . . mammoth heart . . . projected to have well above average fastball." The only part he hurried through was the report's last four words: "has no right hand."

Welke's enthusiasm, on the page and in team meetings, wasn't enough for Toronto to take a real chance on Abbott. The Blue Jays didn't draft him until the 36th round of the 1985 draft and Abbott refused to sign with them. Yet such interest made other teams take notice. Abbott eventually signed with the California Angels after the 1988 Olympics and became only the 15th player since the amateur draft began in 1965 to make his professional debut in the majors. Throughout it all, Welke and Abbott have remained the best of friends. Welke was in Abbott's wedding party. "Don's the first one outside of my family and the ones in Flint," Abbott says, "who really believed in me."

S couts refer to the difference between a quality fastball and breaking stuff (a slider, curveball, or changeup) as range. If the gap between a fastball and the slower deliveries is big enough, then the pitcher has a much better chance for success.

"[Batters] can dial up on that heater," Billy Ripken says. "But Ryan had that nasty hook to go along with the fastball. Randy Johnson has that nasty slider. If a pitcher can throw in the mid to upper 90s and have another pitch that comes in at 80 to 82 [miles per hour], one that he can throw for strikes, you get that kind of package and a guy is pretty much unhittable."

As the 2009 season unfolded, one of the best feel-good stories was Zack Greinke of the Kansas City Royals. After having taken time off due to a social anxiety disorder, the right-hander was back, and one of the things opposing hitters and scouts noticed was how much harder his fastball was. Instead of being clocked in the high 80s, the heater had climbed to 98. When coupled with a curveball timed in the 50s, the combination made the opposition look silly. "That's too big a range even for a major-league hitter," says ESPN analyst Chris Singleton.

After six weeks of the 2009 season, Greinke was 7–1, with a 0.60 ERA. Fernando Valenzuela was the last to have an ERA that low eight games into the season, as he went 8–0, with a 0.50 ERA, to start 1981.

To better ascertain range, let's take a look at the opening lines of Joan Didion's story "Some Dreamers of the Golden Dream":

This is a story about love and death in the golden land, and begins with the country. The San Bernardino Valley lies only an hour east of Los Angeles by the San Bernardino Freeway but is in certain ways an alien place: not the coastal California of the subtropical twilights and the soft westerlies off the Pacific but a harsher California, haunted by the Mojave just beyond the mountains, devastated by the hot dry Santa Ana wind that comes down through the passes at 100 miles an hour and whines through the eucalyptus windbreaks and works on the nerves. October is the bad month for the wind, the month when breathing is difficult and the hills blaze up spontaneously. There has been no rain since April. Every voice seems a scream.

If a scout were recording that sequence, he would mark the first sentence as a quality fastball, maybe a two-seamer in the mid 90s, certainly good enough for that crucial first-pitch strike. The second sentence, the one beginning with "The San Bernardino lies," is as long and loopy as any slow stuff: a curveball, changeup, or even a knuckler well off the outside corner. That sets up another fastball ("October is the bad month") for strike two. Then Didion goes with another short sentence, a fastball perhaps just a few inches off the plate. With the count 2–2, Didion has set up the batter—I mean, reader—for a quick punch-out. And here comes the heat ("Every voice seems a scream"). It may be by us in a rush, but we won't soon forget it.

By alternating between fast and slow, long and short sentences—in other words, exhibiting great range—Didion holds our attention, and that last line is one of her best remembered.

Great range in pitching almost always begins with a quality fastball. From there the other stuff—a curveball, slider, change—can be taught. In essence, that's what David Price went through at Triple-A Durham. Without an epic fastball, though, great range can never really be achieved. No matter how sharp the break on the curve, the difference in speed isn't enough to get decent batters out.

Quality range between the hard and soft stuff is what made Stephen Strasburg, a hard-throwing right-hander out of San Diego State, the number-one pick in the 2009 amateur draft. A fastball that regularly tripped the scouts' radar guns at 100 miles per hour first spread the word. Add a quality curveball to that repertoire and some scouts were saying Strasburg, like Abbott, could make the jump from college ball to the pro ranks.

"He's the best I've seen in quite a while," Ducey says. "With a guy like him, you open the pocketbook and pray everything goes according to plan."

Unfortunately for the Washington Nationals, the team with the first pick in the 2009 draft, things had rarely gone according to plan in their short history in the nation's capital. By the ballclub's fifth season, it had become a cellar dweller, a laughingstock in a town that tends to take everything way too seriously. Complicating things was the fact it's far better to roll the dice on a promising hitter than a promising pitcher, no matter how hard he throws. As Thomas Boswell pointed out in the *Washington Post,* "Strasburg will probably be a .500 pitcher with a 150–150 record, or he'll be a bust. . . . The history of baseball's draft since it began in 1965 is unmistakable. You can project exceptional hitters with about a 50 percent success rate. You can't project No. 1 overall pitchers at all."

From 1965 through the 2008 draft, 102 pitchers have been taken in the first five picks. To date only one (Kevin Brown) has won more than 200 games. Josh Beckett certainly has a shot, but all in all, those guys are the exceptions. The best of the rest are Dwight Gooden, Andy Benes, Tim Belcher, Floyd Bannister, Mike Moore, and Bill Gullickson. In comparison, Paul Molitor, Reggie Jackson, Evan Longoria, Ryan Zimmerman, Chipper Jones, and Alex Rodriguez are just a few of the All Star hitters selected high in the first round.

Strasburg was represented by überagent Steve Boras. He's the guy who brokered Alex Rodriguez's landmark $252-million contract—the biggest deal in the game. His asking price for Strasburg's services? A hefty $50 million for six years. That kind of money was well past the ceiling on top draft picks. Mark Prior had signed for $10.5 million, Price for $8.8 million, with extras. Still, the young fireballer from San Diego appeared worth it, especially to a franchise eager to fill its brand-new downtown ballpark.

Money aside, Strasburg remained an amazing story. At 6-foot-4, a buff 220 pounds, it's difficult to imagine that only a few years ago

Strasburg was so out of shape he was nicknamed "Sloth" and ignored by most scouts. But thanks to his mother, a retired dietitian, as well as a rigorous workout schedule at San Diego State University, with additional yoga classes off campus, the pounds fell away. And the velocity soon soared.

Strasburg's fastball was in the low to mid 90s his freshman year at SDSU. That summer he was clocked at 98 in the New England Collegiate Baseball League, and he hit the century mark for the first time his sophomore year. The kid was living a fairy tale as his collegiate career came to a close. Behind home plate for his final home start against Air Force Academy were members of the Washington Nationals' front office, including acting general manager Mike Rizzo.

In 2006, the Nationals hired Rizzo as assistant general manager and vice president for baseball operations. He had spent the last seven years with the Arizona Diamondbacks, where he helped build one of the best farm systems in baseball. Since coming to the Nationals, Rizzo has made so many trips overseas that his passport ran out of pages; he's been to Japan, Taiwan, Korea, Australia, Mexico, Panama, Venezuela, Colombia, and the Dominican Republic. "I'm on call," he says, "ready to fly out on a moment's notice and sign that next prospect."

But when Jim Bowden resigned as general manager after a scandal involving the team's baseball academy in the Dominican Republic, Rizzo was promoted. One of his first orders of business was what to do with the top pick in the draft, a result of the Nationals being the worst team in baseball the year before. That season the Nationals had failed to sign their number-one pick, a pitcher named Aaron Crow, who didn't throw as hard as Strasburg. The franchise couldn't afford another such failure. Even if it meant dealing with Boras across the bargaining table.

Rizzo had wanted to see Strasburg pitch in person. Like any good scout, he believes he has to look past the radar gun readings. He needed to watch how the young prospect reacted when men got on base, when the phenom was called upon to do something unusual or even extraordinary. The night of Strasburg's final home start proved to be a best- and worst-case scenario for such expectations, as the young phenom was rarely threatened.

Strasburg's first pitch registered 100 miles per hour, and from there he methodically worked through the Air Force lineup. At his best, Strasburg has a deceptively smooth delivery. He doesn't appear to be throwing that hard until the gun shows that his nasty slider is in the mid-80s, his sinking two-seam fastball is in the mid-90s, and his rising four-seam fastball is 100 miles per hour and above, according to the scouts.

That night in San Diego, before a sellout crowd and a college pep band, all of Strasburg's pitches were working. By the seventh inning stretch, everyone in attendance recognized that Air Force had yet to get a single hit off the top pitching prospect in the country. With Rizzo and the Nationals' cadre studying his every move, Strasburg seemed to turn everything up a notch and was throwing his best stuff heading into the ninth inning. Striking out the final Air Force batter, on a called third strike, Strasburg spiked his glove into the ground in front of the mound, his Aztecs teammates rushing onto the field to congratulate him.

"I don't think he really understands what's happened here," San Diego State coach and Hall of Famer Tony Gwynn told the *Washington Post* afterward. "And somewhere along the line he's gonna say, 'Damn, I just threw a no-hitter in front of a packed crowd.'"

The following week *Sports Illustrated* and ESPN reported that Rizzo had decided to make Strasburg the top pick in the June draft. Mike Rizzo had been convinced. "He is Sidd [bleeping] Finch," Strasburg's agent told a baseball executive.

W ell, if we've reached the land of Sidd Finch, the powers that be have certainly gone over the top about somebody's fastball. Welcome to the nightclub where Mystique and Aura are the headliners.

Sidd Finch, of course, was the original fantasy player. A pitcher whose epic speedball was actually a figment of George Plimpton's imagination. Plimpton popularized the Walter Mitty everyman story for *Sports Illustrated*. He got his nose bloodied in the boxing ring by Archie Moore. He played quarterback for the Detroit Lions, which became the book and the movie *Paper Lion*. Early in 1985, Plimpton met with editors Myra Gelband and Mark Mulvoy about a possible April Fools' story. That year the magazine's publication date fell on April 1.

But after getting notes and suggestions from other reporters, Mulvoy, the managing editor, told Plimpton, "Why don't you do your own April Fools' story?"

Within minutes, the three had come up with a tale about a mysterious baseball player who could throw a ball 160 miles per hour. Plimpton was so caught up in the piece's possibilities that after the meeting broke up he walked from the Time & Life Building in midtown Manhattan to his apartment on the Upper East Side in a steady downpour.

"He gave me license to do anything I wanted," Plimpton, who died in September 2003, said in a 1995 interview with the *New York Times*.

Within weeks, Plimpton had come up with a bizarre tale about Hayden Siddhartha Finch, a Tibetan philosophy student who also played the French horn. To pull off the conceit, *Sports Illustrated* needed the cooperation of a major-league club. The New York Mets were more than happy to comply. An extensive photo shoot was set up for the team's spring training complex in St. Petersburg, Florida. Photographer Lane Stewart recruited a friend of his, a junior high school teacher named Joe Berton, to play the gangly yet hard-throwing Finch.

"Mulvoy, Gelband and Plimpton all agreed that the story needed to be played straight throughout," wrote Michael MacCambridge in *The Franchise: A History of Sports Illustrated Magazine*. "Gelband had the idea to make the first letters of the words in the subhead spell out 'Happy April Fools' Day.'"

The actual text read: "He's a pitcher, part yogi and part recluse. Impressively liberated from our opulent life-style, Sidd's deciding about yoga—and his future in baseball."

There were other clues, too. Plimpton pointed out one of the definitions for Finch is "a small lie."

But that's all pretty highbrow for the baseball world. Word soon spread that the Mets had landed the ultimate pitching prospect. A guy whose fastball made Nolan Ryan's look like a change of pace. Everyone became even more curious when it was revealed that Finch always pitched in one work boot and one bare foot, and that he loved to wear his ball cap backward. After Finch was given a cubicle between Darryl Strawberry and George Foster, the *St. Petersburg Times* sent an investigative reporter to the Mets' training camp. The *New York Times* finally tracked down Plimpton, who was traveling, at two in the morning.

"It's a hoax, isn't it?" demanded a *Times* man.

"Of course," answered a sleepy Plimpton.

Sidd Finch, Roy Hobbs, Nuke LaLoosh. Sometimes it's easy to think, especially in light of the steroid era, that baseball's best action heroes have been made up, figments of our imagination. Yet truth does have its merits. In real-life struggles lessons about perseverance remain, as well as a hint of optimism about the future. Consider Sanford "Sandy" Koufax.

From the time that he was little kid, Sandy Koufax could throw hard. As he recounts in his autobiography, *Koufax,* when snowball fights would break out in his old neighborhood in Brooklyn, he would duck into a well-protected place and "pepper the other kids and they couldn't come close to reaching me. Very useful."

But after breaking in with the Brooklyn Dodgers in 1955, Koufax seemed destined to be another hard-throwing prospect who never panned out. For those first half dozen seasons in professional ball, his record was rarely above .500 despite his alluring fastball.

"Of course, this was well before radar guns," says catcher Norm Sherry. "But Sandy easily threw above 100 miles per hour. The key for him, you could say his career really, was him realizing that he didn't have to throw all that hard to be effective. Before he got command of his pitches, he'd just rear back and fire that thing. He really didn't have an idea of where that ball might be going."

That all changed in just one day. The Dodgers had a "B" game in Orlando. A bare-bones squad, which included Koufax and Sherry, was due to take the flight from Vero Beach. The roster got even shorter when one of the other pitchers missed the plane.

"I was catching, and on the way over Sandy told me he was going to use the game to work on some extra pitches, his breaking ball and the like," Sherry recalls. "So we start off in the first inning and I'm mixing in the curve and changeup for him. So he can work on it, like he asked. But Sandy couldn't throw them for strikes. He walked the first two hitters and started to get a little upset. For the third guy, he went back to fastballs, throwing pretty much as hard as he could. So, he walks the third guy. There we are bases loaded with none out.

"I went out to the mound and I told him, 'Sandy, we've only got nine or so guys here to play this game. If you keep this up, you're going to be here a long time. Why don't you take something off the ball? Lay it in there. Let them hit it. We'll catch the ball, get some outs and maybe we'll get out of here at a decent hour. Nobody is going to swing the way you're going now.'

"I went back behind home plate and sure enough Sandy starts to throw them in there, nice and easy. We got out of the inning and when we came off the field I told him, 'Sandy, I'm going to tell you something. And I'm not blowing smoke up your rear end. But you threw harder trying not to then when you were trying to.' I think that registered with him—that his fastball was so good that he could just let it go.

"Sometimes the easier that you do things, the more success you have doing it. Look at the guys who hit home runs. It's kind of the same thing. Most of the time they'll tell you that they weren't trying to hit a home run. They'll say, 'Gosh, I didn't hardly swing.' Everything just worked right. I think it's the same way, especially when it comes to throwing hard. When it works, everything just comes together—your body, your arm. That's when you get the max out of things, rather than when you grunt and groan and throw as hard as you can. Too often when it's done that way things don't ever happen."

A few days later, back at the Dodgers' complex in Vero Beach, it was apparent to anybody watching how far the fireballer had come. Koufax threw to Sherry in what the players called "the string area." This was a series of mounds with string set up near the plates to represent the strike zones. In the past, Koufax had struggled to consistently put the ball inside the strings. But on this day, he was having no difficulty. In fact, he soon told Sherry to cover the plate with dirt. Then he told him to draw a line where the outside of the plate was and another for the inside part.

"After that I just sat on the corners and he hit my glove all day. It was unbelievable how much he changed," Sherry says. "The previous years he hadn't come close to that. Heck, the previous week he couldn't have done it."

In 1961, Koufax broke through, going 18–13, leading the league with 269 strikeouts in 255 ⅔ innings. But that was just a hint of what was to come. He pitched the first of his four no-hitters the following season and led the league in victories and strikeouts in 1963, 1965, and 1966. He was inducted into Cooperstown at the age of 36, the youngest player ever to enter the Hall of Fame.

"With any of these great pitchers, the questions become, 'Can they harness their stuff? Can they pull together what's been given to them sufficiently to become great?'" says Jeff Torborg, who caught Koufax's perfect game in September 1965. "That's not an easy thing to do. Not easy to do on any field, at any time. But these guys show that it can be done."

Sherry agrees that "throwing fast is a God-given talent. That's for sure. But it's not like it's a present with all the bows.

"Sandy's a good example. He was a very determined guy. He was somehow going to make this work and it took a while, but he did. I believe you have to have that: that belief in yourself that it's going to work out somehow."

The old ballpark of *Bull Durham* fame still stands. Unlike such parks in Brooklyn, Detroit, and Pittsburgh, it has been spared the wrecking ball, perhaps because somebody thought enough of it to film a baseball classic there.

On my way out of town, I decided to drive by and pay my respects. Instead of an aging dinosaur, I find Durham Athletic Park to be thriving. On this morning, workmen are painting the front facade and lining the base paths. As part of a $5-million renovation, the DAP now hosts summer collegiate ball, high school games, and professional women's softball.

"If you build it, he will come." Of course, that's the famous line from W. P. Kinsella's novel *Shoeless Joe,* which became the movie *Field of Dreams* starring Kevin Costner, who once played Crash Davis.

Here in Durham, they still come to what should be a forgotten ballpark because of another famous motion picture and characters we almost consider family. Sitting in the stands at DAP, I cannot help thinking of the next Nuke LaLoosh, a kid who somehow possesses the ability to throw thunderbolts from above. No matter how many radar guns are pointed in his direction, no matter how many years fly by, the mystique—dare we say, the fantasy—surrounding a prospective fireballer remains a key element of the game. The next great hurler could be from anywhere, even here, pitching in Nuke LaLoosh's shadow.

By mid-May, David Price had seemed to right himself. After starting the season 1–4, he struck out five and walked none in 4 ⅔ innings, with Andrew Friedman, the Rays' executive vice president for baseball operations, in attendance. His parents flew down from the Nashville area for his next start, against visiting Rochester on May 17. He didn't disappoint, taking a no-hitter through five innings. Despite striking out nine, the Rays treated him like fine china, taking him out after 82 pitches. The no-hitter? It didn't matter. Not at this level.

"We're just trying to be patient," says Debbie Price, who listened to her son's Durham Bulls games over the Internet. "[The Rays] are kind of in a dilemma because if they bring Dave up, who are they going to send back down or trade off? It's the ugly part of the business really."

The Price family often don't talk to one another after David's starts. Perhaps a text message the next day, briefly connecting Durham and the family in Murfreesboro, Tennessee. But Debbie Price says that may be because the season so far hadn't played out exactly as planned.

"Most nights we have the Tampa game on TV," she says. "That's another reason we're rooting hard for him to get back up with the Rays. We went ahead and bought this MLB package and he's not there yet."

The Arm Acceleration

David Price
Photo courtesy of Tampa Bay Rays/Skip Milos

Joe: He walked 18.

Larry: New league record!

Joe: Struck out 18.

Larry: Another new league record! In addition he hit the sportswriter,
the public address announcer, the bull mascot twice . . .

Larry: Also new league records!

—ANNOUNCERS, *BULL DURHAM*

It's a Friday evening at Fenway Park in Boston, with the breeze coming off the Charles River and the CITGO sign beyond the left field wall glowing bright orange and blue. At first glance, it seems to be a perfect night for baseball—until I notice that the teams on the field, the hometown Red Sox and the visiting Angels—are the same ballclubs that took the field during an infamous game decades ago. What happened then, despite advances in equipment, and changes in rules and attitude, could occur again. Once more, I'm reminded how the game can turn evil on any given pitch, especially one thrown by a bona fide fireballer.

In this ballpark, on August 18, 1967, Red Sox slugger Tony Conigliaro was struck in the face by a pitch from the Angels' Jack Hamilton. In an instant, what assuredly was a Hall of Fame career was derailed. Conigliaro suffered a fractured left cheekbone, dislocated jaw, scalp contusions, and a severely bruised eye. The injury caused a cyst to form on the macula, a portion of the retina, resulting in a blurry blind spot. The eye injury would play havoc with his depth perception for the rest of his career, to the point that he became a one-eyed batter. Even though Conigliaro did make several comebacks, he was never the same player.

When I was growing up, Tony C. was one of my boyhood idols. When I signed up for Little League in Gasport, New York, a one-stop-light village between Lockport and Middleport on Route 31, hard by the Erie Canal, I was assigned to the Red Sox. That's how I became a Bosox fan. It was the whim of some adult who assigned me to that particular team as opposed to the Tigers or the Athletics or the Yankees. Of course, this was well before cable, satellite television, or the Internet provided us with highlights and updates 24/7. To root for a team meant tuning in on a transistor radio, often late at night under the bedroom covers so the parents couldn't hear, and studying box scores in the next day's newspaper like they were the Dead Sea scrolls, imagining game sequences from what little information was squeezed into those narrow columns.

That's why that night in 1967 remained part mystery, part nightmare for such a long time to me. I saw the photograph of Tony C. in the morning paper—his left eye socket blackened and bruised almost beyond recognition. But the question of exactly what had happened or, more importantly, how a game I loved and also played for a time could turn so dangerous so easily is what stayed with me through the years. As Rick Wolff, son of broadcaster Bob Wolff and once a sports psychology coach for the Cleveland Indians, told me as my search for the fastest pitcher of all time was just beginning, "You're going to need to discuss the dark side of all this. What happens when a fastball flies out of control."

Long before Ken Griffey Jr., Derek Jeter, or Cal Ripken, there was Tony C. With a smile on his face and with his cocky manner, he was the modern slugger who was ahead of his time both in plate performance and flamboyant lifestyle. He was one of the youngest players to reach 100 career home runs—only 22 when he gained that plateau. Until that night in 1967, it seemed only a matter of time until he hit 400, 500, even 600 dingers.

"He might have been the guy to break [Babe] Ruth's and [Hank] Aaron's record," Hall of Fame pitcher Jim Palmer says. "With that swing, in that ballpark, there's no telling how many he would have hit."

How quickly such promise was taken away—gone in a single pitch. Nearly everyone I spoke with in attendance that evening remains haunted by it.

"The sound is what I'll always remember," Bill Rigney, who was managing the Angels that night in 1967, once told me. "The ball hitting him—it was like a broom smacking the side of a pumpkin. The sound seemed to carry everywhere in that ballpark.

"Of all the things I've experienced in baseball, that's what I can't get out of my head. That's the sound that still wakes me up at night."

An inch or so higher, and Jack Hamilton's pitch would have killed Conigliaro. The tragedy left Red Sox fans wondering what might have been. If Conigliaro had been in the lineup for the 1967 World Series, would Cardinals ace Bob Gibson have had such an easy time sitting down the Boston order? Could the ballclub have had the championship nearly 40 years earlier with its local slugger healthy and still swinging for the fences?

Before dismissing that night at Fenway as another case study from the "Curse of the Bambino," or another example of Red Sox paranoia, consider how memory and time work, how the ripples from a single tragedy can impact lives years and years later. For a moment or two, let's chase the ghost of Tony C. and consider how a baseball thrown with some malice in mind can forever alter one's opinion of high heat.

"He was baseball's JFK," says Dick Johnson, curator of the Sports Museum of New England. "That's why you're still interested in him. That's why there will always be this fascination with him that goes beyond him and the Red Sox. In Tony C., people see their greatest hopes and biggest fears realized in one player, one pitch."

There was something about the way Conigliaro carried himself that immediately won over Johnny Pesky. Pesky was the Red Sox manager in 1964 when Conigliaro arrived at spring training camp fresh from being named rookie of the year in the New York-Penn League. After seeing how the kid could hit the ball, Pesky lobbied hard to have Conigliaro on the major-league roster when camp broke.

"I put my neck out for him," Pesky says. "I knew he was the real thing."

At the plate, Conigliaro exhibited quick hands and a fluid stroke. He appeared taller than his 6-foot-3, 180 pounds when he stepped into the batter's box—a similarity that Pesky remembers Conigliaro sharing with Ted Williams and Joe DiMaggio.

In his initial at bat at Fenway, on the first pitch, Conigliaro proved Pesky a prophet, homering off Chicago's Joel Horlen. Years later, that highlight was included in the video *Red Sox Home Run Heroes,* with Curt Gowdy doing the play-by-play.

"What a thrill that must be for a 19-year-old boy, who a year ago was playing high school baseball," Gowdy says as Conigliaro rounds the bases on the old video. "Look at that smile on his face. Ah, look at that smile."

From the beginning, Conigliaro realized that the way to succeed at Fenway Park was to hang in against inside deliveries and pull everything he could toward left field, toward the Green Monster, only 310 feet, if that, down the line. "He had the perfect swing for Fenway," says Red Sox pitcher Jim Lonborg. "But that swing made him vulnerable to getting hit. It was the price he decided to pay."

Before the tragic beaning in 1967, Conigliaro had already suffered a broken finger, thumb, wrist, hand, and shoulder blade—all from getting hit by a baseball.

"He was a matador," Johnson says. "Nobody had more courage than him. He'd get hit and stick his head right back in there the next time out."

Despite missing six weeks because of injuries, he homered 24 times in 1964, an amazing total for a teenager. Mike Sowell, who wrote *The Pitch That Killed,* the story of Ray Chapman's fatal beaning in 1920, says it "is easy to forget how rough a game baseball can be. You don't see guys getting hit like you do in football. Most of the time, there's a civility to baseball."

Or at least that's what we like to think. But when such rules of engagement are ignored or misunderstood, the consequences can be tragic. Conigliaro wore a helmet, but it didn't have the kind of side flap that players use today. When Sowell hears the sound of a ball ricocheting off a modern helmet, it almost sounds like music to him. "Chapman and Conigliaro didn't hear that," he says. "Maybe that's why I like the sound. Some of the incidents you see today, a guy is hit and in a few minutes is right back up."

Despite such safety measures, beanings have prematurely ended several modern-day careers. The Astros' Dickie Thon was hit in the face with a pitch thrown by the Mets' Mike Torrez in 1984. He missed the rest of the season and half of the next with blurred vision, and he never matched his 1983 numbers of 20 home runs and 79 RBI. The Twins' Kirby Puckett had his jaw broken by the Indians' Dennis Martinez in 1995. He retired the next spring because of vision problems unrelated to the beaning.

Of course, the list of injuries was much longer before helmets and the ear flap (introduced after the Cubs' Ron Santo broke his cheekbone in 1966) became everyday equipment. The notables include Mickey Cochrane (fractured skull in 1937) and Don Zimmer (broken cheekbone in 1956). Orestes "Minnie" Minoso, the first dark-skinned athlete to play in Chicago, the "Latino Jackie Robinson," led the league in getting hit 10 of the 11 years between 1951 and 1961. The lone exception was 1955, when a pitch earlier in the season fractured his skull.

"I tried to take everything as it comes," Minoso says. "I never let the world hurt me. The world didn't break me."

Since the game's origins, pitchers, especially those who throw really, really hard, have used intimidation to win many a battle at home plate.

"My first two times up, he struck me out on six pitches—low and away fastballs," Phil Garner said once about facing Nolan Ryan. "My third time up, the first two pitches again were low and away fastballs for strikes. I decided not to get caught again with a low and away fastball. I leaned out over the plate, hoping to just peck the ball.

"In a flash, in that thousandth of a second, I saw his fastball thrown as hard as he could throw it coming right at my ear. My whole life passed before me. I tried to dig a hole beneath the batter's box 'cause I was scared to death. As he was winding up to throw his next pitch, I was already walking to the dugout. It was strike three for me, and I was just happy to be out of there."

Dick Williams claimed that Ryan rarely threw at anybody, "but he was conveniently wild. His ball just took off."

As later detailed in Ryan's autobiography, Williams remembered slugger Reggie Jackson hitting a line drive off Ryan, which was barely tracked down in the outfield. After Jackson made the turn at first base, heading back across the infield to the dugout, he gave Ryan a playful smack on the butt. The next half dozen games they faced each other, Ryan was "conveniently wild."

Perhaps that's what prompted Jackson years later to say that Ryan was "the only guy who put the fear in me. Not because he could get me out but because he could kill me. Every hitter likes fastballs like everybody likes ice cream. But you don't like it when somebody's stuffing it into you by the gallon. That's how you felt when Nolan was throwing fastballs by you. You just hoped to mix in a walk so you could have a good night."

Dave Duncan, who went on to be a respected pitching coach, says what separated Ryan from most pitchers was that he didn't "just get you out. He embarrassed you. There are times when you've won some sort of victory just hitting the ball."

Brooks Robinson adds that when Ryan was in his prime there was definitely a fear of him. "There's an old baseball saying," the Hall of Fame third baseman said. "'Your heart might be in the batter's box, but your ass ain't.'"

Such sentiment once forced Dodgers shortstop Bill Russell to return to the dugout before his at bat was over. The reason? A fastball delivered by the Astros' J. R. Richard that sailed over Russell's head and splintered a piece of wood attached to the backstop. The wood was a good 30 feet beyond home plate, and Richard's heater was later reported to be 103 miles per hour.

Russell stepped out of the batter's box, thought things over, and then refused to step back in. Dodgers manager Tommy Lasorda tried to console him, but Russell had seen enough. So, Lasorda motioned for Pepe Frias to pinch-hit, which prompted the famous response, "Why do I have to bat?"

Before the start of the 1969 season, the St. Louis Cardinals traded slugger Orlando Cepeda to Atlanta. Cepeda still remembers his first at bat against his old friend and teammate Bob Gibson, and how the rules of engagement changed overnight. "The first time I went to the plate, he knocked me back," he says. "It was mandatory, you know what I mean? In fact, Bob came to my house for dinner after the game, and my son said, 'How come you threw at my dad?' And Bob said, 'It's a game. Baseball.'"

From Ryne Duren to Rob Dibble, pitchers have always employed intimidation. Duren was famous for uncorking his last warm-up pitch to the backstop behind home plate. "I didn't do it as much as people think I did," Duren once said. "But the evil that men do lives after them. Somebody said that once."

Dibble, who along with hard throwers Randy Myers and Norm Charlton was part of the Cincinnati Reds' "Nasty Boys" relief corps, buzzed a hitter or two, especially early in his career. "I've pitched like that my entire career," Dibble told the Associated Press after a 1991 altercation in which he brush-backed the Houston Astros' Eric Yelding, who then came after him and threw his batting helmet at the pitcher. "I didn't hit him. He hit me."

Sometimes even the best intentions can turn heads. When Andy Baylock, who caught Steve Dalkowski in high school, complained about a sore receiving hand, a few adults advised him to get a slab of beef from the local butcher. They told him to cut it thin enough to slide inside the palm of the catcher's mitt to provide another layer of cushion. It seemed like a good idea at the time. What nobody envisioned was that the meat would ooze so much blood and juice that

by the middle innings hitters stepping to the plate against Dalkowski would see red stuff dripping down the catcher's forearm. "It
got a bit out of control," says Bill Huber, Dalkowski's high school
coach. "I had to put an end to that practice, no matter how well
intentioned."

Over the years, a few hitters have found inventive ways to get
even. Jackie Robinson, for example, took a page straight out of Ty
Cobb's playbook. After being decked several times by the Giants' Sal
Maglie, Robinson bunted up the first-base line. The blow was perfectly placed—too far for the catcher to field and not so close to the
bag that the first baseman could take it unassisted. Maglie had no
choice but to field the grounder. As he did so, Robinson, who perfectly timed his dash to first, ran headlong into Maglie. Giants manager Leo Durocher called Robinson's tactic "bush league," and the
incident went all the way up to the league president's office, where
Ford Frick assured everyone that umpires had things under control.
Later, Maglie admitted that throwing at Robinson only "made him a
more aggressive hitter."

Throughout his career, Maglie did more than enough to earn his
nickname, "the Barber." "I couldn't stop throwing the knockdown,"
he said. "That would be the same as if Marilyn Monroe stopped
wearing sweaters."

Yet opposing pitchers soon learned not to throw at another Robinson, Frank Robinson. Head-hunting just seemed to rile him up, to
the point that Phillies manager Gene Mauch finally decided to fine
any of his pitchers $50 who dared challenge Robinson with a little
chin music.

"Pitchers did me a favor when they knocked me down," Frank
Robinson says. "It made me more determined. They say you can't hit
if you're on your back, but I didn't hit on my back. I got up."

Bill Bruton, a career .273 hitter, may have best summed up the
dilemma most batters face when it comes to knockdown pitches and
beanballs. After teammate Eddie Mathews hit three consecutive
home runs in a game, Bruton reluctantly stepped up to the plate,
knowing exactly what was coming. He was hit by the very next pitch

after Mathews's third homer. "What did he pick on me for?" Bruton wondered after the game. "I didn't hit the home run."

Mike Wallace of *60 Minutes* once asked Roger Clemens if he ever threw at a batter on purpose and the Rocket refused to consider the concept. In fact, he demonstrated a similar capacity for stonewalling when he testified before Congress about performance-enhancing drugs years later.

"I don't have to intimidate anybody," Clemens told Wallace. "I don't need it. I don't need anyone to be fearful."

But in the next breath, Clemens said he did need to pitch inside at times.

"That's what power pitchers do," he said.

In the report, *60 Minutes* detailed how Clemens once hit the Mets' Mike Piazza in the head ("I tried to call him and apologize," Clemens explained. "But I was shut down.") and later threw a chunk of Piazza's broken bat at him in an incident during the 2000 World Series.

"Anytime somebody throws the ball at you, it's scary," says the Yankees' Derek Jeter, who seemed to get routinely plunked by Clemens when they were on opposing teams.

Joe Torre, who managed Clemens in New York, told the New York press that the hard-throwing right-hander was "an intimidator."

But with beanballs, what often goes around comes around. Maglie, the old Barber himself, perhaps played a role in Conigliaro's tragedy. After his playing days were over, Maglie became a pitching coach, eventually with the Red Sox. In Boston, he turned "Gentleman" Jim Lonborg into another intimidator on the mound. After going 10–10 in 1966, Lonborg blossomed into a 22–9 Cy Young winner during the Red Sox "Impossible Dream" season. Under Maglie's guidance, he wasn't afraid to come inside on any hitter, and the buzz began that batters needed to be wary against Boston's pitching staff.

By that point Johnny Pesky had been let go as the Red Sox manager, but he still followed one of his all-time favorites. "The night [Tony] was hurt, I was devastated," Pesky recalls. "The only way you can view it is as one of those tragedies in life that happens to everybody, sooner or later. I think of Tony often when I see a young hitter. But none have been as good as him. The closest one was Jim Rice.

"You fall in love with players in this business. In a way, that's what keeps you going. If I live to be 100, I'll never forget Tony."

Mike Andrews was in his first full year on the 1967 Red Sox team. He was one of the first to reach Conigliaro after he had been beaned, along with several teammates and manager Dick Williams. By the time Andrews reached Conigliaro, the Red Sox slugger was motionless near the plate, his left eye almost completely shut. "Right then I knew that this was different than most injuries you see in baseball," Andrews says. "His eye was already swollen up."

While others contemplate what might have been, Andrews finds it amazing that Conigliaro played baseball again. After missing the 1968 season and a brief comeback bid as a pitcher, Conigliaro was back in the batter's box the following season. He hit 20 home runs and collected 82 RBIs in 1969, and he was considered by many to be the American League's Comeback Player of the Year. In 1970, despite ongoing vision problems, Conigliaro had 36 home runs and 116 RBIs.

Even though Conigliaro remained dogged about his comeback, routinely hitting 300 or more balls a day, he was now reluctant to be center stage with a bat in his hands. He liked to take batting practice in private, wanting to get his stroke perfect. Of course, his life would never be perfect again.

"That showed what kind of competitor Tony was," Andrews says. "He wasn't the same Tony. Something was missing. But that didn't stop him from trying. I learned a lot about tenacity and heart by watching him."

The night Conigliaro was beaned, his younger brother Billy and his parents were at Fenway. Billy had been playing for the Red Sox Single-A team in Greenville, South Carolina. But his season had ended prematurely with a torn hamstring.

"I wasn't supposed to be there that night," recalls Billy, who played on the same team with his brother in American Legion and high school, as well as for two seasons later in Boston.

From the family seats, behind the Red Sox dugout on the first-base line, the beaning didn't seem that serious. Conigliaro had a habit of "being dramatic," his brother says. "And from where we were sitting, we didn't hear anything. It wasn't until I got down to the clubhouse that I saw how serious this could be."

Before the game, a slumping Conigliaro had told his brother that he was going to move back up on the plate for this game, and start looking for something inside that he could pull. While Conigliaro was considered a streaky hitter, his brother also remembers his brother "as the best clutch hitter I've ever seen. A lot of players press in a tough situation. For some reason, Tony could relax at those moments."

Conigliaro's clutch hitting helped set the tone for what became the Red Sox "Impossible Dream" season in 1967. Back on June 15, with a man on, he had battled back from a 0-2 count in the 11th inning against the White Sox. His two-run homer into the netting above the left field wall marked the night that many fans in New England began to believe in that magical team. But on that fateful night in August, Conigliaro hardly reacted at all when Hamilton's pitch sailed high and inside.

"Funny, you never go up there thinking you're going to be hit, and then in a fraction of a second you know it's going to happen," Conigliaro later recalled in his autobiography. "When the ball was about four feet from my head, I knew it was going to get me. I knew that it was going to hurt because Hamilton was such a hard thrower."

To this day, Billy Conigliaro, whose birthday is three days before the anniversary of the beaning, hasn't forgiven Hamilton, the man who threw the pitch.

"No doubt that ball was thrown at his head," the brother says. "No doubt."

We can love the brush with danger that high heat provides, the rush we feel when it teases, even momentarily frightens us. It can be the best roller-coaster ride in the amusement park that is the national pastime. But when a fastball bites, we're quick to vilify the pitcher responsible. By then it's too late to change what happened. All we can do is watch the impact of the incident ripple through the game and hope that some good comes of it. That's how it was with

Ray Chapman, still the only hitter at the major-league level to be killed by a pitched ball.

Chapman made a name for himself with his legs, his ability to fly around the bases and snare many a hard-hit grounder in the field. Conigliaro, of course, hit the long ball, but despite the different styles of play, the two were similar in many ways. Both were handsome guys, matinee idols in the towns where they played, and both seemed to have a bright future in the game ahead of them. Regrettably, both became casualties of the game's dark side.

A history existed between Chapman and the pitcher on the mound that muggy Monday afternoon, August 16, 1920. "Carl Mays throws it so he'll dust you off the plate," Chapman is quoted as saying in *The Pitch That Killed*, "but I'll stand right up there. He doesn't bother me. He's not going to intimidate me."

Everyone from Ty Cobb to Chapman's teammates on the Cleveland Indians had become convinced that Mays routinely threw at batters to gain the upper hand. For his part, Mays wasn't in any hurry to disperse any preconceptions.

When Cobb once confronted him, asking Mays point-blank if he threw at hitters on purpose, the pitcher answered, "What do you think?"

According to esteemed sportswriter Shirley Povich, when Cobb replied that his opinion wasn't the point, Mays said, "Well, if you think I do, Ty, that makes me a better pitcher. As long as you're feeling that way about it, I'm more effective."

One could argue that Clemens, Ryan, Randy Johnson, and any of the other top fireballers of the more recent past would have said pretty much the same thing. But there's no getting around the fact that as the Yankees prepared to host the Indians that day at the Polo Grounds in New York, most batters in the game didn't trust the submarine-style pitcher.

But behind almost every tragedy there almost always lies seemingly innocent factors brought into play as if by fate—a chain reaction leading up to what in hindsight appears the inevitable. In the years leading up to the Chapman beaning, the lords of baseball had pledged to clean up the game. At the turn of the last century, it was a more violent sport and there was little question that the ball was often utilized as a weapon. Baseball historian Bill James calculates that about 91 batters were hit by a pitch for every 100 games played in that era. Giving things an added edge, the spitball was often in play despite early attempts to ban it. Putting foreign substances on the ball or scuffing it can make it fly in peculiar, unexpected ways. And as James points out, another result of lathering the ball up with saliva, tobacco juice, or licorice was that it discolored the ball. An off-white ball, of course, is also much harder to see. When these factors are added together, it was only a matter of time before things went wrong.

"By about 1910, a clean ball was never in play," James wrote. Yet with the cost of a baseball rising (according to Sowell they doubled in price in the years before the Chapman incident), umpires were under pressure to keep every last one in play. In fact, Ban Johnson, founder and first president of the American League, issued a directive to the men in blue "to keep the balls in the games as much as possible, except those which [are] dangerous."

The final straw may have been Mays's delivery. James calls Mays a "combination of Dan Quisenberry and Nolan Ryan" because his pitches were the result of an odd sidearm fling that put plenty of speed on the ball.

"Carl slings the pill from his toes, has a weird looking windup and action that looks like a cross between an octopus and a bowler," described *Baseball Magazine*. "He shoots the ball in at the batter at such unexpected angles that his delivery is hard to find, generally, until about 5 o'clock, when the hitters get accustomed to it—and when the game is over."

On the game day, Cleveland was in a slump, but it still held a narrow lead over the White Sox and Yankees in the standings. A light rain had been falling as the game began, but when Chapman stepped up to the plate in the top of the fifth inning the scattered showers had stopped, even though the skies remained overcast.

As Mays went into his windup, delivering the first pitch of the inning, he thought he saw a slight shift in Chapman's feet, like he was squaring around to bunt. Mays said many things in the aftermath of the incident, including the claim that his fastball, high and tight to Chapman, had gotten away from him. He also acknowledged that he had reacted the way any quality pitcher does when he sees a batter squaring to bunt. The proper response is to deliver the ball inside, so the hitter can't get the bat on the ball. Whatever the reasoning that went through Mays's mind at that instant, there's no doubt that his next pitch sailed with stunning speed toward the inside part of the plate, directly at Chapman's head.

As Sowell details in *The Pitch That Killed*, incredibly Chapman just stood there, seemingly transfixed by the pitch's velocity. He made no effort to get out of the way.

"That's the biggest riddle in all of this," Sowell says. "Chapman was an experienced hitter. He was used to getting out of the way. But this time, for whatever reason, none of his talent, that experience of playing at this level, helped him in any way. He was riveted in place and the ball hit him square on."

In an effort to find an explanation, Sowell looked through hundreds of player quotations, many from the time period, trying to find an answer to why an experienced hitter put himself in that kind of situation. Finally, he found a possible explanation from infielder Terry Turner, who played 17 years in the majors, most of them in Cleveland.

"I can still remember vividly how I was fascinated by seeing that ball coming toward my head," Turner said. "I was paralyzed. I couldn't make a move to get out of the way, though the ball looked big as a house. I imagine that a person fascinated by a snake feels much the same way, paralyzed and unable to dodge the deadly serpent about to strike."

Sowell sighs in agreement after the quote is read back to him. "That's why I made it the first thing in the book," he says. "What these guys face up at the plate, being transfixed by fear, is something we can all relate to. It happens every day, everywhere. You're stunned by how things are suddenly turning out, how life can snap around on you, and you can't get out of the way of what's about to happen."

The throw by Mays struck Chapman in the left temple. This was well before batters wore protective headgear, whether it was a shield inside the cap or the helmets that are mandatory from Little League on up today. Medical inquiries would later determine that a fracture three and a half inches long extended along the left side of Chapman's head nearly to the base of his skull. The blow had also caused the right side of his brain to hit against the inside of his skull, resulting in additional trauma.

Witnesses that afternoon reported that a loud crack echoed throughout the ballpark when Chapman was hit. In fact, Mays fielded the ball and went to throw to first, believing that the pitch had somehow ricocheted off Chapman's bat.

Afterward the Indians' shortstop was revived and began the long walk to the clubhouse, which was located past the center field fence at the old Polo Grounds. But approaching second base, he staggered and had to be accompanied the rest of the way by several teammates. Soon after arriving at the hospital, Chapman lost consciousness and died early the next morning.

Four days later, an estimated 2,000 people attended his funeral at St. John's Roman Catholic Cathedral in Cleveland. Player-manager Tris Speaker, who had been Chapman's best man, and outfielder Jack Graney, Chapman's roommate on road trips, were too distraught to attend. The rest of the ballclub, from players to front-office personnel, were there. The legendary fireballer Smoky Joe Wood, now an outfielder with the Indians, was a pallbearer in Graney's absence. Also in attendance were American League president Ban Johnson and several members of the New York Yankees. Mays was not among them.

In the aftermath of Chapman's death, baseball issued a renewed vow to clean up its act. The spitball was outlawed. Baseballs that became discolored, scuffed, or stained were quickly taken out of play. It's estimated that 20 or more balls are discarded in the average professional game today—a direct result of that tragic day at the Polo Grounds. Other safeguards were much longer in coming, however. Days after the incident, a *New York Times* editorial urged that a helmet be developed and soon employed by batters. But such measures would not take effect for another 30 years.

Pee Wee Reese was probably the first major-league batter to wear a helmet when he stepped to the plate in a 1941 spring training game in Havana, Cuba. Late in the 1952 season, Branch Rickey, who was the Pittsburgh Pirates executive, issued fiberglass batting caps to his entire team. "My dad, who was working for the Pirates back then, was one of the guys who stayed up late gluing in the protective foam," says scout Mike Berger.

Initially, the players weren't very fond of Mr. Rickey's protective gear. They were required to wear the helmets anywhere on the field, and some fans dubbed the players coal miners. Joe Garagiola recalls that kids bounced marbles off his helmeted head when he was down in the bullpen. Soon Rickey decided the ballplayers only needed to wear the newfangled helmets when up to bat.

In 1956, batting helmets became mandatory in the National League, and the American League followed suit two years later. The only team that voted against the measure was the Boston Red Sox. Slugger Ted Williams didn't like to wear a helmet.

Today, according to Rule 8.02d of the rule book, umpires can eject any pitcher believed to be guilty of throwing at a batter. Usually this happens after the home-plate umpire issues a warning to both teams. Even though the bylaw asks umpires to be clairvoyant, in addition to calling balls and strikes, it's likely made the game safer.

Helmets and new rules were a long way off for the Cleveland ball-club as it tried to move ahead without Chapman. But after the team strung together a few victories, many of the players believed that their fallen comrade was looking down on them. Perhaps that's so. How else to explain the Indians' rallying down the stretch to take the pennant by two games over the White Sox and three over the Yankees? One of the key players for Cleveland was in fact rookie shortstop Joe Sewell, who replaced Chapman in the everyday lineup. The Indians went on to defeat the Brooklyn Robins in the World Series for their first championship.

As for Mays, he became an outcast, a persona non grata. In the weeks after the incident, several teams, including the Red Sox and Tigers, spoke openly about boycotting games in which the hard-throwing submariner participated. Yet like many such grandstanding gestures, the campaign soon lost momentum. Mays went on to pitch another nine years in the majors, finishing his career with a respectable 207–126 record and 2.92 ERA. In fact, his numbers stack up favorably with those of several hurlers in the Hall of Fame. But Mays would never reach a place of forgiveness and redemption after he retired, let alone a plaque in Cooperstown. To his dying day, he insisted he hadn't hit Chapman on purpose.

"The death of Ray Chapman is a thing I do not like to discuss," Mays later told *Baseball Magazine*. "It is an episode that I shall always regret more than anything else that ever happened to me. And yet, I can look into my own conscience and feel absolved from all sense of guilt. The most amazing thing about it was the fact that some people seemed to believe I did this thing deliberately. . . .

"Suppose a pitcher was moral monster enough to want to kill a batter with whom he can have no possible quarrel. How could he do this terrible thing? Christy Mathewson in the days of his most perfect control couldn't have hit a batter in the temple once in a thousand tries."

Almost 20 years after his book about the Chapman tragedy was published, I ask Sowell how he feels about Mays now. Was he the monster that everybody made him out to be? Or was he simply in the wrong place at the wrong time, throwing the wrong pitch?

"When it first came out, the question I got most of the time was, 'Did you think Carl Mays threw at Ray Chapman on purpose?'" Sowell says. "I don't think so. That opinion hasn't changed much.

"What has changed for me is that I think I have more respect for him. That's what has grown over time. Carl Mays may have not been the friendliest guy in the world. He sure didn't have many friends. But he was loyal to the ones he had and he played the game hard. A lot of players, including Johnny Pesky, admired him, how he went about his business.

"Over time, I've become more convinced that he belongs in the Hall of Fame. His numbers are as good as or better than many pitchers from his era. But there's this one pitch, this one awful mistake. For that he'll probably never be forgiven."

Most fireballers intimidate opposing batters. A select few, such as Robert Moses "Lefty" Grove, who played in the majors from 1925 to 1941 for the Philadelphia Athletics and then the Boston Red Sox, terrified their teammates as well. Growing up in the Allegheny Mountains of western Maryland, Grove pretty much taught himself how to pitch. He, like Amos Rusie before him, gained a reputation for throwing rocks "at anything, moving or stationary." According to the *Baltimore Sun,* sometimes the targets were squirrels and birds, but mostly they consisted of the glass insulators on the telegraph poles. If it hadn't been for baseball, Grove likely would have followed in his family's footsteps and been a coal miner. But he detested going below ground, having to eke out a living that way.

When he was 15, Grove worked with his father in the mines for two weeks. He remembered it being dark when he went down and dark when he came back up. "If it hadn't been for Sundays," he said, "I'd never know if there was any sunshine. After two weeks, I said, 'Paw, that ain't my kind of work and I'm going to get some other job.' . . . I didn't put that coal there and I'm not going to dig it out."

So, Grove went to work at a local glassworks. When it burned down, he found employment at $7 a day at another glassworks and the Klotz Silk Mill. Yet his options were proving to be limited at best. So, in the spring of 1919 legend has it that Grove put on his "store clothes" and pedaled his bike down out of the hills to Martinsburg, West Virginia. The town had a team in the Blue Ridge League and Grove wanted to try out.

After some cajoling, Bill Louden, the manager, gave him a chance. While the kid from the mountains sure could throw hard, too often he had no idea where the ball was going. Still, he made the team.

"[They] offered me $130 a month to play ball over at Martinsburg, more than 50 miles way," Grove later told the *Boston Globe.* "Would I take it? I jumped at that $130 a month just for pitching. My folks told me, 'You'll get homesick,' and I told them, 'I'll not be homesick and I'm never going to be.' I couldn't get away fast enough. And I wasn't homesick, neither."

On or off the mound, Walter "The Big Train" Johnson was an imposing presence.

National Baseball Hall of Fame Library, Cooperstown, NY

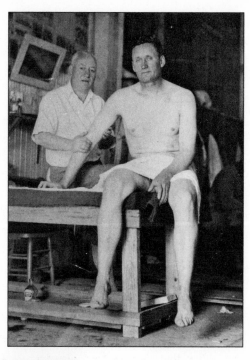

Few had a more violent pitching motion than fireballer Smoky Joe Wood.

National Baseball Hall of Fame Library, Cooperstown, NY

Bob Feller's fastball was clocked at 98.6 miles per hour during this pre-game test in Washington, D.C., in 1946.

Getty Images

Bob Feller and Satchel Paige talk during their barnstorming days. Paige would later join Feller in Cleveland as a member of the major-league Indians.

National Baseball Hall of Fame Library, Cooperstown, NY

Ray Chapman of the Cleveland Indians died tragically after being hit in the head by a pitch thrown by Carl Mays in August 1920.

National Baseball Hall of Fame Library, Cooperstown, NY

Before he was beaned in 1967, nobody had a more promising career than Tony Conigliaro of the Boston Red Sox. Here he swings a bat in the on-deck circle of a spring training game during his comeback bid in 1969.

Jim Hansen, photographer, LOOK Magazine Collection, Library of Congress, Prints & Photographs Division

After six years in the majors Sandy Koufax had a 36–40 record, but over his last six years on the mound he won 129 of 176 decisions, and he would later reach the Hall of Fame.

National Baseball Hall of Fame Library, Cooperstown, NY

Randy Johnson was another fireballer who took a while to find his way. But he went on to reach the 300-victory plateau, an accomplishment that usually lands a pitcher in the Hall of Fame.

National Baseball Hall of Fame Library, Cooperstown, NY

Tommy John shows off his famous arm. Ligament replacement surgery not only saved his own major-league career but the fortunes of many other injured pitchers who followed in his footsteps.

Getty Images

Nobody intimidated opposing batters more than Bob Gibson of the St. Louis Cardinals. He struck out a league-leading 268 hitters and had 13 shutouts in 1968, the so-called "Year of the Pitcher."

National Baseball Hall of Fame Library, Cooperstown, NY

In 1973, Nolan Ryan posted a single-season record for strikeouts (383). In addition, he pitched 26 complete games, four shutouts, and two no-hitters that season.

National Baseball Hall of Fame Library, Cooperstown, NY

Ryan celebrates his fourth no-hitter, which he pitched in 1975 as a member of the California Angels.

National Baseball Hall of Fame Library, Cooperstown, NY

Ryan shows some emotion in the midst of his sixth no-hitter on June 11, 1990, in Oakland. He would record his record seventh no-no the following season against Toronto.

Jose Luis Villegas

Billy Wagner proves that size doesn't matter when it comes to throwing a quality fastball.

National Baseball Hall of Fame Library, Cooperstown, NY

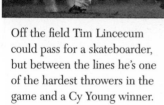

Off the field Tim Lincecum could pass for a skateboarder, but between the lines he's one of the hardest throwers in the game and a Cy Young winner.

Jose Luis Villegas

The top pick in the 2009 amateur draft, Stephen Strasburg signed at the 11th hour with the Washington Nationals.

Ernie Anderson

Steve Dalkowski, shown here in 1959, was a legendary fireballer but never reached the major leagues.

Associated Press

Who says you can't go home again? Steve Dalkowski, center, with several of his boyhood friends at the 2009 spring sports banquet in New Britain, Connecticut.

Tim Wendel

Grove soon gained such a reputation in the Blue Ridge League that Jack Dunn, owner of the Baltimore Orioles, sent his son to Martinsburg for a firsthand look. The younger Dunn was impressed, and one of the most curious deals in baseball was soon completed. One story has it that a recent storm had leveled the outfield fence in Martinsburg. Dunn agreed to pay for a new one—$3,000—in exchange for the rights to Grove.

At that time, the Orioles were playing in the International League, and nobody was better. Under Dunn, the ballclub won seven consecutive pennants, and during his four-plus seasons in town Grove went 108–36. Usually winning makes everybody happy. But several of Grove's teammates in Baltimore appeared to resent his success.

"They used to say that I was mean in those days, but I had a reason," Grove said. "Everybody was mean to me. It was rough on a kid trying to make it in baseball in those days."

So began the often dysfunctional relationship between Grove and his teammates—an uneasy truce that would continue throughout his playing days.

In October 1924, the Orioles sold Grove's rights to Connie Mack and the Philadelphia Athletics for a then-record $100,600. By that point, there were three constants when it came to Grove: (1) His stuff was as fast as anything ever seen in baseball; (2) it was just as wild; and (3) his teammates couldn't stand him. "Hitting off him was like asking to be blindfolded and then trying to swing an ax handle to hit a lump of coal in the darkness of midnight," the *Baltimore Sun* noted.

Under Mack's tutelage, Grove gained better control of his fastball. In his second spring training with the As he got up early every day and started pitching before his teammates showed up.

"I threw for 20 minutes," he later recalled. "I put nothing on any pitch. I merely concentrated on hitting different spots of the plate and I finally got so I could throw strikes blindfolded. After that, it was easy sailing."

So much so that Grove put together one of the most incredible runs in baseball history. From 1929 through 1933, he won 128 games and lost just 33. Yet it was never easy sailing between Grove and his teammates.

"I often was in the need of a helping hand when I came up to the As from Baltimore," he said of his early years with the As, "but I was never offered one. My victories were greeted by silence. My defeats, all due to wildness, brought no advice as to how I might acquire control."

In 1931, Grove was on the cusp of breaking the American League's consecutive-wins record. He had tied Walter Johnson and Smoky Joe Wood by winning 16 straight. The record 17th appeared to be a sure thing as he took the mound in St. Louis against the lowly Browns and their journeyman pitcher Dick Coffman. Before the game, Mack had said that Grove was better than his other heralded left-handers, Eddie Plank and Rube Waddell. The stage was set for a coronation. Instead, Grove was greeted with a debacle.

Besides flattering his superstar pitcher, Mack had allowed Al Simmons, the team's All Star left fielder, to take a few days off. Starting in Simmons's place was backup Jimmy Moore. In the third inning, Moore misjudged a fly ball that gave the Browns a 1–0 lead. Remarkably, the tainted run stood up and Grove lost the game, 1–0.

Afterward, he tore apart the visitors' clubhouse at Sportsman's Park. After that he ripped off his uniform, threw it on the floor, and jumped up and down on it.

"If Simmons had been here and in left field," Grove fumed, "he would have caught that ball in his back pocket."

Grove didn't speak to Mack or his teammates for several days. He never did forgive Simmons for taking the day off and spoiling his potential record breaker.

To help him concentrate and throw more strikes, Mack urged his fiery left-hander to take more time between pitches, to not rush things. The legendary manager told Grove to count to 10, sometimes 15, between deliveries. Opposing crowds soon caught on and chanted the count along with Grove. Despite being prickly with his teammates, Grove didn't let the distraction bother him. In fact, his walk totals steadily decreased throughout his 17-year career.

Such improvement wasn't enough to keep him in Philadelphia, though. Mack was going broke and began to sell off his stars one by one. Before the 1934 season, after he led the league in victories (24), Grove was sent to the Red Sox. He struggled early on and battled a sore arm, especially during the 1938 season. Yet Grove won 105 games in eight seasons with Boston and finished his major-league career with a 300–141 record. (After he retired, Grove would claim that he could have won 400 if he hadn't spent five seasons in the International League with Baltimore.)

Throughout it all, success went hand in hand with his temper tantrums. After player-manager Joe Cronin's error cost Grove a ball-game late in his career, the left-hander followed Cronin into the Boston clubhouse. Cronin hurried into his office and closed the door behind him. But Grove was never put off so easily. Finding a stool, he climbed atop it, so he could reach the wire screen above Cronin's office. From this vantage point, he sneered down at his manager, shouting obscenities about Cronin's inability to field like a major leaguer.

Then Grove wondered why Cronin and Ted Williams, another teammate he traded insults with, didn't attend a party he threw to celebrate winning his 300th game. Talk about a diva.

"That's the kind of bird Mose is," former Red Sox general manager Eddie Collins said at the time. "He may never reach the heights of popularity that Babe Ruth has, but it isn't because he isn't a good fellow. He's naturally shy, like most of those fellows from the mountains, and has a natural distrust of strangers."

Luke Sewell, who batted against Grove for 15 years and later coached in Cleveland, said Grove was faster than the next legend to come down the pike, Bob Feller. "I mean that Grove's fast one actually was past the batter and into the catcher's mitt quicker than Bobby's," Sewell told the Associated Press. "Feller's fast one, though, had more life to it, and, of course, he had a wonderful curve, whereas Lefty had none until after he began to lose speed."

"Lefty Grove was the hardest thrower of his era," Maury Allen wrote in 1981. "[His] fastball would have registered more than

100 miles per hour if the currently used radar gun had been in existence."

Lefty Gomez was once asked who was faster, Feller or Sandy Koufax. His answer was simply, "Grove."

"There was probably no better left-hander who ever pitched," Bill Veeck told the *Washington Star* in 1975. "It's tough to compare different eras and so it is tough to say whether he or Sandy Koufax is better. Certainly no left-hander was better than Grove. His control was his biggest asset. When you throw as hard as he could with his accuracy, you didn't have to do much else."

Perhaps it was Mickey Cochrane, Grove's catcher in Philadelphia, who figured him out better than anybody. When the southpaw got into trouble, Cochrane would forget about reminding Grove to count to 10 or trying to settle him down. Instead, Cochrane would fire the ball back to Grove and shout out an accompanying insult or two for good measure. Grove hated that, the *Christian Science Monitor* reported, and the pitcher "would try to throw the ball right through Cochrane. Meanwhile, the hitters were suffering."

Let's leave it to Red Smith to sum up Grove. "On the mound [Grove] was poetry," Smith wrote in a *New York Times* column in 1975. "He would rock back until the knuckles of his left-hand almost brushed the earth behind him, then come up and over with a perfect follow-through. He was the only 300-game winner between Grover Alexander and Warren Spahn, a span of 37 years.

"He had the lowest earned run average in the league nine different years, and nobody else ever did that more than five times. If the old records can be trusted, Alexander, Christy Mathewson, [Walter] Johnson and Sandy Koufax each won five ERA titles. Some men would say these were the best pitchers that ever lived. Are the records trying to tell us Old Man Mose was twice as good as any of them?"

Two decades after he beaned Tony C. at Fenway Park, Jack Hamilton opened a restaurant in Branson, Missouri. Back then the town of 3,700 was nothing more than a wrinkle in the Ozarks. These days Branson draws more than 6 million visitors annually. They come from far and wide to see what has been nicknamed the "Hillbilly Las Vegas." With 30 music theaters—named for stars from Roy Clark to Japanese-born fiddler Shoji Tabuchi—a 27-acre factory outlet center, and hotels, the traffic is bumper to bumper on Highway 76 through town. And nobody is busier than Hamilton.

"It's nice to know things work out for the best sometimes," says Hamilton, who can be found most days at his restaurant, Pzazz. "We're just down the street from Mel Tillis's and Boxcar Willie's. We work hard, putting in long hours. But in the restaurant business, that's the way you like it."

Most days, after troubleshooting his way through the kitchen, making sure there's plenty of prime rib (Pzazz's specialty), Hamilton can be found out front, greeting customers. Every couple weeks or so, somebody will walk in from Boston or somewhere else in New England. And even though Hamilton wishes he was better known for the one-hitter he pitched or the grand slam he walloped while a New York Met, invariably somebody will ask, "Aren't you the guy who hit Tony Conigliaro?" And with a resigned look on his face, Hamilton will nod and talk about that pitch one more time.

Throughout the 1967 season, it was rumored that Hamilton was throwing a spitball, which had been declared illegal soon after Chapman's death. In fact, early in the game in which Conigliaro was beaned, Red Sox manager Dick Williams complained to the umpires that Hamilton's pitches were behaving strangely. Hall of Famer Bobby Doerr, the Red Sox first-base coach in 1967, noted in his diary for that day that Williams protested Hamilton's offerings in the second inning. Back at the bench, Williams told Doerr that he "was afraid someone would get hurt."

But the Angels' battery denies that Hamilton was throwing a spitter. Catcher Buck Rodgers, who would later manage the Angels, remembers the pitch as "a fastball that sailed."

Hamilton also recalls Conigliaro crowding the plate so much that his head was hanging over it. "No, I wasn't throwing a spitter,"

Hamilton says. "I had two outs in the inning. It was tied. Why would I want to hit anybody in that situation? I was just wild. I was so wild that I couldn't have hit him if I wanted to."

After Conigliaro went down, Hamilton stood on the mound with his arms folded, while many in the Fenway crowd of 31,027 booed. Hamilton started to walk toward home plate, but Rodgers, who had seen the condition Conigliaro was in, blocked his path. After the game, Hamilton tried to visit Conigliaro at Sancta Maria Hospital in Cambridge, Massachusetts, where the Red Sox slugger had been rushed. But Hamilton wasn't allowed in.

"I never did talk with him," Hamilton says. "That's what really bothers me. I didn't get a chance to tell him that it was an accident."

And that's what Hamilton will tell anybody who asks him about the beaning today. It was an accident. "I know that in my heart, I didn't mean to do it," he says. "So, it really doesn't matter what people may say. They don't know. They weren't there. When the anniversaries come around, I know it's going to come up. What are you going to do?"

"I think it's malicious to hit anyone because of your own inadequacies," Jim Palmer says, and Walter Johnson would have undoubtedly agreed.

Legend has it that the Big Train threw at a batter only once in his 21-year career. That declaration comes from several sources, most notably the sportswriter Shirley Povich. Such a reluctance to throw the beanball is attributed to Johnson's outstanding fastball and his easygoing disposition.

That lone beanball incident involving the Big Train occurred against the Philadelphia As in 1912, and if Povich and others are to be believed it wasn't even Johnson's idea. Throughout his career, Johnson told teammates that he was afraid that he would kill a batter one day, and after close calls he often ran toward home plate from the mound out of concern.

The best hitters noticed Johnson's apprehension about coming inside, especially with the hard stuff. The Tigers' Ty Cobb, who would undoubtedly look for an edge against his own grandmother, saw how Johnson winced when he fired the ball too close to the batter's head and shoulder. That's when the Georgia Peach began to crowd the plate, confident that Johnson wouldn't dare bust him too far inside.

"I'd crowd that plate so far that I was actually sticking my toes on it when I was facing Johnson," Cobb later told Povich. "I knew he was timid about hitting a batter, and when he saw me crowding the plate, he'd steer his pitches a little bit wide. Then, with two balls and no strikes, he'd ease up a bit to get it over. That's the Johnson pitch I hit. I was depending on him to be scared of hitting me."

Perhaps that's a major reason why Cobb was the all-time hits leader for so long. He could use such reverse psychology against even the best in the game. Other hitters didn't think things through to such a degree or, if they did, didn't have enough confidence in their conclusion to actually try it out against Johnson. But occasionally some did have success.

One of them was the Athletics' Frank "Home Run" Baker. He hit so consistently off the Big Train that the Senators' trainer, Mike Martin, finally confronted Johnson.

"That Baker has been ruining us all season," Martin told Johnson. "If you don't knock him down, I'll always think you've got no guts."

Why the Big Train bothered listening to the team trainer is anybody's guess. But for whatever reason the criticism hit home. When Baker next came to bat, Johnson vowed he would intentionally throw at his head.

With Baker in the batter's box, Johnson went into his windup with malice on his mind. The pitch, as Povich later recalled, was "a high, hard one, inside, that barely missed Baker's skull and sent him foundering and pale into the dirt. Johnson, white with terror, was the first to reach him. He was a happy man when Baker stirred, glowered, and told him, 'Get back there and pitch!'"

Years later, Johnson told Povich, "The moment I threw the pitch, I wished I had it back."

In the twilight of his career, Johnson did an extended interview with *Baseball Magazine*. In the piece, he left little doubt on where he stood on the subject of the beanball, calling it "the meanest thing in baseball."

He explained that the "bean ball is one of the meanest things on earth and no decent fellow would use it. I shall not attempt to judge anyone, but there are pitchers, I am convinced, who do resort to the bean ball intentionally.

"Such a ball to be effective must be pitched fast. The bean ball pitcher is a potential murderer. If I was a batter and thought the pitcher really tried to bean me, I would be inclined to wait for him outside the park with a baseball bat, or I wouldn't be averse to spiking him as I slid into first base when he was covering the bag. I don't think any treatment of such actions is too severe."

For a moment, the Big Train sounds an awful lot like his old adversary Ty Cobb.

When so much is on the line, the thought process of pitcher and batter becomes very intriguing. Before Cobb rationalized correctly that Johnson would never throw at him on purpose, he went to great lengths to not only convince himself to step up to the plate but to do his utmost against a fireball pitcher like Johnson.

"I reasoned with myself. I said, 'I am up here to make a success and must overcome this foolish fear,'" Cobb later explained to *Baseball Magazine*. "'The worst that can happen to me is that Walter Johnson will hit me. If he does hit me that it is all part of the risk I assume playing ball, a risk that is peculiar to my profession. . . .'

"So I ignored my fears. I not only refused to back away from the plate, but I crowded the plate. I was determined to conquer Johnson's fastball. And that season I batted nearly .700 against him, a higher average, I believe, than anyone else ever made at his expense."

In essence, Conigliaro and nearly every successful batter from Cobb's era to the present day have made the same pact with themselves.

Four days after Tony Conigliaro came home from the hospital, the Red Sox signed outfielder Ken "Hawk" Harrelson. The Hawk replaced Tony C. in right field, collecting a league-high 109 RBIs the following season. In 1970, Conigliaro was traded to the Angels, Hamilton's former team, where his eyesight continued to diminish. Midway through the 1971 season, Tony C. retired at the age of 26. In 1975, he attempted one more comeback with his Red Sox. But it ended after just 21 games.

After taking broadcasting jobs on the West Coast, Conigliaro came home for the final time. In 1982, after he had auditioned for a broadcasting spot with the Red Sox, he suffered a heart attack. Although his heart recovered, his brain went too long without oxygen. He lived out the rest of his days with his family and at a chronic-care hospital outside of Boston, where he required 24-hour care. Bumper stickers throughout New England read, "I PRAY FOR TONY C." He died in 1990 at the age of 45.

"I don't know how my mother and father did it," Billy Conigliaro says. "Each day was a struggle and you just took it a day at a time. I know that's what killed my father. Seeing his son suffer like that."

Really nothing else in baseball can be as sudden or as shocking as a pitch that can kill. Even though nobody at the major-league level has died directly from a beaning since Chapman, baseball can still be deadly. Researchers Bob Gorman and David Weeks calculate that 9 minor leaguers and 111 amateur baseball players, some as young as eight years old, have died as a result of beanings since 1887. And despite the best in equipment, from lighting to helmets to a fresh baseball put in play at almost every turn, the game still has its dark side.

Consider another Friday night, April 17, 2009, at Fenway Park. The Red Sox are hosting the Baltimore Orioles when seemingly out of nowhere Danys Baez's 93-mile-per-hour fastball to Boston's Kevin Youkilis gets away from him. The high heat tails inside, head high, with such ferocity that all Youkilis can do is turn his head ever so slightly away. An instant later, the ball smacks off his helmet and Youkilis falls to the ground. On the mound, both of Baez's hands reach for his head, as if he cannot believe what he's done. For a long moment or two, the Fenway faithful hold their breath.

Thankfully, Youkilis is soon on his feet, walking to first base as the cheers build throughout the ballpark. Baez nods his head in Youkilis's direction, as if in apology.

"Hitting somebody in the head is frightening," says Jim Palmer, now a broadcaster for the Baltimore Orioles. "Not only for the guy who's hit, but for the guy who threw the ball, too."

L egend has it that before a spring training game between the Baltimore Orioles and the Boston Red Sox at the old Miami Stadium, Steve Dalkowski was throwing to a few hitters while a group of reporters and players watched. Among those in attendance was Ted Williams of the Red Sox, the last guy to ever hit better than .400 in a season, the guy renowned for his keen vision, the one who didn't like to wear a batting helmet. After studying Dalkowski, Williams couldn't help himself. He was tantalized by this epic fastball, so he picked up a bat, ready to take a few hacks against the young left-hander.

According to lore, Williams took three practice swings, cocked his bat, and nodded for Dalkowski to give him his best shot. Dalkowski went into that abbreviated motion of his. The next thing everybody knew the ball was in the catcher's glove, only a few inches below Williams's chin. "The Splendid Splinter" looked from the glove, back out to Dalkowski, and then walked out of the batting cage. He told reporters that he never would bat against that kid again. It was too dangerous—the way the ball seemed to disappear and then reappear only when it was already past him.

Of course, Teddy Ballgame could have just asked some of the kids who faced Dalkowski back in New Britain, Connecticut, to know how terrifying the experience could be. "If he'd hit someone in the head, he might have killed them," Len Pare, Dalkowski's high school catcher, once told the *Baltimore Sun*. "Fortunately, he never did. But once a game, he'd throw a ball behind the batter. That put the fear of God in everyone. Then the next three pitches would be way outside because he was afraid of hitting the guy.

"He didn't have to worry about brushing people back. They never dug in. They just wanted out of there. They'd swing at anything. Steve struck out tons of guys without throwing the ball over the plate."

In the closing chapters of his professional career, Dalkowski came as close as he ever would to becoming a complete pitcher. In a remarkable piece of luck, he had hooked up with Earl Weaver, a manager who could actually help him. The two of them came together for the 1962 season in Elmira, New York, and for the first time, Dalkowski began to throw strikes. During one stretch, over 53 innings, he struck out 111 hitters and walked only 11.

Many considered it only a matter of time until Weaver was the head man at the parent club in Baltimore, which did happen in 1968. Under his direction, the Orioles won the American League pennant four times and the World Series once. Weaver wasn't afraid to speak his mind and was known for his rants against umpires as well as his own players. And deep down, Weaver had a profound respect for what a power arm could mean to a team, how a quality fastball could even turn a season around. Growing up, Weaver had seen Bob Feller pitch. He remembered being in awe of how fast the ball traveled to the plate. Later in his managing career, Weaver witnessed firsthand what Nolan Ryan could do. And when he first laid eyes on Dalkowski, he saw that in terms of pure speed, the unassuming left-hander was easily one of the best.

That season in Elmira, Weaver attacked with the tools of a social scientist the riddle of why Dalkowski couldn't throw strikes. Weaver learned that Dalkowski was the son of a blue-collar background. He listened to his young phenom tell the story about hitting that batter in Kingsport in his rookie season, how Dalkowski had visited the kid in the hospital and how that incident still depressed him. From others in the organization, Weaver learned about Dalkowski's adventures with the "Lost Boys"—Bo Belinsky and Steve Barber.

"By the time he got to me, Steve was in bad shape," Weaver says. "He was well on his way to being an alcoholic. He'd lost track of who really could help him and who was just along for the ride."

Tough love was heading Dalkowski's way and he sure didn't like it—at least at first. "He's one guy that I never really got along with," Dalkowski says. "In fact, for a long time, I hated Earl."

Weaver soon discovered that liquor and lousy friends weren't Dalkowski's only problems. That season in Elmira Weaver gave all his players the Stanford-Binet Intelligence tests. When the results came back, Dalkowski's score was the lowest on the team—an IQ of about 65.

"That meant we were going about it all wrong with him," Weaver says. "We were telling him to hold the runners close, teaching him a changeup, how to throw out of the stretch. The problem was he couldn't process all that information. We were overloading him. Those tests showed that if you had something to teach 100 people, Steve would be the last to learn."

In an effort to save the prospect's career, Weaver took his training in the opposite direction. He told Dalkowski to throw only two pitches—his fastball and slider—and simply concentrate on throwing the ball over the plate. Dalkowski went on to have his best year ever. In his final 57 innings of the 1962 season, the left-hander gave up one earned run, struck out 110 batters, and walked only 21.

"Maybe it was the slider," Dalkowski later told Pat Jordan, a pitch that reaches the plate five to eight miles per hour slower than the fastball and usually breaks laterally and downward. "I began throwing a lot of sliders that year. I threw it as hard as my fastball and I could throw it for strikes. I'd just hit the black part of the plate with it when I was right. I struck out Ken Harrelson five times in one game and he said to me, 'I don't believe it! I don't believe it!'"

As the final piece of the puzzle, Weaver worked up another technique to help with Dalkowski's control. The left-hander was under strict orders to take some heat off the fastball, and go with the slider some, until he got two strikes on the batter. Then Weaver would whistle from the dugout. That was Dalkowski's go-ahead that he could throw as hard as he wanted. Weaver remembers that Dalkowski loved to hear that whistle.

Despite the newfound success between the lines, Dalkowski's antics off the field continued to escalate. Once Andy Etchebarren, Dalkowski's catcher in Elmira, began riding him, telling Dalkowski that his fastball was overrated. Etchebarren motioned at the wooden outfield fence and said that if Dalkowski's fastball was so good, why didn't he just throw it right through that fence? Dalkowski already owed his catcher $20, so for that amount and a few extra dollars the bet was made on the spot.

Etchebarren handed Dalkowski a ball. The fireballer stepped back and proceeded to throw it right through the wooden fence. It was a feat that harked back to the glory days of Amos Rusie.

Convinced that the ball must have hit a knot or that the fence wasn't very strong in the first place, Etchebarren tried to duplicate the feat. But his attempt only bounced off the wall, directly back at the two of them.

"But that's not my favorite one," Etchebarren says, shaking his head, recalling another Dalkowski story. "No, that has to be about [Dalkowski] and the cop car. Poor Dalko—he tried to drink everything in sight."

The tale involves Ray Youngdahl, another Orioles farmhand led astray, and another evening spent howling at the moon. Youngdahl joined Dalkowski at a bar one evening, eager to drown his sorrows after striking out four times with men on base. Youngdahl had a few drinks and then went outside and fell asleep in the backseat of his Cadillac. Come closing time, Dalkowski was once again three sheets to the wind. Somehow he was in possession of the car keys, so he stumbled outside, started the vehicle up, and began to drive home— with Youngdahl still asleep in the back.

Soon Dalkowski was sighted driving down the middle of the road by a policeman, and the cop pulled him over. Dalkowski didn't have a driver's license, so the cop told him to follow him back into town. By then Youngdahl was wide awake, even though he probably wished he wasn't. Because that's when Dalkowski put the car into reverse and bashed into the police cruiser.

Pat Gillick, who would later lead three teams to World Series championships (Toronto in 1992 and 1993, and Philadelphia in 2008), was a young pitcher in the Orioles' organization when Dalkowski came along.

"I first met him in spring training in 1960," Gillick says. "The minors were already filled with stories about him. How he knocked somebody's ear off and how he could throw a ball through just about anything. He had a great arm but unfortunately he was never able to harness that great fastball of his.

"His fastball was like nothing I'd ever seen before. It really rose as it left his hand. If you told him to aim the ball at home plate, that ball would cross the plate at the batter's shoulders. That was because of the tremendous backspin he could put on the ball."

In Elmira, Weaver had Dalkowski bunked in a private home with several other Orioles pitching prospects, including Gillick. The fiery manager told the others to do what they could to keep Dalkowski in line. But that proved far more difficult than anybody, including Weaver, expected.

"It was very tough to have him make any kind of curfew, to toe the line in any way," Gillick recalls. "Steve had a mind of his own. We know now that alcoholism ran in his family. He was certainly susceptible to the bottle. About all we could hope to do was keep him on the straight and narrow the night before he pitched."

Despite having to play babysitter to the pitching phenom, Gillick insists nobody in the Orioles' camp was envious of Dalkowski's magic arm—wondering why such a gift was wasted on a guy with a propensity for hard liquor and fast times.

"I wasn't jealous of him. I don't think anybody really was," Gillick says. "We were all rooting for him to make it to the majors. All you had to do was see how he threw—so hard, able to pitch all day—that if he had made the majors we'd be talking about him as one of the most dominant arms ever in the game. Even back then you saw what was at stake."

Between Weaver's tough love and the support of teammates like Gillick, Dalkowski turned the corner pitching for Elmira. His final line there was 160 innings pitched, 192 strikeouts, 114 walks, and a 3.04 ERA. Better yet, in the second half of the season, he walked only 11 batters in 52 innings. Weaver remembers at bats where the hitters went three or four innings lucky to foul off a pitch. After years of being lost in the wilderness, Dalkowski suddenly had a future in the Orioles' organization.

In 1963, at spring training, he struck out 11 batters in 7 ⅔ innings. The myopic left-hander with thick glasses was slated to head north with the parent club as the Orioles' short-relief man. He was even fitted for a big-league uniform. Yet in his last spring appearance, on March 22, disaster struck.

Dalkowski scholar John-William Greenbaum says trouble had been coming from a long way off. Dalkowski's elbow started to bother him while he was pitching winter ball in Puerto Rico and Venezuela. Why a top prospect like Dalkowski wasn't examined and steps weren't taken at the first hint of arm trouble seems downright criminal today. By the time the left-hander reached spring training, Orioles teammates noticed that he didn't have the superhuman speed of past seasons. In fact, he was pulled for a March 17 game due to a sore arm.

But five days later, for a Grapefruit contest against the Yankees, Dalkowski was back on the mound. Everything started off beautifully that day. He fanned Roger Maris on three pitches. He struck out four in less than two innings. But when Dalkowski threw a slider to New York's Phil Linz, he felt something pop in his elbow. Despite the pain, Dalkowski, like countless pitchers before and after him, tried to carry on. Yet when he pitched to the next batter, the Yankees' Bobby Richardson, the ball flew to the screen behind home plate. With that Dalkowski came out of the game. A few days later, in Vero Beach, he tried to warm up but it was no good. The pain was still there.

"That was it for his great speed," Greenbaum says. "If Steve was pitching today, he wouldn't have pitched in excess of 65 innings, from winter ball through spring training, with an injured elbow. They would have shut him down. It would have been different."

When the Orioles broke camp, headed north for the start of the regular season, Dalkowski didn't go with them. Instead, he started the season in Rochester and couldn't win a game. From there he was demoted back to Elmira, but by then not even Weaver could help him. In what should have been his breakthrough season, Dalkowski won two games, throwing just 41 innings. His legendary fastball was gone.

"Damn, I can't believe that day in Miami," Dalkowski later told *Inside Sports* magazine. "Why then, after all those years? I never had a sore arm. I think I know why. The night before I pitched against the Yankees I went out drinking. I met this broad and took her back to my room. Maybe that's where I lost it.

"She had a half-pint of vodka in her purse. The next morning I got up, and I was hung over. I don't know. I threw that first pitch to Richardson and the ball just took off and hit the screen.

"I think a higher power took it away from me when I had it all together. I'm not mad. It was my own fault."

The Release

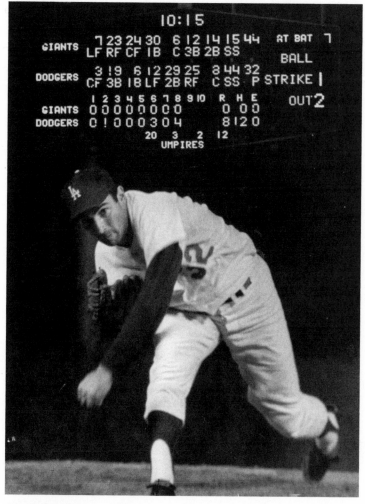

Sandy Koufax
Photo courtesy of the National Baseball Hall of Fame Library, Cooperstown, NY

Gentlemen, we can rebuild him. We have the technology.

—*THE SIX MILLION DOLLAR MAN*

I f Steve Dalkowski had been injured a few decades later, undoubtedly science would have tried to rebuild his arm. When the
surgery and rehab was over, perhaps he wouldn't have possessed
the great velocity that seemed to be his birthright: a thunderbolt
handed down from Zeus himself that became the gossip of minor-
league ballparks nationwide. But he might have been able to take the
mound again, thanks to another left-hander, Tommy John.

Halfway through the 1974 season, John was 13–3, only a few
victories shy of his best season to that point in his career. On a Los
Angeles Dodgers' pitching staff that included Andy Messersmith,
Don Sutton, and Mike Marshall, then the top closer in the game,
John didn't take a backseat to anybody. There was even talk of him
enjoying a 30-win season. But all of that almost ended on one pitch
to Montreal Expos first baseman Hal Breeden on July 17.

Even though Breeden would play only five years in the majors, a
career .243 hitter, his was a face that John would always remember.
"I threw him a sinker," John says. "I'll never forget that pitch or Hal
Breeden as long as I live."

As soon as John let go of the ball, he says he felt a "crazy sensation" in his left elbow. For an instant, the joint felt like it was coming
apart. Afterward John shook his arm, pretending it was nothing more

than a cramp. For the umpteenth time in his career, he told himself that pitchers sometimes have to pitch hurt.

"I remember thinking, 'Gee whiz, that was really foul. Did I get out of synch or something with my arm slot or delivery?'" he says "That's what I figured it must have been, so I tried not to think anything of it."

John went ahead and uncorked another pitch. Once again his elbow went totally out of kilter, feeling like it was "flying out somewhere to right field. . . . It happened again when the arm was coming through, in the same motion, as I was driving to the plate. The sharp pain was back and I knew this wasn't like anything else I'd had before."

With that John called time and walked off the mound. Dodgers manager Walter Alston came out of the dugout.

"What's wrong?" he asked.

"I hurt myself," John replied.

In the dugout, John put on his warm-up jacket and the word was spread to find Dr. Frank Jobe, the Dodgers' physician, who was in attendance that day. After the game, Dr. Jobe examined John in the trainer's room as teammates and reporters milled about, asking questions that John couldn't really answer. Of course, this was before magnetic resonance imaging, or MRI, so Dr. Jobe and other medical experts were flying blind.

The next day Dr. Jobe reexamined John's elbow again. The joint, swollen and sore, was loose to the touch when manipulated. After icing the elbow for another day, taking X-rays, and a visit to Dr. Herb Stark, an expert in tendon injuries, Dr. Jobe concluded that John had torn the left elbow's medial collateral ligament, which ties the arm's two largest bones, the ulna and the humerus, together. The pitching motion puts tremendous force on the elbow joint, where the medial collateral is located. Repeated pressure causes the joint to deteriorate over time. Medical experts say it's akin to a rope that gradually frays due to great force. The pain that John felt on those last two pitches to Breeden was the result of his arm tearing apart at the elbow.

Back in 1974, such a diagnosis meant retirement. Up to that point in its history, baseball was filled with pitchers who had felt something snap in their arm—a moment that ended their playing days forever. In John's case, the pitching arm was further compromised by surgery he had undergone two years earlier to remove bone chips. Immediately after hearing the diagnosis, John realized that the odds were against him. "For a pitcher, having arm operations is a little like gambling," he says. "You may win once, but each time you take a chance, hurt the arm again, you're coming closer to losing everything."

Unfortunately for John, plenty was on the line. His wife, Sally, was due with the couple's first child in a few weeks. With one pitch, John had gone from being the family's breadwinner, perhaps pitching for a play-off share, to being out of baseball as a player. Dr. Jobe advised John to look for another line of work. Realistically there was no way that John would ever throw a ball with much velocity again, let alone deliver it hard enough to get major-league hitters out.

"I had the option to hang it up," John says. "I spoke with the Dodgers about possibly managing. But I also kept talking with Dr. Jobe about what could be done, if I was willing to take a chance."

Hypothetically, Dr. Jobe said, it was possible to transplant a tendon from elsewhere in the body and string it through the damaged joint. Holes could be drilled in the ulna and humerus bones, and the elbow joint could then be knitted together with the new tendon. Back in the 1970s, such scenarios sounded like science fiction. Still, John wanted to hear more.

"You need to understand what I was thinking at that time," John says. "I couldn't imagine my life without baseball. I still can't. It's all I've ever known, so I was open to any and all ideas Dr. Jobe came up with. Even when he started to talk about transplanting a tendon from elsewhere in my body to the damaged elbow, I was ready to go ahead. I was ready even after I asked about the chances of this succeeding and he said, 'One, maybe two chances in a 100.' I said OK because that's how much I still wanted to play ball at the highest level."

From such desperate straits, the left-hander became the poster boy for an operation that has now become commonplace in baseball. The first operation on John's elbow was performed in mid-September 1974. During that time the worst fears were confirmed. Not only was the ligament holding the elbow together torn, but the muscles surrounding the joint had separated, and the nerve itself had been severely traumatized.

"Considering the long odds with the surgery, what Dr. Jobe had told me about finding another line of work, I figured I better have a serious backup plan when it came to playing baseball," Johns recalls. "So, I called Hoyt Wilhelm at his home in Sarasota. I asked him if he could teach me how to throw a knuckleball. He seemed to think I'd have no problem learning it. Sometimes I think maybe that's the way I should have gone. If so, I'd still be pitching. I'd be baseball's Methuselah."

John never followed up with learning Wilhelm's knuckler. Many believe that's because the ligament surgery was a success right off. In reality, the radical procedure almost didn't work.

In the weeks after the operation, scar tissue compromised the surrounding nerves and paralysis began to set in. Tommy Lasorda says that John's "ring finger and little finger had curled up into his palm. It had atrophied into the hand of a cripple. All he felt was pain and numbness."

After John scalded himself, due to increasing numbness in his fingers, he returned to Dr. Jobe. "Something had to be done. The arm was dying," John explains. "By this point, I had no choice but to keep going down this path."

A few weeks before Christmas 1974, a second operation was performed to clear away the scar tissue. Afterward John's left arm was placed in a cast for several weeks. Never one to mince words, John says his left hand resembled "a monkey paw" when the cast was taken off. That didn't stop him from giving his wife a softball mitt for a game of catch in the backyard. Despite hot-water therapy and squeezing Silly Putty, the arm was slow to respond. To hold a baseball, John needed to pick the ball up with his good right hand and place it in his lifeless left hand. To keep it from falling out, he had to curl the fingers around the ball, sometimes taping them in place.

Even though John couldn't really grip a ball at first, he insisted on attending spring training at the Dodgers' complex in Vero Beach, Florida. Several of his teammates thought he was crazy; just another washed-up pitcher in denial. None of the catchers wanted anything to do with him, so John took half a dozen balls every day down to a concrete wall at the Dodgers' facility, where pitchers practiced their pickoff moves. There, with nobody watching, he tried to throw as best he could.

"What I tell guys who've had this surgery done is that it's like learning how to pitch all over again," John says. "You have to resign yourself to the fact that you're going to have good days and a lot of bad days. No avoiding it because of the steep learning curve involved. You have to accept it. Some days you're going to be horrible out there."

John says about the only people who believed in him at this point were Dr. Jobe, Lasorda, and Dodgers scouting director Ben Wade. Throughout the 1975 season, John was on the Dodgers' bench, charting pitches and trying to make the best of things. "I believe that the injury was God's way of testing me," he says. "Adversity can result in patience and discipline, even character."

John would need all of that and then some to make it back to the pitching mound at the big-league level. Dr. Jobe had told him that nerves regenerate at the rate of an inch a month. So, during that season of purgatory, he kept an eye out for any signs of progress. One morning, when he was driving to the ballpark, John noticed he was able to raise his left pinkie finger, ever so slightly, off the steering wheel. That became another milepost on the road to recovery. In such small steps his body was healing itself. During this time he embraced a line of scripture that he heard at church—"For with God nothing shall be impossible," Luke 1:37.

"Slowly I was gaining momentum," he says. "It was coming back together for me. The key was throwing—a lot. That was the only way we knew of to build up strength in my arm again. So I started to throw every day, often off the mound to a catcher. Before all of this,

I had never been a big believer in throwing every day. In fact, my old pitching coach, Johnny Sain, had told me back in 1971 that I should be throwing every day, but I hadn't paid any attention to him."

What many don't realize is that time almost ran out on John. If anybody needed to go through the routine of spring training, it was the guy recovering from landmark surgery. Yet time in the Florida and Arizona camps was cut short by a labor dispute between the players and owners. By the time it was settled, John had pitched in only three spring training games.

Throughout John's comeback attempt, the Dodgers had been supportive. They let him chart pitches on the bench, even though his teammates thought he was fooling himself. Yet as the 1976 regular season got under way, Dodgers manager Walter Alston began to lose patience. In his first start, John gave up a three-run homer to the Atlanta Braves. Before his next game, just his second start of the season, Alston told John that this could be his last chance. Unless he really showed something against the Houston Astros, the ballclub was of a mind to release him.

With that as the backdrop, John took the mound. When the first two Astros hitters singled, Alston ordered the bullpen to start warming up. No doubt about it. John was on a short leash. The left-hander appeared to be out of trouble when Houston's Cesar Cedeno hit into what was a sure double play. But the relay was thrown away and only Dodgers first baseman Steve Garvey pegging a runner out at the plate kept the Astros off the scoreboard. A wild pitch had moved Cedeno to second with two out.

When John went 3-and-0 to the Astros' Bob Watson, his comeback bid appeared to be nearly over. Catcher Joe Ferguson called time and came out to the mound to talk things over with John. "Now we're gonna find out what you're made of," he told John. "Forget about the hand, forget about the elbow, forget everything. I want to see smoke. Gimme your best fastball. Throw as hard as you can—let 'em rip."

As Johns recalls the moment decades later, "So there I was, one pitch from adios. And I did exactly what Ferguson ordered. I threw three heaters, right down the pipe."

Watson struck out and John never looked back. He finished the season with a 10–10 record and was named Comeback Player of the Year by the *Sporting News*. He would go on to pitch 14 more seasons after his surgery, winning 164 games over that period.

Much has changed medically since John's operation. In 1974, Dr. Jobe rated the chances of his success at 1–2 percent. Today, the chances of complete recovery are 85–90 percent. The injury and resulting surgery have become common in kids as young as 10. And an unexpected benefit of the surgery was discovered. Pitchers who undergo the procedure can often actually throw the ball harder and faster when they return.

A study by the American Orthopedic Society found that 83 percent of athletes at all levels who had Tommy John elbow reconstruction surgery returned to action at "the same or better level of play."

"Today there's little if any downside to having the surgery," says scout Don Welke. "It's become commonplace at the professional level and more than a few seem to be adding some speed to their fastball because of it."

John says he wasn't sure if he threw harder after coming back from the surgery. He was more concerned that his delivery was balanced and the arm came through at the proper angle. Only then could he maintain enough velocity to stay in the game.

In other sports, the limits of performance are methodically broken and shaved away. Thanks to Usain Bolt and Michael Phelps, marks in track and swimming were shattered at the 2008 Summer Games in Beijing. But the gold standard in baseball has long been 100 miles per hour.

"It's a number that is recognized as the elite," says Nolan Ryan, the all-time strikeout king. "So when someone throws at that level, it gets people's attention."

It's also a good way to get hurt. Experts at the American Sports Medicine Institute (ASMI) in Birmingham, Alabama, where pitchers with sore arms are routinely sent for examination, confirm what Tommy John felt that day in 1974: The harder a guy throws, the more violence can be done to the arm. Pitchers can lift weights, even skirt the rules by doing steroids, but their ligaments and tendons remain prone to injury.

"You ready to throw?" says Glenn Fleisig, tossing a hardball in my direction.

Actually, I look better suited for a pickup game of softball in the park. I try to snag the ball nonchalantly, which is pretty much impossible with the softball glove I've brought along. It's so old it's been endorsed by Ted Williams—yes, the vintage model from Sears. I'm dressed in black spandex biker shorts, white ankle socks, and running sneakers. Also, I'm bare-chested—my red Washington Nationals T-shirt draped over a nearby chair, well out of camera range.

As part of the search for the secrets behind high heat, I traveled to ASMI early in the summer of 2009. Located on the St. Vincent's medical campus, a few blocks east of downtown Birmingham, Fleisig and his staff work in conjunction with Dr. James Andrews, the most famous orthopedic surgeon in sports. His office lies only a short walk away, where framed autographed jerseys from Drew Brees, Clinton Portis, and Carmelo Anthony line the hallways. But this afternoon, we're in the cavernous motion laboratory, the domain of Fleisig and his research crew.

I'm bare-chested because 21 reflective markers have been attached to the end points of the bones used for pitching. I sport three on my right pitching wrist and hand alone. Overhead, eight cameras on the ceiling are ready to record my every move at 240 frames per second. The high-speed cameras will be electronically linked, with the data flowing into a single laptop.

Soon it becomes apparent to everybody watching that my catcher, Wesley Pennington, can put a lot more on the ball than I can. Only later do I learn that Wesley played intercollegiate ball. Right now he's humming the ball back to me with attitude, as big leaguers say. His throws have such bite that I can feel my palm, barely protected by the Ted Williams softball mitt, already beginning to ache.

"Tim looks ready enough," Fleisig says. "Let's go."

I've asked to undergo ASMI's basic pitching evaluation. The cost ranges from $500 for youth players to $1,000 for elite players. Fleisig has agreed to do this for free. In some ways, I'm the comic relief for the afternoon.

I step atop the portable mound and peer in at Wesley, 60 feet, 6 inches away. He's wearing shin pads but no mask. He doesn't seem concerned about my fastball catching him in the noggin. The plan calls for me to throw 10 pitches, as hard as I can, and then do three more, under the bright lights, for a video.

Before my first delivery, I find myself flashing back to Steve Dalkowski. No wonder he couldn't throw a strike during that infamous session at the Aberdeen Testing Grounds. A guy feels alone out here, with everybody ready to measure his every move.

"I'm a little self-conscious," I shout to Fleisig.

"Self-conscious?"

"You know, self-conscious, with everybody looking at you?"

"The good ones aren't," Fleisig replies.

I nod, taking that in.

"Try not to move the hat," Fleisig adds. "It could affect the readings."

I nod more slowly, remembering that I have four reflective sensors attached to the white ASMI ball cap I'm wearing.

"All right," Fleisig says. "We're ready when you are."

My first delivery skips a foot or so in front of the plate and Wesley stabs it with a hint of disdain. The way he flips the ball back to me I can tell he isn't impressed.

My second attempt rides only slightly out of the strike zone and Wesley doesn't have to scramble too much to catch it. My next one actually hits the glove with a resounding crack. I'm not doing too badly for the shape I'm in. I awoke at five this morning, flew to Atlanta, and drove two and a half hours down Interstate 20 to get here.

Maybe it's my mind wandering. Whatever the reason, I'm becoming wild in a hurry. In an effort to keep my throws accurate I decide to really concentrate on Wesley's glove, to shorten up my delivery, make it more compact. Too late I realize that's exactly the wrong thing to do. In compromising everything for accuracy, my velocity plummets. My windup becomes more ragged, really out of whack, and as a result I don't even hit 50 miles per hour on the ASMI radar gun.

G rowing up in Rockland County, north of New York City, Glenn Fleisig loved to play baseball. In fact, his car sports a Mets license plate and a hardball atop the stick shift. His real aptitude, though, was for how the world moves and fits together. He attended Massachusetts Institute of Technology (MIT), studying mechanical engineering. His plan was to find a job in that field and play ball on the weekends.

He worked hard at MIT, on track to earn his degree in three and a half years. The only thing standing in his way was the senior project, a schoolwide requirement back in 1983. At first, Fleisig wasn't sure what to do. But then he wandered into the biomechanics lab and a whole new world opened up to him.

"They were applying the laws and mechanics of physics to human motion," he says. "Basically, that's biomechanics. Before then I'd never heard the word. Here they were not just building cars and bridges, but seeing how people move. I thought this was really cool. In the lab, they were breaking down the components of a golf swing. I thought that if I have to do some schoolwork, I might as well do it about a golf swing."

Fleisig became so enthralled with biomechanics that on the eve of graduation he asked his professor where he could find a job in this field. The prof only smiled. Biomechanics was so new in the mid-1980s that there were no real jobs to be had. One of the few places serious about such work was the U.S. Olympic training center in Colorado Springs. Fleisig was lucky enough to land an internship there in the summer of 1984, when the center was ramping up for the Summer Games in Los Angeles. Barely an afterthought much of the time, the Olympics moves front and center in the years the games are held. And that's when Fleisig found himself studying the biomechanics of top American athletes about to compete on the world stage.

But such heady times ended almost as soon as they began. Soon after the Olympics, Fleisig's internship in Colorado Springs ended, and once again he was looking for a job. He heard about an up-and-coming orthopedic surgeon, Dr. James Andrews, and the two of them spoke over the phone.

"I want to apply biomechanics to baseball," Fleisig said.

"That's exactly what I want to do," Dr. Andrews replied. "But I'm not ready yet."

Nobody else in the country was as enthusiastic about applying rules of physics to sports, really investigating how the basic motions we've done since childhood can be honed and improved to lessen injury and heighten performance. So, Fleisig began to pursue his master's in mechanical engineering and got work building missile defense systems for a firm based in New Jersey. On Thanksgiving Day 1986, two and a half years after his conversation with Dr. Andrews, the phone rang at Fleisig's parents' house. After rising through the ranks, Dr. Andrews was ready to open his own practice, and he wanted Fleisig on board.

"He asked, 'You remember us? You still want to do this?'" Fleisig recalls. "Of course, I did. I couldn't think of anything else in the world I more wanted to do."

From such impromptu beginnings, a sports biomechanical empire has flourished in the hills above Birmingham. Here, the doctors rely on the information discovered in Fleisig's lab, as well as the data from a more grisly setting. Within easy walking distance of the motion laboratory and the doctors' offices, down a narrow hallway, lies the metal vault, where the cadavers are kept cold.

Instead of full torsos, ASMI requires joints—shoulders, elbows, and knees. Almost regardless of sport, these are the pivot points where things start to break down. To determine how well and how long a surgically repaired elbow can hold up, for example, the operation is performed on a cadaver joint and then put to the test. Drills and a vice are the tools of the trade found in this windowless room.

On this day, two knee joints sit on a small table. Holes have been drilled into the side because Dr. Andrews and his staff are debating the best entry point for anterior cruciate ligament (ACL) operations.

"It's the only way to determine what really works," says Becky Bolt, a biomechanist at ASMI.

Perhaps I've seen *Young Frankenstein* one too many times, but I can't help asking her if it's difficult locating such body parts for testing.

"Most of them come from people in their 50s," she replies. "We'd love to have younger ones, but they're tough to procure."

Is it just my imagination or does Bolt keep flashing looks at my knees and elbows? Hopefully she has my chart for the evaluation. I'm older than I look. Honest.

The next morning, Fleisig and his staff meet with me to analyze my pitching motion. To throw a ball with any velocity or command requires a series of movements, sometimes working in opposition to each other, to be adeptly performed in a set order. Fleisig calls these motions "the kinetic series," a sequence composed of The Windup, The Pivot or Balance Point, The Stride, The Release, and The Follow-Through.

"If any of these factors fall out of alignment, isn't doing its job, then whatever energy has been built up quickly dissipates," Fleisig says. "Picture that we're out skating and Wes is on the end. We want to send him flying, really propel him. So, we join hands and if each of us puts some effort into it, that energy is passed down the line, with Wes being the beneficiary."

What the ASMI research director has described, of course, is "crack the whip," the childhood game played on frozen ponds and roller rinks across the country.

"But if everyone doesn't give a little push," Fleisig adds, "or worse yet, the chain is broken—we drop hands—then the energy isn't transferred. No matter how hard Wes skates he cannot go as fast as the rest of us could propel him. The same process happens with throwing a baseball."

We've gathered around a large-screen television. Freeze-framed on it is an image of me—about to go into my windup. Thanks to video and computer analysis, every step of my motion has been broken down and compared to the steps of pitchers of all levels, from youth to the elite. The reflector sensors allow the data to be crunched into a biomechanical report.

The first stage is The Windup. For the evaluation, I decided to go with a complete delivery. No going out of the stretch as pitchers do with a man on base. As I bring my left leg up, begin to turn at the waist, everything flows well enough. As I reach the point where I stop turning, in effect trying to turn my body into a human catapult, Fleisig pauses the video.

Here I've reached The Pivot or Balance Point. After moving away from the plate, the pitcher gathers himself here before picking up speed and throwing toward the catcher. Even though I'm on one foot here, looking like a flamingo about to take flight, I'm pretty well balanced. Despite leaning back a shade, the staff agrees, so far I'm doing the job. Unfortunately, my kinetic chain is about to go headlong into the ditch.

Soon comes The Stride, and mine is way too short. Instead of looking like Tom Seaver, who stepped toward home plate with such purpose that he routinely scuffed the knee of his back, drive leg, I look like I'm hopping, rather daintily, over a mud puddle. Until this point, I've been within "the normative range" throughout the evaluation. But now the data fades from black to red numbers, meaning I'm screwing up—bad.

My stride should be slightly less than my height (69 inches). Instead, it's a lackluster 55 percent of my height. In comparison, elite pitchers are in the 78 percent to 87 percent range. In addition, the position of my lead left foot isn't right. Quality pitchers plant that foot directly in front of the pitching rubber, with the toes slightly to the side. Instead, I've come down too far to the side and my toes are toward the catcher. On top of it all, my elbow, as I cock the ball, is a bit low.

"The energy that you gathered during The Windup is now being lost," Fleisig says. "So much of throwing hard comes from the legs.

You hear that all the time. What it means is that what you generate from the lower half of the body needs to be transferred to the arm and ultimately the ball. Here, that connection, the link, is lost. Any strength from the legs is gone. From now on, you're trying to generate all your power just with your arm."

Wesley Pennington adds, "Pitching effectively is an elaborate system of pauses, stops and starts. If one thing is off, it doesn't matter how well you do the rest."

From here on, my pitching motion becomes a runaway train on a downhill track. As a result of my short stride, my elbow doesn't flow back far enough. That results in my release point being too far above my head. The speed of my arm when my elbow extends should be 2,200–2,681 degrees per second. Mine is a pedestrian 1,707. In my Follow-Through, my pelvis should slow by 23–38 meters per second. I'm still flying off the handle at 11. A pitching motion that began with such promise now resembles a Rube Goldberg drawing—all bad angles and poor intentions.

The staff's consensus? If I pitched like this on a regular basis, I'd end up on the disabled list, or at least at my chiropractor, in a few weeks. I decide not to tell them my shoulder has been pretty achy since yesterday's session.

In reviewing the data, I realize that my mind-set was completely off, too. In trying so hard to control the ball, I ended up aiming it. Almost pushing the ball toward the plate like a guy at the local pub would propel a dart. In essence, I'd throttled back on how hard I could throw simply to get the ball across the plate. As a result, I gave away whatever real talent I'd brought to the table. The real pitching geniuses among us may be the ones with enough confidence to keep throwing hard, no matter the consequences or initial results. They certainly make adjustments (what I'd give to throw at ASMI again with a longer stride off the pitching rubber), but they never compromise or stop believing in themselves.

After a biomechanical analysis at ASMI, pitchers receive an 11-page report and a DVD. The older ones then huddle with their strength and pitching coaches. Specific exercises can be prescribed, and everyone keeps an eye out for the same bad habits.

A few hours after my evaluation, a local dad brings his nine-year-old into the ASMI motion lab. (To my ever-lasting dismay, the kid is clocked two miles per hour faster than me.) After watching the video, the father pays mostly in cash, so his wife won't be the wiser. If that seems a tad excessive, you haven't been around youth sports much.

The days when kids marked the seasons by sports—football in the fall, basketball and hockey in the winter, and track and baseball in the spring—are pretty much gone. From New England to California, kids have become pint-sized specialists, playing just one sport year-round.

"We have reached the point of saturation—a vicious revolving door of never-ending seasons," says Fred Engh, president of the National Alliance for Youth Sports, in his book *Why Johnny Hates Sports*. "Children cannot even take a couple of months' hiatus from a sport for fear of falling behind their peers and being excluded from teams the following seasons. Those elite teams, all those trophies—that's what the parents want."

In fact, the number of kids who specialize has grown to such proportions that the American Academy of Pediatrics (AAP) issued a policy statement a decade ago warning that serious health risks come with concentrating too much, too early on a single sport. "More injuries, more signs of psychological stress and more cases of early burnout" are the results, says Steven Anderson, the chair of the academy's committee on sports specialization in children. "The returns for this early investment of time and energy do not seem to justify the costs."

According to the AAP, signs of overload include chronic injuries and illnesses, weight loss, sleep disturbances, and falling grades in school. When any of these problems present themselves, Anderson says, "the sport, the intensity, the source of motivation and the fun level need to be closely examined."

At ASMI, Fleisig fields calls from concerned parents, and he often agrees with the AAP and other youth experts: Specializing too early in one sport doesn't make much sense when it comes to biomechanics.

"In generations past, when kids got tired they usually played a little more and then went home," he says. "But now you have the guys in the uniforms, the supervising adults, saying, 'Oh, no, we have three more innings to pitch.' In generations past, little boys' bodies were calling the shots. Now we're listening to the adults, not the kids."

Fleisig says that any rigorous sports activity produces "microtears" in the muscles, tendons, and ligaments. That's normal, and when we allow the body to rest it will repair itself.

"We're alive—we're not cars or bridges," the research director adds. "The body has a great feedback system, the ability to repair itself. It works great, if we listen and pay attention.

"I tell people major-league baseball players don't play year-round. They play in a cycle—preseason, regular season, perhaps postseason, and then the off-season. But somewhere along the line, in this past generation, more kids have started to specialize in one sport and play it year-round. As a result, they are really stacking the deck for injury."

Compare the experiences of today's pint-sized pitchers with the way Walter Johnson or Bob Feller was raised. In many modern-day households, the exceptional athlete is elevated to what author Mary Collins calls "performer status." Weekends and after school tend to revolve around the star child athlete. These kids often don't have daily chores to do, as Johnson and Feller did.

"By Little League, the better kids are on select teams," Nolan Ryan says. "What do we do with the kid who shows the ability and coordination and timing to pitch at an early age? We overthrow them. As a result, it used to be college kids, but now it is high school kids who've had Tommy John surgery."

Although Feller had his own "field of dreams"—a backyard ball field he built with his father—neither he nor baseball was placed above the family's daily routine. While Sundays during the summer were spent playing ball at the Oakview ballpark, the rest of the week Feller and his sister, Marguerite, helped out around the farm, and Saturdays were spent going to town and selling "the grain, corn, hogs and livestock," he says.

Sports psychologist Rick Wolff says in *Coaching Kids for Dummies* that "excelling in sports has become as much a part of the

American dream for parents as getting their kids into the best schools and living in the best neighborhoods."

Certainly playing baseball for a living, reaching the major leagues, was a dream of Feller's from an early age. But he shakes his head when discussing the lengths kids and their parents will go in pursuit of an athletic scholarship or a professional contract a half century later.

"At some basic level, you have to keep it fun," he says. "I mean that's why you play the game in the first place. That's what I did."

Feller emphasizes that while baseball was always his first love, reluctantly agreeing that some would consider his father overindulgent for helping him build his own personal field, he adds that things were somehow different back then. Feller also played basketball at Van Meter High School. In fact, he was a starter. His sister was on the girls' basketball team and the state champion in table tennis.

"We had success, but it was a part of our regular life," Feller says. "No matter how well I pitched or played, there were still chores to be done. I'd say it was the same with Walter Johnson, probably most players coming up until recent years. And you know, looking back on it, thank God for that farm work. I may have hated it at the time, but it made me strong. I could pitch all day after doing those chores."

Fleisig nods as I tell him about Feller's upbringing. "He did different sports; his body had a chance to recover," the ASMI research director says. "His was a more reasoned approach than what we see happening today. Somewhere the next Bob Feller or Nolan Ryan is growing up, but I doubt if he's playing baseball 12 months out of the year."

A nybody who followed baseball during the 1990s realizes that they were lied to. Nearly all of us covering the game during that period can probably look back on at least one moment or interview where we allowed the wool to be pulled over our eyes when it came to the steroids issue. Mine came in 1998, when I covered what was then billed as "The Great Home Run Chase" for *Baseball Weekly*. I bought into much of the hoopla surrounding Mark McGwire and Sammy Sosa. Once upon a time, the thread of epic home-run hitters—Babe Ruth, Hank Greenberg, Roger Maris, Hank Aaron—held together different eras of the game. Now the stain of performance-enhancing drugs extends from McGwire and Sosa to Barry Bonds, Alex Rodriguez, and Manny Ramirez. For a long time, steroids and supplements were thought to benefit only hitters. It took a topflight fireballer—Roger Clemens—to prove otherwise.

In 1998, Clemens was enjoying a season for the ages with the Toronto Blue Jays. When I caught up with him late that summer he was well on his way to not only winning a record fifth Cy Young Award, but to capturing pitching's Triple Crown (victories, ERA, and strikeouts) for the second consecutive year as well. Despite his being almost 36 years old, scouts marveled that he was throwing harder than ever. His fastball, which was topping out at 92 miles per hour his last season in Boston, was close to the century mark on the radar gun.

It was an amazing turnaround from the start of the season. Eleven starts in, Clemens had gone 5–6, with an ERA of 3.50, and was still trying to win three games in a row, let alone repeat as Cy Young champion. But from the end of May through the rest of the season, Clemens went 15–0 in 22 starts with a 2.29 ERA. After failing to reach double figures in strikeouts in his first 11 starts, he reached that plateau 11 times afterward, averaging 11.02 strikeouts per every nine innings.

As the summer got hotter, so did the Rocket. During a stretch in late August he almost single-handedly led the Blue Jays back into wild-card contention, pitching three consecutive shutouts against Seattle, Kansas City, and Minnesota.

"Sometimes I stop and shake my head," Clemens said after that third shutout. "I feel I've been in a zone. All the work I did in April, May, and June is paying off."

What was actually paying off for Clemens was the regimen he was employing. According to the Mitchell Report and later detailed by Jeff Pearlman in *The Rocket That Fell to Earth*, Clemens had begun to shoot up with Winstrol, a synthetic anabolic steroid. That's the same stuff sprinter Ben Johnson tested positive for in the 1988 Summer Olympics. Down the road, baseball sluggers Rafael Palmeiro and Barry Bonds would be accused of using it. By the end of the season, Blue Jays strength and conditioning coach Brian McNamee was injecting Clemens with Winstrol every third day.

Of course, Clemens didn't mention that particular part of his fitness plan. Instead, he preferred to talk about his role as an elder statesman, a would-be Zen master to the promising Blue Jays hurlers, who included Pat Hentgen, Roy Halladay, and Chris Carpenter. Carpenter grew up in Raymond, New Hampshire, 40 minutes from Fenway Park. "Roger was my hero back then," he told me at the time. "Now I get to watch him every day. How he prepares."

Ah, the downside of hero worship. The epic season that enthralled us all was soon suspected to be tainted. As were many of the seasons that followed. More than a decade later, with Clemens still in denial about any involvement with steroids or human growth hormones, investigations indicated how improbable those Cy Young seasons were in Toronto. "The arc of Clemens' career is upside down," wrote Eric Bradlow, Shane Jensen, Justin Wolfers, and Adi Wyner in the *New York Times* in 2008. "His performance declines as he enters his late 20s and improves into his mid-30s and 40s."

Anybody who's seen *Damn Yankees* knows that ballplayers will make a pact with any devil to improve performance. It's nothing new. A century before Clemens, Pud Galvin drank a concoction of glycerin and ground-up animal testicles to give his fastball more staying power. "If there still be doubting Thomases who concede no virtue of the elixir," the *Washington Post* reported in 1889, "they are respectfully referred to Galvin's record in yesterday's Boston-Pittsburgh game. It is the best proof yet furnished of the value of the discovery."

Despite Galvin's and the *Post*'s claims, there is no magic potion or elixir that will transform a pedestrian pitcher into a fireballer. But that hasn't stopped players from going to great, sometimes superstitious, sometimes dangerous and illegal, lengths to take their game to the next level or, in the case of veterans, delay Father Time. Clemens managed to throw hard into his 40s, but that still wasn't even close to one of the greatest, most prolific fireballers of all time.

The incomparable Satchel Paige pitched well into his 50s, even though his exact age was always up for debate. A skinny kid growing up ("If I turned sideways, you couldn't see me"), Paige was still a beanpole when he began to star in the Negro Leagues. He would always be embarrassed by his skinny legs and often wore two pairs of socks to flesh out his lower silhouette. But Paige knew the value of being physically fit. He regularly warmed up by fielding bunts, shagging flies, taking infield at third base. He tried not to throw hard "until every muscle, every single one, was all loosened up." On game days, which were pretty much most days when Paige was barnstorming, he took a hot bath after he woke and often a hotter one after the game.

Many of Paige's fitness tips would play as well today as they did three-quarters of a century ago. In his autobiography, Paige outlined his keys "for staying young." Such tips included:

- "Avoid fried meats which angry up the blood."
- "If your stomach disputes you, lie down and pacify it with cool thoughts."
- "Keep the juices flowing by jangling around gently as you move."
- "Go very light on the vices, such as carrying on in society—the social ramble ain't restful."
- And the tip that would become his calling card, "Don't look back. Something might be gaining on you."

Phil Pote once asked Bob Feller, excluding himself, who was the fastest pitcher ever. Feller replied, "Satchel Paige."

Feller and Paige barnstormed together during the 1940s and many came away believing that Paige's fastball was a touch quicker.

"[My] fastball looks like a change of pace alongside that little pistol bullet Satchel shoots up to the plate," Dizzy Dean once wrote in his newspaper column. "And I really know something about it because for four, five years I tour around at the end of the season with all-star teams and I see plenty of Old Satch.

"It's too bad those colored boys don't play in the big leagues because they sure got some great ballplayers."

If the search for the fastest pitcher wasn't complicated enough, consider that several of the top hurlers ever to play the game were forbidden from appearing in the major leagues due to the color of their skin. They played in the old Negro Leagues, in what passed for baseball's parallel universe, underpublicized and too often unnoticed by much of the country, until Jackie Robinson broke the color barrier in 1947. Paige was eventually afforded the opportunity to pitch at the game's highest level, making the big leagues in 1948 at the ripe old age of 42.

"Age is a question of mind over matter," Paige once said. "If you don't mind, it doesn't matter."

To this day, Paige remains the most famous pitcher to come out of the Negro Leagues (he struck out 21 major leaguers in one exhibition game) and he made the Hall of Fame in 1971 as the first Negro League inductee. Lost in his shadow, though, stand such other quality fireballers as Smokey Joe Williams, Leon Day, and Wilber "Bullet" Joe Rogan.

In an effort to recapture the past, Buck O'Neil once wrote up several scouting reports on the old Negro Leaguers. They now reside at the Hall of Fame in Cooperstown. O'Neil was a player and manager in the Negro Leagues, and in his later years he scouted for the Chicago Cubs and Kansas City Royals and was the star of Ken Burns's television series *Baseball*. The scouting reports O'Neil assembled are in his handwriting, on Royals letterhead, and they have become a tribute to what might have been.

For right-hander Leon Day, O'Neil notes that he would have been a "front-line starter" in the major leagues. "Everything quick," O'Neil writes. "Strikeout pitcher. Very durable. Worked with three days rest. Played second base or left field between starts. Top athlete. Very desirable."

O'Neil becomes more laudatory in his look back at Bullet Rogan. A pitcher with little or no windup, who came right at hitters, Rogan was maybe 5-foot-5, 155 pounds, proving that little guys could bring the heat well before Tim Lincecum and Billy Wagner.

What exactly did Rogan's no-windup delivery look like? Allow historian Paul W. Fisher to describe the scene:

> Every eye is trained on the mighty Rogan. He is a trim, square-shouldered, deep-chested man, with slim legs and hips. He brings his hands softly to his belt buckle, his hips begin to pivot slowly right, the hands come slowly and softly toward his face and then—
>
> His right arm has swept back quicker than the eye, whipped around and over and at slightly less than three-quarters motion. In the yellow afternoon, a mote of white light flies from his black hand. The fortunate among the thousands caught its split-second speed; even at the far reaches of the roped outfield, they heard its crash into [Frank] Duncan's big glove. WHAP!

What we have here is a pitcher intent on getting batters out in a hurry.

"Live high fastball and hard sharp breaking curveball that we called a drop ball," O'Neil says of Rogan. "Strikeout pitcher. Excellent athlete. Hit fourth in the lineup when he played the outfield. Very desirable. Bob Feller type."

Was he better than Paige?

"I don't know," Bobby Williams, a veteran shortstop in the Negro Leagues told John Holway. "He was good, but I wouldn't say he was greater than Paige. But Rogan was another infielder when he was pitching, he could play outfield, he could hit. Paige couldn't do anything but pitch."

For much of his career, even though it rarely showed on the field, Paige was bothered by an upset stomach, especially in high-pressured games. He nicknamed his stomach troubles "the miseries," and initially the condition was blamed on big-game stress and fast living. Several doctors wondered if he had ulcers. It wasn't until late in his career, between the 1948 and 1949 seasons, that the real culprit was discovered—lousy teeth. Paige's choppers were literally rotting away, so he had all of them pulled and went the rest of his days with ill-fitting dentures.

"When your whole life may be depending on your stomach, you don't worry about having no teeth," he later wrote. "You'll do about anything, even if you got to put a bunch of sticks in your mouth."

After Paige got used to his "store teeth," he prayed and waited to see if the old stomach ailments would return with the same vengeance. "But those pains weren't coming back like they used to," he said. "They were there, but not like they'd been all through the last season."

Teeth problem aside, what made Paige unusual among legendary pitchers was his miraculous comeback from a bout of arm trouble that would have ended most careers and perhaps reduced him to a footnote in the search for the top fireballer of all time.

In 1938, Paige was arguably at his peak. He had just returned from the Dominican Republic, where he and other Negro League stars—Josh Gibson, Schoolboy Griffin, and Cool Papa Bell—had led Cuidad Trujillo to the championship. That team had been bankrolled by the country's dictator, Rafael Trujillo. Before the championship game, against Estrellas de Oriente, Paige's ballclub was sequestered in a guarded hotel. After they fell behind in the early innings, Trujillo's troops began to surround the diamond.

"You better win," the Trujillo City manager told his all-stars.

They rallied for a 6–5 victory. Paige was on the mound, where he took a look around at all the weaponry and figured he was pitching for his life.

After that near-death experience, Paige and the others hurried back to the United States. While the other Negro League all-stars stayed close to home, Paige was looking for another big payday, so he ducked out of his agreement with the Pittsburgh Crawfords and headed to Mexico.

"Being greedy like that just about ended my career," he wrote, "and just about cost me a couple or three times the money I was making for those few games in Mexico."

Three games into the season, Paige felt what was at first a burning sensation in his arm. A few days' rest didn't help. In fact, the burning gave way to numbness. Paige began to run a fever, and soon after he couldn't even lift his arm above his head.

In desperation, he went down to the stadium and, without bothering to change into his uniform, tried to throw. The ball only traveled a few feet and Paige headed home the next day. He was examined by several specialists. One told him he would never pitch again.

Paige was only 32 years old. A typical ballplayer would usually have several more years in him. But in the world of high heat, the fall from star to mere mortal can be sudden and unexpected.

"I didn't want to see nobody," Paige later said in his autobiography. "I could see the end. Ten years of gravy and then nothing but an aching arm and aching stomach. Oh, I had my car and shotguns and fishing gear and clothes.

"I had those, all right, and they were all mighty fine. But you got to make money to keep them and when you ain't making money and when you ain't saved money, they go fast.

"Mr. Pawnshop must have thought I was a burglar the way I kept coming back to see him with another shotgun or another suit."

Sucking up his pride, Paige got a job as a pitcher/first baseman on the Kansas City Monarchs' barnstorming squad. With another Negro League season under way, the team was essentially a backup squad. They toured the Northwest and Canada, playing whenever they could. Paige often heard it from the crowd when he took the mound. They came to see the fabled fireballer and instead all he would deliver was soft stuff, sidearm and even underhanded. When Paige's arm showed no sign of coming around, he was moved to first base. His goal was to save up some money before returning home to Mobile, Alabama.

But one day, before the next game, Paige began to warm up on the sidelines. Even though he was playing first base, a position that didn't require much throwing, Paige threw repeatedly in warm-ups. It was the only way to push the pain in his arm toward numbness.

But on this day, there was no pain when he threw. He called the catcher over and began to throw harder to him. Knut Joseph, the manager, was summoned and proceedings shifted to the pitching mound. There, Paige threw pitch after pitch, putting more and more effort into each one, beginning to kick his leg toward the heavens in that classic pitching motion of his. With each delivery, the velocity increased and, more importantly, the pain didn't return.

The catcher and manager were both grinning by now. That evening Joseph called J. L. Wilkinson, the Monarchs' owner back in Kansas City. Even though Paige was eager to rejoin the parent club, Wilkinson, to his credit, refused to rush things. He told Paige to stay with the backup club for the rest of the season, to get back in shape. It wasn't until the spring of 1939—at the age of 33—that Paige's comeback began.

"After my arm first came back, I didn't know for sure I could blaze away until I got back into some games and really had to," Paige said in his autobiography. "I could. That hummer of mine sang a sweet song going across the plate. It was the finest music I'd ever heard."

Paige would later call his recovery "a miracle." With his arm better than ever, he rejoined the Kansas City Monarchs for the 1939 season and finally got his chance to play in the major leagues nine years later.

The scar has long ago faded to just a thin white line, riding the inside of the elbow joint on Tommy John's famous left arm. After retiring as a player in 1989, with a 288–231 record and 3.34 ERA, John still found ways to stay in the game. He was a coach, a broadcaster, and, as the 2009 season began, in his third season as the manager of the Bridgeport (Connecticut) Bluefish in the Atlantic League. Over the years, he's had several players on his teams who've had the operation he made famous. In fact, one guy even had Tommy John surgery twice.

Such notoriety hasn't brought him any closer to the National Baseball Hall of Fame in Cooperstown, however. Before the 2009 season began, it was announced that John received only 31.7 percent of the votes from the baseball writers, well below the 75 percent required for induction. The bid was his last attempt. While John could someday gain entry through the Hall of Fame's Veterans Committee, he isn't counting on it.

"It is what it is," he says as his Bluefish take batting practice. "It's not something I have any control over, so why worry about it? The guy who I'd really like to see make it to Cooperstown is Dr. Jobe."

John tells how it was Dr. Jobe's idea to cut along the original incision made to remove the elbow chips in 1972. How it made sense to follow that "road map," as the doctor told him, and leave the surrounding muscle areas undisturbed. Over the years, John has come to believe that it was such subtleties and attention to detail that made all the difference.

"I was lucky," he says. "I happened to be on a team with the best doctor in the world to do such a thing. He rolled it all out for me, never kept me in the dark about what was going to happen. Now the surgery has become almost run of the mill—young kids are even getting it. But it sure wasn't run of the mill back then. All of us were taking a huge chance."

Someday John would love to coach at the big-league level. Yet he wonders at age 66 if he's perceived by baseball's powerbrokers as being too old, just another baseball lifer past his prime. The surgery, that stroke of genius when an unnecessary tendon from John's right wrist was used to reconstruct his left elbow, will be the headline on his obituary, and he knows it.

"And that's fine," John says. "Maybe that's how it should be. In an ideal world, the procedure should really be named after Frank Jobe. He's the one who drew it up. I was just the guy who needed it."

But then he smiles, adding, "That said, I wouldn't mind a hundred bucks for every one that's been done since I went under the knife. That would be OK with me."

The Follow-Through

Steve Dalkowski
Photo courtesy of the National Baseball Hall of Fame Library, Cooperstown, NY

*I am convinced that life is 10 percent what happens to me
and 90 percent how I react to it.*

—CHARLES SWINDOLL

Show a little faith, there's magic in the night.

—BRUCE SPRINGSTEEN

Tornadoes were sighted in the Dallas suburbs last night, and now in the morning dark clouds ride the western horizon. The gusting winds cause the lights to flicker inside Nolan Ryan's executive office. The man they call "Big Tex" in these parts barely acknowledges the ongoing cracks of thunder and flashes of lightning. From his perch high above the playing field at Rangers Ballpark in Arlington, Texas, he wants nothing more than to get in tonight's game against the visiting Toronto Blue Jays. The previous night's contest was canceled. So much rain fell that not even the Rangers' high-tech field, capable of siphoning off up to 10 inches per hour, could keep up with the onslaught from Mother Nature.

As the tempest rages outside, Ryan glances at the scouting reports for his ballclub's 2009 top picks. A few days ago, baseball's annual draft was held, with fireballer Stephen Strasburg going to the Washington Nationals as the first selection overall. As president of the Texas Rangers, Ryan has a major hand in his team's draft strategy. The old baseball assertion that you can never have enough pitching rings

195

as true today as it did a century ago. With that in mind, Texas selected a pair of pitchers—Matthew Purke and Tanner Scheppers—as its first two picks. Purke fits the desired profile (left-handed, fresh out of high school). In comparison, Scheppers was a roll of the dice. After starring at Fresno State, he suffered a shoulder injury prior to last year's draft. As a result, he fell to 48th overall. Instead of signing, Scheppers pitched for the St. Paul Saints in the independent American Association. That's where Don Welke, the scout who championed Jim Abbott, and who now works for the Rangers, became convinced Scheppers could play at the big-league level.

"Don's definitely in his corner," says Ryan, who is just the third Hall of Fame player to serve as president of a major-league team. John Montgomery Ward (1912) and Christy Mathewson (1923 and 1925) are the others. "If it wasn't for Don Welke, we probably wouldn't have taken Scheppers, at least not that high. But when a scout with a track record like Welke's makes the case for somebody, you have to listen."

But even if the science and the majority of scouting reports stack the deck against such a move? Unlike other team presidents, Ryan admittedly has a soft spot for scouts who wear their hearts on their sleeves. They remind him of Red Murff, the scout who years ago believed in him when the rest of the Mets' scouting staff had wanted to draft just about anybody else.

Here, in the days following the annual amateur draft, Ryan knows as well as anybody that the real challenge for any organization has only just begun. "The biggest thing young pitchers have to learn is to believe in themselves," he says. "They don't have to possess the most remarkable arm to succeed. But they need to realize, very quickly, how important it is to throw strikes, to trust their stuff."

Mike Maddux, who was brought in as the Rangers' pitching coach under the Ryan regime, often talks about "pitching with conviction," which he defines as "acting wholeheartedly on what you believe in, what you know to be true."

"The question is always, can you put it together?" Ryan says. "Over the years, I've seen a lot of kids who had unbelievably great arms but never made much of it. They either got injured or were unable to master the principles of throwing. When you get to this level, the major leagues, there's not a lot of separation in the physical ability of players. It's the mental approach to the game that separates people.

"There are times that you need to will the ball over the plate. Those are situations where you have to throw strikes and it has to be in a certain location. You have to believe in yourself because the game is on the line. That's what separates people at the highest levels."

Such traits and characteristics remain almost impossible to gauge and decipher, even by the best of scouts. Pure speed, on the other hand, is something tangible. And yet, judging speed has always been more complicated than taking simple measurements.

In 1997, Matt Anderson was that year's Stephen Strasburg. The pitching phenom regularly hit 100 miles per hour on the radar gun, and scouts charted his every start at Rice University. When word got back to Ryan, who had retired a few years earlier, he decided to check out the hard thrower, himself.

In person, it was clear Anderson did in fact have plenty of giddyup on his fastball. And at first Ryan was excited by what he saw on the mound. But then he noticed that just about every batter was able to foul off Anderson's famed fastball. Eager for a better look, Ryan left the seats behind home plate, where the radar guns were assembled, and walked over to the left field line. There he studied Anderson's delivery and determined that the phenom was opening up toward the plate too quickly. No matter how hard he threw, the batters were able to catch a good glimpse of his high heat. When a scout asked Ryan what he thought, looking for confirmation of Anderson's promise, the Hall of Famer stunned him by mentioning a flaw in the prospect's delivery.

"I'm not qualified to say if it's correctable or not," Ryan said. "But it's a big concern of mine."

The Detroit Tigers selected Anderson with the first pick in the 1997 amateur draft. After posting a 5–1 record the following season—a rookie year in which he struck out 44 in 44 innings—he blew out his shoulder in 2002 and would never be the same.

Most of the time science serves us well. Time and time again we're reassured by its ability to explain so much, to tie it all together with a fancy, empirical bow. But when things don't add up, when the deluge does arrive, we're reminded how much remains unfathomable. How the world can still surprise.

As the rain continues to fall outside Ryan's office, our conversation turns to epic fireballers, the fastest of the fast. For Ryan, the best ones had something more in their favor than correct elbow angle or significant leg stride. Sandy Koufax, Bob Gibson, Bob Feller are among his favorites because they went beyond sheer ability. They "were willing to make the commitment," he says.

Perhaps with that in mind, Ryan adds another name to his short list.

"Billy Wagner," he says. "I think he threw as hard as anybody I've ever seen."

In 2003, Wagner's fastball was clocked at 101 miles per hour at Turner Field in Atlanta. That made him one-tenth of a second faster than Ryan's 100.9 miles per hour, which was recorded in 1974. Of course, there's no real barometer for throwing the high heat. Radar guns weren't around when Johnson, Paige, or Feller played. And to this day, Major League Baseball doesn't recognize radar speeds as an official statistic. There's also little consensus among the game's statistical services—Elias Sports Bureau, STATS Inc, and the *Sporting News*. But what's just as interesting when it comes to pitchers like Wagner is another set of numbers—height and weight.

According to *The Baseball Encyclopedia,* the self-proclaimed "complete and definitive record of Major League Baseball," Wagner is 5-foot-11 and 170 pounds. As they say in television, he looks a lot bigger on the screen. In another sport, Wagner's size would be a huge strike against any prospect and sometimes still is in the baseball world, where most scouts favor huge, strapping guys over punks any day. Yet if you can throw a baseball, hard, sooner or later, you'll probably get your chance.

"You see little guys who are capable of throwing cheese," says right-hander Tim Lincecum of the San Francisco Giants. "That stigma of being too small is always there, though, I suppose. Everybody still seems to love the big guy. But that doesn't mean us little guys can't bring it."

After his junior year at the University of Washington, Lincecum stood 5-foot-9 and weighed 160 pounds. In large part that's why the first nine teams passed on him in the amateur draft. They did so even though Lincecum was a two-time Pac-10 pitcher of the year and had struck out more batters in conference play than Tom Seaver, Mark Prior, and Randy Johnson.

After joining the Giants' organization, Lincecum soon made it clear to the front office that the minor leagues were a waste of time. He pitched only 13 times down on the farm, allowing seven earned runs and striking out 104 batters. His fastball was consistently clocked in the high-90s. In May 2007, Lincecum got the call to join the big-league club and didn't miss a beat. He threw 30 quality starts in his first 40 games for the Giants. Since 1956, only six other pitchers have done that at the big-league level. Still, respect can be so elusive. On the road, team secretaries have to keep an eye out because more than one security guard has tried to run him out of the stadium. Lincecum looks more like a skateboard punk than the ace of his team's pitching staff.

"That's why somebody like Billy Wagner will always be somebody I look up to," Lincecum says. "In the past few years, I've been catching up on the history of guys who could throw hard. I've seen footage of Feller. He had a higher leg kick than me. He was longer with his follow-through. My delivery is more like Sandy Koufax's. It's about the right weight transfer at the right time. I've got more of Luis Tiant, that hip roll, in me. But you're only talking slight differences there. Anybody who can throw hard can look at somebody else who throws hard and see the familiarities. It's kind of like we're talking the same language. That's why I can't figure out why so many scouts and baseball people mess up. If you can bring it, why worry about what a guy looks like, how he does it?"

If we were out on the playground, picking teams, Wagner would appear to have little in common with Ryan, Feller, Walter Johnson, or even such contemporary fireballers as Joel Zumaya, Ubaldo Jimenez, or David Price. But there's something about not only the way his fastball once crackled but also what he went through just to reach the pitching mound.

For his part, Wagner cannot fully explain why or how his fastball registered above 100 miles per hour 18 times during the 2005 season alone. He talks about it having something to do with heart with a large dollop of anger, and then agrees that a big part might have to do with how he grew up. That a rocky childhood can perhaps result in the gift of an epic fastball.

As he walks in from the bullpen, with the game on the line, you wonder: How can this little guy get anybody out? Billy Wagner is often listed at 5-foot-11, but he is easily an inch or two shorter. This has to be some kind of joke, right?

But then Wagner begins his warm-up throws. His windup is compact and quick, and the ball flies out of his hand, making a beeline for the plate. Throughout the warm-up, Wagner shows little emotion. Off the field, he invariably draws a crowd in the clubhouse, a team spokesman even though he pitches only a few innings at best in big games. Yet, on the mound, Wagner becomes a tight-lipped assassin—ready to take on the world all by himself.

With Wagner in mind, imagine a lineup, like they have at a police station, complete with height markers on the wall, of the hardest throwers in baseball history. At first glance, they would seem to have little in common. If we're gazing at the crew from the far side of the one-way glass, somebody like Walter Johnson, the famed "Big Train," would tower over Wagner or the bespectacled Steve Dalkowski. Unlike in other sports, no prototypical model exists for being able to fire a baseball better than 100 miles per hour. All shapes and sizes are eligible, but only a few will ever be blessed. And many of those expected to live up to the assumed success and heightened demand that come hand in hand with the gift of firing a baseball with such velocity will wonder if it was indeed a curse in disguise. For it is one thing to be able to throw hard. It can be quite another to throw the high heat consistently for strikes.

Wagner was the first legitimate fireballer in his prime that I ever saw in person. It was 1997 and the diminutive left-hander had just become the closer for the Houston Astros. Many considered him a short-term solution to the Astros' bullpen woes. After all, how long could this baby-faced kid last in one of the most demanding jobs in sports? It just so happens, a good long time. After all, he was armed with one of the most electric fastballs in the game. After nine years and 225 saves in Houston, Wagner went on to pitch for the Philadelphia Phillies and New York Mets.

Still, Wagner already knew that a career is often defined by a few key moments. "Either you do it or you don't," he says. "The rest doesn't add up to anything unless you let it do that to you. I learned a long time ago not to let that happen to me."

Many will remember Wagner for one night, at the old Astrodome, where he came in to pitch the ninth inning in front of the hometown crowd. Staked to a 2–1 lead, Wagner had to face the heart of the Florida Marlins' batting order. The previous season, Wagner's rookie year, the Marlins had lit him up for two home runs, including a game winner. If that wasn't enough to get the heart pumping, there was his previous outing, four days before. Against the Colorado Rockies, Wagner had allowed his first earned run of the season: a Ruthian blast by Vinny Castilla that fell well back in the left field bleachers.

Due up in the Marlins' half of the ninth inning that night was Bobby Bonilla, Moises Alou, and Jeff Conine. The later had homered the first time he ever faced Wagner. All were certainly capable of tying the game with one swing of the bat. That evening, as the crowd rose to its feet, Wagner paused briefly behind the mound, his face mostly hidden behind his black glove.

In this pause before the first pitch, Wagner often allows the old nightmares to again sweep over him, drawing out the realization that he deserved something better growing up. He remembers that period of his life when he was so mad at the world that throwing a baseball, over and over again, was his only escape from heartbreak. He had no real home. He barely had adults interested in his life and what he could grow up to be. Gradually, he learned to channel that anger and frustration toward a higher purpose. So effectively, in fact, that now, in these quiet moments before he steps on the mound to pitch, we have to get ready to hurl science out the window. Because sometimes the presence of demons can elevate an average fastball into one of most dynamic pitches in baseball. And over the course of a major-league career such a gift can transform a kid once forgotten by family and friends into one of the best relievers in baseball.

"It's funny," says Larry Dierker, his former manager. "With Billy, the bigger the situation, the bigger the crowd, the better he seems to like it. Most guys run from that kind of pressure. They're afraid of failure and the times when everything seems to be on the line. But for Billy, it almost seems like some kind of relief for him. It's like he's found something he's been waiting a long time for."

Bonilla flicked his angry bat, ready to go. The Astrodome faithful roared, and Billy the Kid stepped onto the pitching slab, ready to draw. Closing out a ball game—even facing the four-five-six hitters— can be paradise compared to the hell that passed for Billy Wagner's childhood.

Wagner's parents divorced when he was five years old. For the next nine years, he was as wanted as an unpaid bill. Looking back on it, he says his parents' marriage was "a mismatch . . . doomed from the start." There was never enough money. They argued, with the incidents escalating in the years after his father returned from a tour of Vietnam.

"Those were tough times," says Yvonne Hall, Wagner's mother. "That doesn't change the fact that we had responsibilities, that we had children. But when a marriage starts to go bad, kids kind of get pushed to the side."

After the split, Wagner and his younger sister, Chastity, bounced from relative to relative. Growing up, Wagner attended 15 different schools through junior high. Only an average student, he regularly took his aggressions out on the field. The rougher the game, the more he liked it.

He broke his right arm playing football. As soon as it had healed, he promptly shattered it again, playing football. "I kind of got used to breaking things," he says.

Wagner began life as a right-hander. Even today he still writes and eats with his right hand. But after he broke the arm and during a prolonged time in various casts, he began to throw left-handed. Balls, rocks, anything—it didn't matter. Wagner discovered that one of the few things in his life he could control was the accuracy and velocity of any available projectile. It felt good to throw hard.

Born in Tannersville, Virginia, Wagner was shuffled around southwestern Virginia, moving from his father's, to his mother's, and on to both sets of grandparents, before doing it all over again. His childhood reads like a map of battlefields from the Civil War—Lynchburg, Concord, Marion, Appomattox. "Back then the world was on my shoulders and I was mad at anybody who talked to me," he says. "I wasn't so mad about being moved around. I just felt like my sister and I weren't getting a fair shake. That we weren't getting treated like we should be treated as kids."

Indeed, Wagner found himself having to act more and more like an adult. When his mother remarried, his new stepfather was a drunkard and physically abused Yvonne. One hot summer afternoon, when Billy was nine years old, the family went swimming at a local pond. While they were in the water, the stepfather became enraged at Billy's mother. He held Yvonne's head underwater, almost drowning her, until Billy began to pound on his back and head with his small fists.

"That was enough to save me," Yvonne says. "That's why my son will always be my hero. He's my heartthrob. I'm so proud of him and what he's done with his life. He can take the worst situation and find something good in it. But I saw, after a while, he couldn't grow up the way he should with me. I had to let him go."

Yvonne was a waitress at the Golden Corral Steak House in Lynchburg, Virginia, and Billy's baseball games were often miles away from her work. Between the unstable home life and the inability to get Billy to his games and practices, his mother decided Wagner would move in with his aunt and uncle, Jack and Sally Lamie. At the age of 14, Billy's wandering days were over and he was officially adopted by the Lamies. His cousin Jeff became his stepbrother.

Jeff Lamie was a sports star, and Wagner tagged along after him; joining many of the same teams. But while Lamie had an athlete's physique, Wagner was a runt. In high school, he was maybe 5-foot-7, tipping the scales at 140 pounds. He was so small that he was overlooked for the Virginia High School All-Star Game his senior year despite impressive statistics.

When no universities expressed much interest in him, Wagner followed Lamie to nearby Ferrum College. The day Billy tried out, he was fortunate to simply make the team. Pursuing an outfield spot, he didn't hit very well. As a last resort, Ferrum coach Abe Naff suggested he throw off the mound. Although Wagner had never gotten his fastball out of the mid-80s in high school, that day he threw harder than he ever had.

"That's when God said, 'It's time for you to throw a little harder. Make a life for yourself,'" he remembers. "I had to be throwing 91, 92 miles per hour that day. I had never thrown that hard before."

Because the Ferrum team couldn't afford a radar gun, exactly how hard Wagner could bring it wasn't determined until his sophomore year. When an Atlanta Braves scout passed through town, checking out several of the college's senior pitchers, Naff asked him to clock Wagner.

"He about fell over," Naff says. "Billy was consistently putting the ball over in the low- to mid-90s. He just couldn't believe it."

Wagner averaged an NCAA (National Collegiate Athletic Association) record 19.1 strikeouts per nine innings as a sophomore. In the summer, he starred in the Cape Cod League, where he caught the attention of a number of baseball pundits, including ESPN's Peter Gammons. In three seasons at Ferrum, he struck out 327 batters—then a Division III record.

"At the cut of the grass and the dirt," says Naff, "his ball just explodes. Always has. You can't figure how a guy that small can throw the ball that hard."

The Braves never got a chance to draft Wagner. He was taken in the first round, 12th overall, in 1993 by the Houston Astros. Wagner, like Lincecum, quickly rose through the organization. He made the major leagues for good after just two years in the minors.

But the nightmare, at least when it came to family, wasn't quite over. This time it was a quick blow to the heart instead of a slow numbing squeeze of the soul.

Two days after the Astros added Wagner to their 40-man roster— May 16, 1995—he received a late-night phone call from his girlfriend, Sarah Quesenberrry. Her voice was frantic and edgy. At first he thought it was some kind of a joke. Then she told him that her father and stepmother had been shot and killed outside a Hillsville, Virginia, apartment complex. The Quesenberrys were helping Sarah's half sister move when her estranged husband arrived on the scene. During a heated argument, Steven and his second wife, Tina, were gunned down in cold blood. Once again being on the mound, no matter how pressurized the situation, proved to be a sanctuary for him. "There's no explanation for why things happen sometimes," Wagner says. "But baseball has been a blessing in disguise for me. No doubt about that. It's allowed me to move on with my life."

Driving Route 29 from the Washington, D.C., suburbs toward Charlottesville, Virginia, can be like a trip back in time. The road dates back to the 1700s and was the same route that James Madison and Thomas Jefferson traveled to meet with the other Founding Fathers back when the nation was being born. Somewhere near Culpepper the last of the subdivisions that line the rolling turnpike out from Washington finally gives way to farmland, and out on the horizon looms the rolling outline of the Blue Ridge Mountains. Near Charlottesville, Wagner lives on a 200-acre farm with Sarah and their four children. After the baseball season ends, he comes home to this spread, complete with alpacas grazing in the fields. From a distance, they could pass for small llamas. During the offseason Wagner usually travels the alpaca circuit, showing and selling the animals.

But after the 2008 season, Wagner had more pressing concerns. That year, as the Mets battled in the National League East, he had been forced to spend several weeks on the disabled list because of a sore elbow. Then the injury was deemed more serious. After 14 years in the majors, it was determined he needed to have Tommy John surgery. Afterward, he spent much of the 2009 season, his last of a four-year, $43-million deal with the New York Mets, rehabbing the injury. He returned in time to finish the season as a setup man for the Boston Red Sox.

Theories abound about how a little guy like Wagner can generate as much velocity to compete with the big boys. Former Astros pitching coach Vern Ruhle once said that Wagner's powerful legs were "the foundation for everything he does." Dierker says the way Wagner snaps his wrist during his follow-through toward home plate may be the key. If so, Wagner shares the company of Roger Clemens and Steve Dalkowski, who were also known for such techniques.

For his part, Wagner believes that the reasons may extend past physical ability. "I think a lot of it has to do with my heart," he replies.

Despite a childhood straight out of Charles Dickens, struggling to prove himself in a game that regularly turns to bigger guys for the heavy work, Wagner remains remarkably self-confident. Long ago he learned when to keep the demons under lock and key and when to turn them loose.

"There are a lot of days that I've thought about my childhood or what happened to [Sarah's] dad, and I'll take it on the field with me. I'll admit to that," he says. "It makes me stronger. I'm a little bit more intense. I'm a little bit tougher when I'm out there.

"When you're 18 years old, it's time for you to make your own way in the world. It doesn't have to be bad anymore. For 18 years it may have been, but after that it's your life. You can take it and make it anything you want. That's what I really believe in. You can make it anything you want."

Before missing much of the 2009 season due to Tommy John surgery, Wagner had proven himself in game after game, season after season, establishing himself as one of the top arms in the game despite his small stature. Some maintained he belonged among the greatest fireballers ever—Bob Feller, Walter Johnson, Sandy Koufax, Steve Dalkowski. Some, like Nolan Ryan, believed that in his prime Wagner may have found his way to the head of that class. Could he have been the fastest ever?

"That's for somebody else to decide," says Wagner, who signed with the Atlanta Braves for the 2010 season. "But I'm proud of what I've done, how I've gone about my business. For the most part, it's been, 'Here's my fastball. Can you hit it?' It's been as simple as that."

That's certainly the way it was years ago when I first saw him, on that night in the Astrodome, when Wagner was first becoming Billy the Kid. After getting Bobby Bonilla to ground out, Wagner got two strikes on Alou. But the Marlins' outfielder fouled off several pitches down the right field line before looping a single into center.

That brought up the dangerous Conine. Wagner decided to give him nothing but heat. In fact, over the years, the closer figures that 90 percent of his pitches at the big-league level have been fastballs. Wagner, like many relievers, remembers how, during the 1996 World Series, the Braves' fireballer Mark Wohlers got beat with his third-best pitch on the game's largest stage.

"If I'm going to lose," Wagner said, "it will be with my best stuff."

Conine fanned on nothing but high heat.

Catcher Charles Johnson represented the Marlins' last chance. He jumped on Wagner's first pitch, driving the ball deep into right field, where an outfielder tracked it down.

Afterward, in the home clubhouse, Wagner sat in front of his locker. His left arm, from the shoulder on down to the wrist, was wrapped in ice bags and Ace bandages—an omen of the stress put on his arm and the injury still years away.

"Nobody was up there just trying to spoil pitches," he said afterward in the clubhouse. "They were swinging hard, at every pitch. One mistake and they could have hit it out, easy. It just came down to strength against strength. That's the way it should be, but you know sometimes it just isn't."

M y home phone rings and it is Phil Pote on the other end. The man must be telepathic. Almost every time this search for the fastest pitcher starts to stall, he gives me a call.

"Who have you been talking to?" he asks.

"Billy Wagner," I reply, "and Tim Lincecum."

"The little guys."

"Who can throw hard. Nolan Ryan has Wagner on his all-time list."

"I can't argue with that," Pote replies. "But remember that the old Astrodome had a fast gun. The pitchers loved to waste one there just to see what showed up. Word had it that the old Dome added a few clicks, especially if a ball was high in the strike zone."

"So, you're saying Wagner was the beneficiary of that."

"Listen to the hotshot writer using the five-dollar words."

"But that's what you're saying, isn't it?" I say.

"I'm not taking anything away from Billy Wagner," Pote said. "If I could have thrown that hard back in my day, I'd be living at a much higher station in life than I am now. All I'm saying is consider both ends of the spectrum. If you're going to focus on Wagner and the like, make sure you remember the big guys."

"J. R. Richard."

"There's one. How about tall guys who couldn't get out of their own way for a spell? Sometimes you wonder how they ever put it together."

"Like Randy Johnson?"

"Now you're talking," Pote says. "Sometimes the mechanics of pitching, all the science involved, can be just as difficult for them."

"El Rando Grando" steps from behind the velvet curtain. He's dressed in a white puff-sleeved shirt, gold-colored vest, and red satin pants that look like they're out of the Arabian Nights.

As the crowd cheers, he briefly acknowledges his fearless assistant, Impalea, who is strapped to a spinning circular platform. Red lines converge toward her body like crosshairs on a rifle's telescope. El Rando Grando—aka Randy Johnson—gingerly picks up a pearl-handled knife and begins his act.

His first attempt strikes a bit too close to Impalea for comfort, drawing gasps from the audience. Although his second pitch soars off camera, there's little doubt what has happened. An ugly splat is heard, followed by loud groans. Poor Impalea is history. Such wildness doesn't faze El Rando Grando, though. He shakes his head and moves on, already poised to deliver the next knife.

This television commercial aired in the Seattle market for Mariners season tickets in the mid-1990s. Other spots included manager Lou Piniella as an unsympathetic psychiatrist, outfielder Jay Buhner as a lousy stand-up comic, and pitcher Chris Bosio as a crazed tooth-pulling dentist. But everyone's favorite was Johnson as El Rando Grando. That's because this was the era when Johnson arrived as one of the most dominant pitchers in the game, a fireballer who would reach the 300-victory plateau nearly 15 years later. After years of struggling with his control he was finally ready to humble hitters. A transition mirrored by the shift of his nickname from "Big Bird" to "Big Unit," and a career punctuated by one of the most bizarre events in fireballer lore—the exploding bird. In March 2001, during a spring training game at Tucson, Arizona, Johnson was on the mound with the Giants' Calvin Murray at the plate. As Johnson delivered a fastball that was estimated to be traveling at upward of 95 miles per hour, a dove swooped down low between the pitching mound and home plate. In odds that were later calculated to be 1 in 13 million, Johnson's offering struck the bird.

"[It] just exploded," Murray told the Associated Press. "Feathers everywhere. Poof."

The official call? No pitch. The incident remains a favorite on YouTube today.

If it wasn't for Nolan Ryan and Tom House, it's likely that Johnson's legacy would have centered on a few odd pieces of baseball trivia rather than a successful career of All-Star and postseason appearances. During the 1992 season, the Rangers were in Seattle, and Ryan and House watched Johnson battle through a poor workout.

"It was obvious he was having trouble with his control," House recalls. "I got to asking Big Tex what he would do about the kid's delivery. I threw in some suggestions. It's something we did anyplace we were—watching other players, trying to figure out what makes them tick."

Even though so much in baseball is secret, House prides himself on being "a teacher first and everything else second." After the workout, he overheard Johnson complaining about his wildness. In response, he invited Johnson to meet with him and Ryan the next day in the Rangers' bullpen.

House had spotted a flaw in Johnson's delivery. As the left-hander completed his follow-through, he wasn't driving toward the plate. At least not driving as hard as, say, Nolan Ryan. In fact, the winter before, through his work with the Bio-Kinetics Co., House had analyzed several pitchers' windups, including Johnson's. He remembered that Johnson's delivery was in so many different pieces, the different stages refusing to work together, that somebody such as Jim Abbott, who is seven inches shorter than Johnson, was almost a foot and half closer to home plate when he released the ball.

"It was a coaching moment," House says. "Maybe Randy was more receptive because Nolan was there. I'm sure he had been given similar information before. But on that day we had a kid who was ready to listen."

"Everybody said Nolan Ryan had a big influence," Johnson says of his change in form, "but Tom House was the one who worked on my mechanics."

Where Ryan helped was with the mental part of the game. He and Johnson then went over how to set up hitters. And more importantly,

Ryan told the hard-throwing but erratic southpaw not to worry about the walks. Control would come in time. He should go with his strength—the heat.

Johnson likes to compare himself with Ryan. The two rarely played on contenders and as a result, Johnson believes, hardly ever received fair shakes in Cy Young races. "A lot of people look at him as having all these individual accomplishments and being only a .500 pitcher," says Johnson, who changed his number to Ryan's for a day when the Express retired. "But he was only on a .500 team or below. So, you can only go out there and do so much."

O f course, sometimes science can only do so much, as well. Despite the latest in testing and the best of intentions, a fireballer can be misunderstood. As a result, a career can be forever altered.

Almost from the beginning, James Rodney Richard was a formidable presence on the mound. In Vienna, Louisiana, where he grew up, Richard went an entire season of high school ball without allowing an earned run. By the time he reached the Houston Astros in 1971, he stood 6-foot-8, and his slider was faster than many pitchers' fastballs. He struck out 15 batters in his first National League start, tying Karl Spooner's record set in 1954. Richard went on to strike out 313 hitters in 1979. Many a hitter caught wind of that résumé, snuck a peek at Richard out on the mound, and considered himself pretty much out before he even stepped into the batter's box.

"When you've got a guy out there who throws the ball 98 miles per hour like James Rodney, the batters don't do too much joking around. It's all business," Astros catcher Alan Ashby once told Cox News Service. "When a batter steps into the box against J.R., the comments don't vary much. Usually, they just look there and say, 'Well, no chance this time.' And afterward, you just see the guys turn around slowly with this look of despair on their face, kind of an expression of helplessness. Against J.R., you see it all the time."

Yet along the way, Richard was also called a loner, a problem player, and a malingerer. In the end he would become yet another fireballer with a tragic closing act as his career, which began with so much promise, so much velocity, was derailed well before the intimidating right-hander had any chance at reaching the Hall of Fame.

Richard grew up in a farm family, one of six kids. The Richards ate the vegetables they grew, and after chores the boys played ball in the fields, with tennis balls and broom handles for bats. At Lincoln High School, Richard had several games for the ages, including pitching a no-hitter in which he also hit four home runs and drove in 10 runs. Signed by Houston, he struggled in the Astros' farm system for many of the same reasons Randy Johnson labored initially.

"Because of his size, J.R. had to work harder than most people," Hub Kittle, the team's old pitching coach, told the *Houston Chronicle*. "Because he was so tall, we had to change his delivery in the very beginning. At first, he tried to come straight over the top—and he was just so tall, he didn't have any leverage."

Despite his striking out 15 in his big-league debut, the Astros sent Richard down to the minors to gain more experience. So began an uneasy relationship between the player and ballclub, which would soon border upon the dysfunctional. By 1975, Richard had made the team for good and appeared ready to settle in as the team's ace. Richard, like Koufax nearly two decades earlier, had seemingly solved his control problem almost overnight. And he threw hard. So hard that his slider was in the low- to mid-90s, with a fastball that "topped 100, with gusts up to 104," columnist Mickey Herskowitz wrote in the *Houston Chronicle* in 2004.

"So what does that make J.R. in his prime?" Herskowitz added. "We can answer that one easily. It made him Randy Johnson with a chest. . . .

"J.R. was an intimidator who might have been bigger than the Hall of Fame. That is, whether or not he had the kind of years that land a player in Valhalla, he was going to be legend, the kind of pitcher the old-timers talk about as one of a class."

Unfortunately, so much of that disappeared in a great hurry, leaving incriminations and finger-pointing in its wake. As the 1980 season began, Richard was acknowledged by many to be the top pitcher on a deep staff that included Ryan. Even though he had pitched no fewer than 267 innings in any of the previous four seasons, Richard felt out of sorts that season.

His ailments ranged from an upset stomach to blurred vision to losing feeling in his fingers to a tired arm. A visit to Dr. Frank Jobe, who had performed the first ligament replacement, or Tommy John surgery, was arranged with no medical cause or injury found. There certainly didn't seem to be any preexisting condition as that season progressed. Only a few days before the doctor's visit, Richard had pitched two scoreless innings in the 1980 All-Star Game, in which he struck out Reggie Jackson. The Astros' team physician publicly advised Richard to get more sleep. Several of his teammates grumbled that Richard was a slacker. Richard didn't do himself any favors when he complained about Ryan's new contract. Richard was making $850,000 at the time, while the Astros had just made Ryan baseball's first $1-million man.

"Am I bitter? Yeah, you might say that," Richard said at the time. "I think it's life in particular, baseball some—but life in general. I've been through a whole lot of things in my life, a little bit of everything. Prejudice. You name it, I've been looking at it."

He was about to be looking at a whole lot more. Sixteen days after the Astros' doctor told him to get more sleep and cut down on his social life, Richard suffered a devastating stroke. On July 30, 1980, he was playing catch with teammate Wilbur Howard before a game at the Astrodome when he collapsed. Rushed to the hospital, he fought for his life while doctors removed a blood clot from his neck. Due to the stroke, Richard suffered paralysis to the left side of his body, including his arm. Through rehabilitation Richard would regain use of his arm and leg, moving well enough to attempt a return to the Astros, but he would never be the pitcher he once was.

Instead of getting a bronze plaque in Cooperstown, Richard became a cautionary tale for ballplayers of his era. Another reminder that being blessed with a rocket arm could be as much a curse as it was good fortune.

"They didn't believe J. R. Richard because they didn't want to," Jim Palmer told the *Los Angeles Times* days after Richard left the hospital. "If you're J.R., you're 10–4 with a 1.89 ERA and you say you're hurt. They're in a pennant race and he's their top pitcher. . . . Obviously some people thought he was unhappy that Nolan Ryan was getting more money. People want to make all kinds of insinuations."

Richard received a reported $1.2 million in a medical malpractice suit. But that wasn't enough to stabilize his life and to fill the void left by not playing baseball. His first marriage broke up, lousy investments were made, and in 1993 Richard was found by a *Houston Post* reporter living under an overpass, not too far from the Astrodome, where he once starred.

Richard eventually found a home for himself in south Houston, conducting baseball clinics and becoming a minister at the Now Testament Church. In 2004, before the All-Star Game in Houston, Richard signed 6,000 autographs in two hours. Unlike many of today's players, he reveled in the attention—delighted that people still remembered him.

"I don't have any velocity," he said after *Sports Illustrated* asked how hard he could still throw, "but I can still throw strikes. You never forget how to pitch—it's like riding a bicycle."

Well, maybe not. Sometimes throwing a baseball never quite becomes second nature, no matter how much science and psychology can be brought to the equation.

Pittsburgh Pirates pitcher Steve Blass remains the classic example of somebody who came down with such a dramatic case of nerves, or the "yips," that he couldn't throw a strike to save his life. As a result, Blass went from pitching two complete games in the 1971 World Series to disappearing from the playing ranks by the age of 32. To this day, Blass says, he has no idea what really happened to his form and delivery. "But I learned that life goes on," he says. "It is what you make of it. I just feel fortunate to enjoy the success I had before it was taken away from me."

Other players have been bitten by the yips bug. Because of it, for a time second baseman Steve Sax couldn't throw accurately to first. Dale Murphy had to shift his position from catcher because too many of his return throws to the pitcher ended up in center field. Mackey Sasser came down with the same mental block. But among the fireball community, the one everyone remembers is Mark Wohlers.

As the closer for the Atlanta Braves, he once clocked at 103 miles per hour. If in doubt, he went with the heat, in the mold of Goose Gossage, Jonathan Papelbon, and Billy Wagner.

The first sign of trouble appeared when Wohlers began to throw wildly to first base on routine fielding plays. In the Braves' dugout, pitching coach Leo Mazzone told manager Bobby Cox that they better hope such wildness didn't carry over to Wohlers's pitches to home plate. Soon enough, though, Wohlers started to walk batters. Then some of his deliveries were flying past the catcher, sailing all the way to the screen. Overnight he had morphed into the second coming of Steve Dalkowski.

Ironically, Wohlers's wild streak only affected his fastball. His slider and split-finger fastball remained accurate enough. But soon hitters realized that the right-hander couldn't throw strikes with his lightning-quick fastball anymore and began to sit on the slower stuff. After saving 97 games in three seasons, Wohlers was sent down to the minors in 1998. Despite a comeback bid with the team's Triple-A affiliate in Richmond, sessions with therapists, and the efforts of a personal trainer, he was never the force he once was. When asked what went wrong, Wohlers told the *New York Times*, "I wish I knew."

E ven though science failed to forecast the emergence of Wagner and Lincecum and couldn't put Richard back on the mound, ballclubs nevertheless still attempt to quantify the gift and mystique of the fastball.

By Memorial Day 2009, David Price was back up with the Tampa Bay Rays—this time he hoped for good—and made his season debut against the Cleveland Indians. He came out firing. Scouts said his first dozen or so pitches were all four-seam fastballs, in the 94- to 98-mile-per-hour range. But when the Indians' Jamey Carroll drew a leadoff walk, followed by Grady Sizemore's flare hit down the left field line, Price was facing two men on base with none out.

He then began to mix in his hard slider, clocked at 86 to 88 miles per hour. This was the pitch Price lost for a time down in Durham because he was working so much on his changeup. Using the slider to set up the fastball, he struck out Victor Martinez, Jhonny Peralta, and then Shin-Soo Choo. For a brief moment, the sky appeared to be the limit for the 23-year-old phenom.

In the second inning, though, things went downhill in a hurry. Staked to a 5–0 lead, Price walked the leadoff batter on four pitches. From then on, he fell behind too many hitters. By the time he was lifted with one out in the fourth inning, he had already thrown 90 pitches.

"I didn't have a feel for anything," Price told the Associated Press afterward. "I've got to do a better job than that. I was averaging 10 pitches an out. That's not good enough."

In his next start, the left-hander struck out 11 and recorded his first major-league victory of the season against the Minnesota Twins. He followed that with two no-decisions against the New York Yankees and Los Angeles Angels. On June 16, in his fifth start, Price managed to make it into the seventh inning but was on the losing end of a 5–3 loss to the Colorado Rockies.

Sports Illustrated's Tom Verducci wrote that Price "may have the stuff of an ace, but the Rays' left-hander is a long way from being an ace." At the same age (two months shy of turning 24), Price's progress paled when compared to that of somebody like CC Sabathia of the New York Yankees. Price had a single victory and had never thrown 110 pitches or more in a game. In comparison, Sabathia already had 45 victories and 29 110-pitch games by that point in his career.

Rays manager Joe Maddon maintained that the organization was waiting for "a moment of epiphany" when it came to Price. After that switch goes on, "he'll be [the next] Sandy Koufax."

Although Maddon wanted Price to go deep into ball games, the young left-hander rarely got past the sixth inning during this initial run through the league. The culprit? Perhaps pitch counts.

Tampa Bay, of course, has a lot riding on Price's long-term success. As a result, like many pitching prospects, he's allowed to throw only 100 pitches or so a game.

"It's a different era," Phil Pote says. "Quite honestly there's a lot more money involved, and nobody's too interested in talking about the ramifications of it all."

I don't understand what Pote means by "the ramifications of it all."

"OK, think this through with me now, partner," Pote replies. "Say somebody like David Price is pitching today and there's a 90-pitch count on him and, god forbid, he ends up getting hurt and he throws 89 pitches; everybody is probably OK with it. At least how it happened. He didn't exceed the predetermined pitch counts."

"All right."

"But if somebody like David Price throws 91 pitches, somebody's going to ask the pitching coach, the manager, what's going on." Pote continues, "That's just the way it works. You have agents, general managers, ownership, trainers involved. Everybody is in this thing. Is it right or is it wrong? The answer is, it's just different."

As a result, for many teams pitch counts have become standard operating procedure. Except down in Texas. The same week Price was lifted after 4 ⅓ innings and 105 pitches against the Angels, Nolan Ryan sent a directive throughout the Rangers' organization: From this day forward, pitch counts were banned.

"He wants us to toughen up," says Texas ace Kevin Millwood, "go deeper in ball games. He knows there's no reason we should be using five or more pitchers to pick up the victory."

If anything, Ryan was trying to lead by example, in a retroactive fashion. As the *Philadelphia Daily News* pointed out, Ryan threw 5,684 pitches in 333 ⅔ innings in 1974, his seventh full season in the majors. He averaged 135 pitches a game and went on to play another 19 seasons in the big leagues. But not even that number represents the limits the human body can come close to enduring. In a throwback to the heyday of Pud Galvin and Amos Rusie, the Red Sox Luis Tiant threw an incredible 163 pitches in winning Game Four of the 1975 World Series.

ASMI's Glenn Fleisig says pitch counts are necessary at the youth levels, but pitchers at the minor- and major-league levels "shouldn't have strict pitch counts. They have coaches who should know what to look for, as opposed to Little League.

"You have to remember pitch counts weren't around 15 years ago. Now the pendulum may be swinging back. There's an awareness that these guidelines don't need to be set in stone. Most people coming to me now ask, 'Don't you think [professional pitchers] have been babied too much?'"

In reaction to the ban, Bill James recently told *Sports Illustrated* that "what Ryan is doing is the clearest and boldest example of challenging the conventional wisdom from within the system that I've seen in years, and I'm applauding it."

Sitting behind his mahogany desk, the late-morning sky finally clearing beyond his office window, Ryan doesn't look like a revolutionary or rabble-rouser.

"I'm just trying to bring what I've learned back to the game," he says. "What I was taught worked pretty well in my day. Can it work again? I believe so."

After nearly making the Baltimore Orioles' major-league roster in 1963, only to suffer a serious elbow injury just before heading north with the parent club, Steve Dalkowski was never the same. Even though he went on to post only his second winning record, playing for Elmira, Stockton, and Columbus, the velocity was gone.

At Stockton, Dalkowski went 8–4, and that's where Phil Pote, who was just beginning his career as a big-league scout, caught up with him. But after all the buzz, all the talk, Pote came away disappointed.

"What I saw didn't match the legend I had heard so much about," Pote says. "He was still throwing hard, or at least trying to. But I couldn't help feeling that I had been cheated somehow. I never saw his best stuff."

The following season, 1965, Dalkowski struggled in spring training and the Orioles shipped him to Tri-Cities (Pasco, Washington), one of the lowest rungs in their system. Dalkowski's arm still hurt and his fastball came in on a straight line, no longer rising to the heavens as it neared home plate. He wasn't able to blow the ball by hitters anymore. Even though Tri-Cities manager Cal Ripken Sr. would become one of the standard-bearers for Dalkowski's legend, he could only take so much of the left-hander's antics. After Dalkowski hit a bar that the club had deemed off-limits, his career with the Orioles' organization was over.

"I was the one who released him [from Tri-Cities]," Ripken later told Pat Jordan. "Yet there's not a soul in the world who didn't like him, including me. He just didn't give himself a chance.

"Why, in spring of 1965, he was sent from the Triple-A camp in Daytona [Florida] to the minor-league camp in Thomasville, Georgia, and it took him seven days to make a few-hour trip. Harry Dalton got pissed off, and was going to release him, but I told him I'd take Steve with me to Tri-Cities. I told him he had to be in bed early the night before he pitched. That lasted two weeks and then he drifted the other way."

After being released by the Orioles, Dalkowski signed with the California Angels and reported to their minor-league team in San Jose. He pitched only six games there, though, going 2–3. The Angels sent him to Mazatlán of the Mexican League in 1965. After being assigned back to the Mexican League for the 1966 winter season, he retired from baseball.

At loose ends, Dalkowski began to work the fields of the San Joaquin Valley in California. Places like Lodi, Fresno, and Bakersfield. He became one of the few gringos, and the only Polish one, among the migrant workers. And during this time he developed a new addiction to cheap wine—the kind of hooch that goes for pocket change and can be spiked with additives and ether. White port was Dalkowski's favorite. In order to keep up the pace in the fields he often placed a bottle at the end of the next row that needed picking.

"The guys there all picked fruit and drank wine, so I tried it and got hooked on it," he later told the *Sporting News*. "The wine they drink isn't like dinner wine. It's got a lot of chemicals. It can kill you."

Dalkowski chopped cotton, dug potatoes, and picked oranges, apricots, and lemons. He married a woman from Stockton. After they split up two years later, he met his second wife, Virginia Greenwood, while picking oranges in Bakersfield. But none of it had the chance to stick, not as long as Dalkowski kept drinking himself to death. He was arrested more times for disorderly conduct than anybody could count. He was sentenced to time on a road crew several times and was ordered to attend Alcoholics Anonymous. For years, the Baseball Assistance Team, which helps former players who have fallen on hard times, tried to reach out to Dalkowski. This was how he lived for nearly a quarter century—until he finally touched bottom.

In 1991, the authorities recommended that Dalkowski go into alcoholic rehab. But during processing he ran away and ended up living on the streets of Los Angeles. "At that point we thought we had no hope of ever finding him again," says his sister, Pat Cain, who still lived in the family's hometown of New Britain, Connecticut. "He had fallen in with the derelicts and they stick together. We thought the next we'd hear of him was when he turned up dead somewhere."

On Christmas Eve 1992, Dalkowski walked into a laundromat in Los Angeles and began talking to a family there. They soon realized that he didn't have much money and was living on the streets. The family convinced Dalkowski to come home with them. In a few days, Pat Cain received word—her big brother was still alive. Soon he reunited with his second wife, Virginia Greenwood, and they moved to Oklahoma City, trying for a fresh start. But within months Virginia suffered a stroke and died in early 1994.

"That's when I knew I had to get Stevie back home," Cain says. "It was his only chance. He ended up in the hospital in Oklahoma City due to his drinking. I started to work with them to get him back here, back to New Britain. That finally happened in March 1994. That's when he came home for good."

Dalkowski moved into the Walnut Hill Care Center, near where he used to play his high school ball.

"When we brought him home from Oklahoma City, the doctors told us not to get our hopes up," Cain says. "They said he probably didn't have much time left and if you looked at him, tried to talk to him, you'd understand why. Steve wasn't in very good shape."

Slowly, though, Dalkowski showed signs of turning the corner. One evening he started to blurt out the answers to a sports trivia game the family was playing. Bill Huber, his old coach, took him to Sunday services at the local Methodist church until Dalkowski refused to go one week. His mind had cleared enough for him to remember he had grown up Catholic.

Less than a decade after returning home, Dalkowski found himself at a place in life he thought he would never reach—the pitching mound in Baltimore. Granted, much had changed since Dalkowski was a phenom in the Orioles' system. Home for the big-league club was no longer cozy Memorial Stadium but the retro redbrick of Camden Yards. On September 7, 2003, before an Orioles game against the Seattle Mariners, Dalkowski threw out the ceremonial first pitch. His friends Boog Powell and Pat Gillick were in attendance.

"I bounced it," Dalkowski says, still embarrassed by the miscue. Yet nobody else in attendance that day cared.

"He was back on the pitching mound," Gillick recalls. "Back where he belonged."

Five and a half years later, in the sweet afterglow of the first warm day of spring, Dalkowski arrives at the St. George Church's social center in New Britain. He's come for the town's Sports Hall of Fame Annual Induction Dinner. Dressed in a mock turtleneck, gray pants, and dark blazer, he enters the room, taking slow steps, with his sister by his side. Without much fanfare, they find a table in the back row of the banquet room, one of the 27 under golden chandeliers that have been trimmed out in linen tablecloths and enough food, plates, and utensils to feed a small army. Although Dalkowski and his sister don't move too far from the table they've selected, soon word spreads that the pitching legend has made an appearance, and old friends begin to gather around. Most of them have known Dalkowski for ages. At Pat's urging, several of them sit down, and the conversation—a rehash of the good old days, a remembrance that makes things larger than life—soon bubbles forth.

In recent years, New Britain has struggled. In 2007, the median household income was $36,681—barely half the state average. Yet the institutions of community, church, and family remain strong and vibrant in the town of 71,000.

"Stevie couldn't have done this, just sat around and talked, a few years ago," Pat Cain says, smiling. "Every year he gets a little bit better when it comes to memory. This town, his friends—I really believe coming back to New Britain has saved him."

At the table, Dalkowski has been joined by Len Pare, John Arduini, and Bob Barrows. All of them grew up on New Britain's west side and played Little League ball.

"I was on the Red Sox," Dalkowski says.

"Me, too," Barrows says. "I caught you and everybody else, too."

"I know," nods Dalkowski, who now sports a closely cropped gray beard. Gone are the thick glasses and the youthful countenance that was all smiles in posed minor-league photographs. "I remember. How could I forget the guys who caught me?"

"Same goes for us," says Pare, who once had his finger broken catching a Dalkowski heater.

"I know, I know," Dalkowski says in a soft voice.

Pat Cain asks Arduini what Little League team he was on.

"The Dodgers," he says, bringing the conversation to a brief halt.

"The Dodgers?" Dalkowski repeats as if it's the most ridiculous notion he's ever heard.

"I thought we were all on the same team in '50," Barrows says. "The Red Sox."

"Most of the time we were," Arduini says, "except for that first year. Then I was on the Dodgers."

For a moment, nobody says a word. They contemplate that even in New Britain, a place that prides itself on its sports, to the point that several speakers who step to the podium this evening will call it the best sports city in all of New England, things weren't always quite the way everyone remembers them to be.

"Well, that's OK," Dalkowski begins.

"That's right," Barrows adds. "You were with us soon enough."

"That's what I'm trying to tell you," Arduini says.

Throughout the evening, people drop by Dalkowski's table to say a few words. When it's my turn, I ask him what advice he would give to young pitchers.

"Throw strikes," he replies. "And run. That's good for the legs, you know."

Then Dalkowski pauses, ready to deliver the punch line. "And don't drink," he adds, smiling.

Yes, alcohol and great expectations nearly killed arguably the hardest thrower ever. Yet on this spring evening, among this band of brothers, such troubled times seem a long time ago. A few weeks after the 2009 banquet, Dalkowski turned 70 years old. Many in the baseball world believed that he had died years ago. But here he is, talking baseball with the friends he's known since childhood.

"New Britain never forgets its own," says coach Bill Huber, dropping by the table to shake hands with his old star. "I'm happy he's back. I'm happy this town has again reached out to him."

The Call

Nolan Ryan

Steve Dalkowski

Bob Feller

Walter Johnson

Sandy Koufax

Billy Wagner

Satchel Paige

Joel Zumaya

Amos Rusie

Goose Gossage

Bob Gibson

J. R. Richard

W̶e remain a land fascinated by speed. In large part, that's why baseball's top pitch, the fastball, has held the public's attention since the game's beginnings more than a century ago. Go to a ballpark today and it is still the fastball, now clocked by stadium radar and spelled out on the JumboTron scoreboard at the big-league locales that gets the crowd buzzing. Often in baseball lore, pitchers like Ryan and Feller, Johnson and Dalkowski, Tim Lincecum and David Price, are cast as loners, individual players forever set apart by their gift. But if we again gather them together in a lineup, and then take a step back to look at the group as a whole, we can see that the lives and career trajectories of these athletes are often intertwined. When it comes to the question of who is the fastest of the fast, finding an answer takes more than simply assessing them individually. It requires a larger perspective, a sense of what separates but also what binds these players together.

The names above form a top-12 list of the fastest pitchers of all time—a consensus of the experts I spoke to in writing *High Heat*. Now it also serves as the homestretch in a journey that took me from

Brooklyn to Cooperstown, Birmingham to Los Angeles, Durham to Dallas. Everywhere along the way, I asked for a rundown of the top fireballers ever. Some that I interviewed complained that it's next to impossible to compare pitchers from different eras and levels of competition. Others protested that there is no definitive way to measure a phenomenon that often borders upon the supernatural. These concerns are certainly valid.

"It's not an easy question to answer," says Phil Pote. Once again we're on the phone, talking baseball. "Folks probably hemmed and hawed about giving you answers."

"Some did."

"But in the end they still had an opinion, didn't they? It's always been that intriguing a proposition. The game's ultimate can of worms."

Indeed, almost everyone I spoke with, from historians like John Thorn to Hank Thomas, and former players like Jeff Torborg and Tommy John, came up with a list of the top fireballers ever. With that in mind, let's consider once again perhaps the most arbitrary and yet captivating of baseball questions: Who is the fastest of all time? To reach a conclusion we need to navigate a few more twists in the road, answer a few additional remaining questions.

First, would Walter Johnson be a star in today's game? For much of his career, the Big Train got big-league hitters out with nothing but a fastball. It can be argued that in baseball, unlike in other sports, one actually can compare stars from different eras. Until the steroids scandal made headlines, you could discuss Babe Ruth, Roger Maris, Mark McGwire, and Barry Bonds in a conversation about the best home-run hitters ever. Yet even before performance-enhancing drugs began to take over such conversations, some maintained that the stars of yesteryear don't measure up to superstars of the modern era. The old-timers weren't as big physically and they didn't benefit from today's modern training techniques.

"Outside of Rod Carew and Tony Oliva, I didn't have to worry about the kinds of hitters that you find throughout the game today," says Dick Bosman, who pitched at the major-league level and now coaches in the Tampa Bay Rays organization. "You're looking at the very best athletes who ever put on a uniform right now. The steroids issues aside, they're bigger, they're stronger, better nourished, and hopefully they're better informed and better coached."

Bosman adds, "The way they teach hitting is so different now, too. They teach them to wait on the ball, let it travel back into the strike zone more. An example is Derek Jeter's inside-out swing. It's damn hard to pitch to a guy like that. I had plenty of guys I pitched to— Harmon Killebrew, Bobby Allison—they were looking to do one thing and one thing only and that was to drive a ball out of the ballpark. You knew if you made your pitches low and away to those guys, you'd probably get them out."

While others agree that the approach at the plate has changed, with hitters usually more disciplined and much better prepared, they maintain Johnson would have been just as successful today as he was in the 1910s.

"He not only threw the ball hard, he won," says Washington Nationals broadcaster and historian Phil Wood. "To me, he's still the greatest pitcher who ever lived."

"Walter Johnson would have adapted to today's hitters," adds author Peter Golenbock. "He was an incredible fireballer. That talent translates down through the years."

If you agree with Wood, Golenbock, and those in that camp, you have your answer. There's no need to go any further. But if any sliver of doubt remains, let's move on to the next fork in the road.

Do we underestimate Bob Feller? At first, that question seems to border upon the ridiculous. After all, how can anyone underestimate a Hall of Famer who finished his career with a 266–162 record, leading the American League in strikeouts seven times?

Yet World War II cost "Rapid Robert" nearly four seasons in the majors. Unlike other ballplayers who kept playing until they were drafted, Feller enlisted in the U.S. Navy soon after Pearl Harbor. He had won a league-leading 25 games the season before and returned to strike out a league-leading 348 in 1946. Who knows what he could have accomplished without the time away from home? It's likely that he would have easily surpassed 300 career victories and perhaps even put up another no-hitter or two.

"Bob Feller threw as hard as anybody," Nolan Ryan says. "You cannot forget about him."

But for many, Feller was, perhaps inadvertently, knocked down a peg or two by Johnson. Soon after Feller came up with the Cleveland Indians, sportswriter Shirley Povich asked the Big Train to assess the new phenom. Was Feller as fast as him? Johnson studied Feller and finally replied, "No." No matter that Johnson also said, "That kid sure is fast." Povich, who often championed the Big Train's accomplishments, made sure the world knew of Johnson's verdict. If that statement rings true, then the case is closed. But again, if you're still uncertain, let's continue along to the next question.

If we don't give Feller enough credit, do we perhaps give Steve Dalkowski too much?

The bespectacled left-hander gained a mythic reputation for his exploits on and off the field in the Baltimore Orioles' farm system. By studying still photographs of Dalkowski (to date no footage has been found of the fireballer in action), John-William Greenbaum calculates that this phenom threw as hard as 105–109 miles per hour. Dalkowski's great promise and even his epic failures speak to something deep inside all of us. Dalko was the lovable loser so many of us can identify with.

"Based on the comments I've heard, based on the other contenders, those being Bob Feller, Herb Score, Sandy Koufax, Nolan Ryan, Bob Gibson, I would believe that Steve was the fastest ever, prior to his 1963 arm injury," Greenbaum says. "He's my choice."

But even those who were in Dalkowski's corner during his struggle to reach the major leagues wonder if he really belongs on the top rung.

"I believed in Steve Dalkowski as much as anybody," says longtime Baltimore Orioles manager Earl Weaver. "With some better luck, I'm certain he would have been remembered as one of the best, maybe even *the* best, hard-thrower in baseball history.

"It was like he never got comfortable with this remarkable gift that he had been given. He didn't give it a chance. He wasted it all. Because of that you can't say he was the fastest ever. He didn't reach the big leagues."

Pat Gillick, who was once Dalkowski's roommate and went on to be the general manager for the world champion Toronto Blue Jays and Philadelphia Phillies, agrees with his old manager. "Nobody wanted him to succeed more than the guys who played with him," Gillick says. "Even though I have no doubt that Steve Dalkowski was a hard thrower, he didn't quite make it."

Such comments prompt Greenbaum to reply, "OK, I can say he was the fastest professional pitcher. . . . Think a left-handed Joel Zumaya, only a bit faster."

Yet even Ron Shelton, who transformed the tall tales he heard while in the Baltimore Orioles' farm system into the movie *Bull Durham,* has second thoughts about rating Dalkowski as the top fire-baller ever. "That is what haunts us," he wrote in the *Los Angeles Times* in July 2009. "He had it all and didn't know it. That's why Steve Dalkowski stays in our minds. In his sport, he had the equivalent of Michelangelo's gift but could never finish the painting."

Perhaps, in a way, that's why all these fireballers enthrall us so. In this realm of the surreal, often the inexplicable, each struggled to find a way to make all the pieces fit, and none of them had a perfect path to the top. Satchel Paige spent his prime in the separate and unequal domain of the old Negro Leagues. Amos Rusie and Jim Creighton pitched more than a century ago, in a netherworld that's now difficult to comprehend. Sandy Koufax's dozen years in the major leagues were split almost evenly between pedestrian and then Hall of Fame numbers.

During the 2009 season, the year of my search, David Price reached the majors on Memorial Day, but even though the promising left-hander often pitched well, especially at home, Tampa Bay Rays manager Joe Maddon was still waiting for that "moment of epiphany." Meanwhile, the Detroit Tigers' Joel Zumaya was once again sidelined by injury, and Billy Wagner returned from Tommy John surgery only to find he would be joining the playoff hunt with the Boston Red Sox in the unaccustomed role of setup man. And yet elsewhere, newcomer Neftali Feliz of the Texas Rangers was clocked at 101 miles per hour in his major-league debut; teams were lining up to bid for the services of Cuban defector Aroldis Chapman,

whose fastball hit 102 miles per hour; and phenom Stephen Strasburg signed at the 11th hour with the Washington Nationals, finaliz-
ing a record-breaking deal that arguably placed the weight of the
franchise squarely on his shoulders. The allure of speed, however
fleeting or capricious, remained one of the game's constants. It was
still, as it had been for much of the game's history, very much the
coin of the realm.

Ironically, few of the pitchers featured in these pages asked for
the largesse of high heat. Due to the expectations and pressure of
possessing such rare talent, arguably more have suffered and even
failed than have succeeded. If what binds them all together is the gift
they've been provided with, then what truly separates them is the
ability to harness and to honor it. And so, after glancing down this
lineup of fireballers for the ages, adjusting our focus to get a sense of
the bigger picture, perhaps that is what our final question should be
about: gifts and blessings, curses and missed opportunities. Who per-
severed the most with what was bestowed upon them?

Years ago, before the Baltimore Orioles moved to Camden Yards,
I often drove up to old Memorial Stadium before the Sunday
home games. It was a good time to do interviews as the players had
time on their hands. During the 1992 season, the Texas Rangers
were in town, and after talking with several players in the visiting
clubhouse, I went up the tunnel to the dugout. A steady drizzle had
soaked the field and nobody was sure if the afternoon's game would
be played. A few of us sat there, watching the storm clouds roll in.

That's when I noticed two figures out in center field. They were
running, doing calisthenics, in the gray mist. Due to the elements
and distance, I couldn't make out who it was and finally asked one of
the players sitting nearby.

"It's Ryan," he replied. "He's out there with the trainer."

Even though Ryan had pitched and won the night before, he was
the only one making sure he got his workout on this gloomy morning. Perhaps that's why so many of today's young guns drop his name
when the talk turns to throwing hard, with purpose and intention.

Umpire Ron Luciano once said that Ryan's fastball left the pitcher's mound "as big as a golf ball." Yet by the time it reached home plate, the sheer velocity caused an optical illusion to take place. The ball seemed to explode "into a million blinding white specks," and after it smacked into the catcher's mitt the batters would look back at Luciano in disbelief.

"So Ryan's your guy?" Pote asks. "Your top choice? The fastest of all time?"

"Look at what he went through," I reply. "How close he came to quitting in those early years, how he made himself into a Hall of Fame pitcher. It was like he wasn't going to let this greatness he was given slip away. Now, I know you love Dalkowski and think the world of Paige and Feller. But I don't see how they're ahead of Ryan. Not when you consider what's been given and how that gift has been honored, so to speak."

There is a pause on the other end of the line.

"Sounds like you've done some serious thinking during your travels," Pote finally says.

"I guess I have."

"They say that's what traveling is good for, babe," Pote adds. "See some of the world, put your thoughts together. I like your criteria— the gift given and all. Nolan Ryan? You'll find no argument from me on this one, partner. Not with a guy who could throw with that kind of velocity."

Hanging up the phone, I know I'll soon be hearing from Phil Pote again. Our conversation about fireballers is far from over, and that's probably how it should be.

Still, I'm comfortable with my choice. When it comes to the gift of high heat, and what can truly be accomplished with such a boon seemingly handed down from above, none did better than "the Express."

The Top Twelve

NOLAN RYAN

- Nicknamed "The Express"

- Recorded seven no-hitters and 12 one-hitters

- Struck out a record 383 in 1973

- Hall of Fame: 1999

- President of Texas Rangers

Photo courtesy of the National Baseball Hall of Fame Library, Cooperstown, NY

Year	Team	W	L	ERA	SO	SV
1966	NY-N	0	1	15.00	6	0
1967	in minor leagues					
1968	NY-N	6	9	3.09	133	0
1969	NY-N	6	3	3.53	92	1
1970	NY-N	7	11	3.41	125	1
1971	NY-N	10	14	3.97	137	0
1972	CAL-A	19	16	2.28	329	0
1973	CAL-A	21	16	2.87	383	1
1974	CAL-A	22	16	2.89	367	0
1975	CAL-A	14	12	3.45	186	0
1976	CAL-A	17	18	3.36	327	0
1977	CAL-A	19	16	2.77	341	0
1978	CAL-A	10	13	3.72	260	0
1979	CAL-A	16	14	3.60	223	0
1980	HOU-N	11	10	3.35	200	0
1981	HOU-N	11	5	1.69	140	0
1982	HOU-N	16	12	3.16	245	0
1983	HOU-N	14	9	2.98	183	0
1984	HOU-N	12	11	3.04	197	0
1985	HOU-N	10	12	3.80	209	0
1986	HOU-N	12	8	3.34	194	0
1987	HOU-N	8	16	2.76	270	0
1988	HOU-N	12	11	3.52	228	0
1989	TEX-A	16	10	3.20	301	0
1990	TEX-A	13	9	3.44	232	0
1991	TEX-A	12	6	2.91	203	0
1992	TEX-A	5	9	3.72	157	0
1993	TEX-A	5	5	4.88	46	0
Totals		**324**	**292**	**3.19**	**5714**	**3**

STEVE DALKOWSKI

- ○ Nicknamed "White Lightning"
- ○ Never reached the major leagues
- ○ Was the basis for the character Nuke LaLoosh in the movie *Bull Durham*

Photo courtesy of the National Baseball Hall of Fame Library, Cooperstown, NY

Year	Team	Class	W	L	ERA	SO	BB
1957	Kingsport	D	1	8	8.13	121	129
1958	Knoxville	A	1	4	7.93	82	95
1958	Wilson	B	0	1	12.21	29	38
1958	Aberdeen	C	3	5	6.39	121	112
1959	Aberdeen	C	4	3	5.64	99	110
1959	Pensacola	D	0	4	12.96	43	80
1960	Stockton	C	7	15	5.14	262	262
1961	Kennewick	B	3	12	8.39	150	196
1962	Elmira	A	7	10	3.04	192	114
1963	Rochester	AAA	0	2	6.00	8	14
1963	Elmira	AA	2	2	2.79	28	26
1964	Elmira	AA	0	1	6.00	16	19
1964	Stockton	A	8	4	2.83	141	62
1964	Columbus	AAA	2	1	8.25	9	11
1965	Tri-Cities	A	6	5	5.14	62	52
1965	San Jose	A	2	3	4.74	33	34
Totals			**46**	**80**	**5.57**	**1396**	**1354**

BOB FELLER

- Nicknamed "Rapid Robert"
- Pitched three no-hitters and 12 one-hitters
- Led the American League in victories six times
- Hall of Fame: 1962

Photo courtesy of the National Baseball Hall of Fame Library, Cooperstown, NY

Year	Team	W	L	ERA	SO	SV
1936	CLE-A	5	3	3.34	76	1
1937	CLE-A	9	7	3.39	150	1
1938	CLE-A	17	11	4.08	240	1
1939	CLE-A	24	9	2.85	246	1
1940	CLE-A	27	11	2.61	261	4
1941	CLE-A	25	13	3.15	260	2
1942	Served in World War II					
1943	Served in World War II					
1944	Served in World War II					
1945	CLE-A	5	3	2.50	59	0
1946	CLE-A	26	15	2.18	348	4
1947	CLE-A	20	11	2.68	196	3
1948	CLE-A	19	15	3.56	164	3
1949	CLE-A	15	14	3.75	108	0
1950	CLE-A	16	11	3.43	119	0
1951	CLE-A	22	8	3.50	111	0
1952	CLE-A	9	13	4.74	81	0
1953	CLE-A	10	7	3.59	60	0
1954	CLE-A	13	3	3.09	59	0
1956	CLE-A	4	4	3.47	25	0
1956	CLE-A	0	4	4.97	18	1
Totals		**266**	**162**	**3.25**	**2581**	**21**

WALTER JOHNSON

- Nicknamed "Barney" and "The Big Train"
- Part of the original class in the Hall of Fame—1936
- Won 417 games, often with a losing team behind him

Photo courtesy of the National Baseball Hall of Fame Library, Cooperstown, NY

Year	Team	W	L	ERA	SO	SV
1907	WAS-A	5	9	1.87	71	0
1908	WAS-A	14	14	1.65	160	1
1909	WAS-A	13	25	2.22	164	1
1910	WAS-A	25	17	1.36	313	1
1911	WAS-A	25	13	1.89	207	1
1912	WAS-A	33	12	1.39	303	2
1913	WAS-A	36	7	1.14	243	2
1914	WAS-A	28	18	1.72	225	1
1915	WAS-A	27	13	1.55	203	4
1916	WAS-A	25	20	1.90	228	1
1917	WAS-A	23	16	1.90	188	3
1918	WAS-A	23	13	1.27	162	3
1919	WAS-A	20	14	1.49	147	2
1920	WAS-A	8	10	3.13	78	3
1921	WAS-A	17	14	3.51	143	1
1922	WAS-A	15	16	2.99	105	4
1923	WAS-A	17	12	3.38	130	4
1924	WAS-A	23	7	2.72	158	0
1925	WAS-A	20	7	3.07	108	0
1926	WAS-A	15	16	3.63	125	0
1927	WAS-A	5	6	5.10	48	0
Totals		**417**	**279**	**2.17**	**3509**	**34**

SANDY KOUFAX

- Had four no-hitters in four years, capped by a perfect game in 1965

- Fanned 18 in a game twice

- Hall of Fame: 1972

Photo courtesy of the National Baseball Hall of Fame Library, Cooperstown, NY

Year	Team	W	L	ERA	SO	SV
1955	BLN-N	2	2	3.02	30	0
1956	BLN-N	2	4	4.91	30	0
1957	BLN-N	5	4	3.88	122	0
1958	LA-N	11	11	4.48	131	1
1959	LA-N	8	6	4.05	173	2
1960	LA-N	8	13	3.91	197	1
1961	LA-N	18	13	3.52	269	1
1962	LA-N	14	7	2.54	216	1
1963	LA-N	25	5	1.88	306	0
1964	LA-N	19	5	1.74	223	1
1965	LA-N	26	8	2.04	382	2
1966	LA-N	27	9	1.73	317	0
Totals		**165**	**87**	**2.76**	**2396**	**9**

BILLY WAGNER

- Knicknamed "The Kid"

- Played at Ferrum College, where he averaged a record 19.1 strikeouts per 9 innings pitched

- Randy Johnson taught him how to throw a slider

Photo courtesy of the National Baseball Hall of Fame Library, Cooperstown, NY

Year	Team	W	L	ERA	SO	SV
1996	HOU-N	2	2	2.44	67	9
1997	HOU-N	7	8	2.85	106	23
1998	HOU-N	4	3	2.70	97	30
1999	HOU-N	4	1	1.57	124	39
2000	HOU-N	2	4	6.18	28	6
2001	HOU-N	2	5	2.73	79	39
2002	HOU-N	4	2	2.52	88	35
2003	HOU-N	1	4	1.78	105	44
2004	PHI-N	4	0	2.42	59	21
2005	PHI-N	4	3	1.51	87	38
2006	NYM-N	3	2	2.24	94	40
2007	NYM-N	2	2	2.63	80	34
2008	NYM-N	0	1	2.30	52	27
2009	NYM-N/BOS-A	1	1	1.72	26	0
Totals		**40**	**38**	**2.39**	**1092**	**385**

LEROY "SATCHEL" PAIGE

- Due to the color barrier, didn't reach the majors until the age of 42

- Helped pitch Cleveland to the 1948 pennant his rookie season

- Hall of Fame: 1971

Photo courtesy of the National Baseball Hall of Fame Library, Cooperstown, NY

Year	Team	W	L	ERA	SO	SV
1927	B Barons	8	3	unavailable	80	1
1928	B Barons	12	4	unavailable	112	0
1929	B Barons	11	11	unavailable	184	3
1930	Bar/Bsox	12	4	unavailable	95	1
1931	Cub/Craw	5	6	unavailable	24	0
1932	Crawfords	14	8	unavailable	109	2
1933	Crawfords	5	7	unavailable	57	0
1934	Crawfords	13	3	unavailable	97	0
1935	Monarchs	0	0	unavailable	10	0
1936	Crawfords	7	2	unavailable	59	0
1937	Stars	1	2	unavailable	11	0
1938	Mexico	unavailable				
1939	Monarchs B Team	no data				
1940	Monarchs	2	0	unavailable	18	0
1941	Monarchs	8	1	unavailable	61	0
1942	Monarchs	6	6	unavailable	42	0
1943	Monarchs	9	13	unavailable	72	1
1944	No data available					
1945	Monarchs	4	6	unavailable	30	0
1946	Monarchs	5	1	unavailable	23	0
1947	Monarchs	1	1	unavailable	no data	0
1948	CLE-A	6	1	2.48	45	1
1949	CLE-A	4	7	3.04	54	5
1950	Did not play at major-league level					
1951	STL-A	3	4	4.79	48	5
1952	STL-A	12	10	3.07	91	10
1953	STL-A	3	9	3.53	51	11
1965	KC-A	0	0	0.00	1	0
ML Totals		**28**	**31**	**3.29**	**290**	**32**

JOEL ZUMAYA

- Was clocked at 104.8 miles per hour in Oakland in 2006

- Has spent much of early career on the disabled list

Photo courtesy of Getty Images

Year	Team	W	L	ERA	SO	SV
2006	DET-A	6	3	1.94	97	1
2007	DET-A	2	3	4.28	27	1
2008	DET-A	0	2	3.47	22	1
2009	DET-A	3	3	4.94	30	1
Totals		11	11	3.15	176	4

AMOS RUSIE

○ Knicknamed "The Hoosier Thunderbolt"

○ Led National League in strikeouts five times and led or tied for most shutouts five times

○ The top fireballer of the 19th century

○ Won 20 or more games eight consecutive times

○ Hall of Fame: 1977

Photo courtesy of the National Baseball Hall of Fame Library, Cooperstown, NY

Year	Team	W	L	ERA	SO	SV
1889	IND-N	12	10	5.32	109	0
1890	NY-N	29	34	2.56	341	1
1891	NY-N	33	20	2.55	337	1
1892	NY-N	32	31	2.88	288	0
1893	NY-N	33	21	3.23	208	1
1894	NY-N	36	13	2.78	195	1
1895	NY-N	23	23	3.73	201	0
1896	out of baseball					
1897	NY-N	28	10	2.54	135	0
1898	NY-N	20	11	3.03	114	1
1899	out of baseball					
1900	out of baseball					
1901	CIN-N	0	1	8.59	6	0
Totals		**246**	**174**	**3.07**	**1934**	**5**

RICHARD "GOOSE" GOSSAGE

○ Rated the top fastball reliever of all time by Rob Neyer

○ Rated to have the second-best fastball for 1975–1984 (behind Nolan Ryan) by Bill James

Photo courtesy of the National Baseball Hall of Fame Library, Cooperstown, NY

Year	Team	W	L	ERA	SO	SV
1972	CHI-A	7	1	4.28	57	2
1973	CHI-A	0	4	7.43	33	0
1974	CHI-A	4	6	4.15	64	1
1975	CHI-A	9	8	1.84	130	26
1976	CHI-A	9	17	3.94	135	1
1977	PIT-N	11	9	1.62	151	26
1978	NY-A	10	11	2.01	122	27
1979	NY-A	5	3	2.64	41	18
1980	NY-A	6	2	2.27	103	33
1981	NY-A	3	2	0.77	48	20
1982	NY-A	4	5	2.23	102	30
1983	NY-A	13	5	2.27	90	22
1984	SD-N	10	6	2.90	84	25
1985	SD-N	5	3	1.82	52	26
1986	SD-N	5	7	4.45	63	21
1987	SD-N	5	4	3.12	44	11
1988	CHI-N	4	4	4.33	30	13
1989	SF-N/NY-A	3	1	2.95	30	5
1991	TEX-A	4	2	3.57	28	1
1992	OAK-A	0	2	2.84	26	0
1993	OAK-A	4	5	4.53	40	1
1994	SEA-A	3	0	4.18	29	1
Totals		124	107	3.01	1502	310

BOB GIBSON

- Had a basketball scholarship to Creighton University

- Played a season with the Harlem Globetrotters

- Recorded 13 shutouts during the 1968 season

- No-hit the Pittsburgh Pirates in 1971

- Won nine consecutive Gold Gloves (1965–1973)

- Hall of Fame: 1981

Photo courtesy of the National Baseball Hall of Fame Library, Cooperstown, NY

Year	Team	W	L	ERA	SO	SV
1959	STL-N	3	5	3.33	48	0
1960	STL-N	3	6	5.61	69	0
1961	STL-N	13	12	3.24	166	1
1962	STL-N	15	13	2.85	208	1
1963	STL-N	18	9	3.39	204	0
1964	STL-N	19	12	3.01	245	1
1965	STL-N	20	12	3.07	270	1
1966	STL-N	21	12	2.44	225	0
1967	STL-N	13	7	2.98	147	0
1968	STL-N	22	9	1.12	268	0
1969	STL-N	20	13	2.18	269	0
1970	STL-N	23	7	3.12	274	0
1971	STL-N	16	13	3.04	185	0
1972	STL-N	19	11	2.46	208	0
1973	STL-N	12	10	2.77	142	0
1974	STL-N	11	13	3.83	129	0
1975	STL-N	3	10	5.04	60	2
Totals		251	174	2.91	3117	6

J. R. RICHARD

- Passed on 200 basketball scholarships to sign with Houston
- Fanned 15 batters in his major league debut
- Led the National League in strikeouts in 1978 and 1979
- Suffered a stroke in 1980

Photo courtesy of the National Baseball Hall of Fame Library, Cooperstown, NY

Year	Team	W	L	ERA	SO	SV
1971	HOU-N	2	1	3.43	29	0
1972	HOU-N	1	0	13.50	8	0
1973	HOU-N	6	2	4.00	75	0
1974	HOU-N	2	3	4.15	42	0
1975	HOU-N	12	10	4.39	176	0
1976	HOU-N	20	15	2.75	214	0
1977	HOU-N	18	12	2.97	214	0
1978	HOU-N	18	11	3.11	303	0
1979	HOU-N	18	13	2.71	313	0
1980	HOU-N	10	4	1.89	119	0
Totals		107	71	3.15	1493	0

Afterword

Once in a blue moon, a debut actually turns out better than the hype. Such was the case when Stephen Strasburg, perhaps the most heralded pitching phenom in a generation, strode to the mound for the first time in Washington, D.C. In a performance for the ages, the right-hander electrified an overflow crowd in the nation's capital, striking out fourteen batters, one shy of the record for a major-league debut.

Overnight Strasburg had seemingly placed himself along such epic fireballers as Bob Feller, Sandy Koufax, and Nolan Ryan. The accolades—"14-K gold," "National Treasure," and "Merry Strasmas"—rained down from all corners. The game was instantly heralded as one of greatest moments in Washington sports history.

But before we knew it, the exhilarating ride was over—or at least seriously derailed. With five weeks left in his rookie season, Strasburg headed to the sidelines with a torn ulnar collateral ligament in his pitching elbow. Whether he would ultimately be recognized as an All-Star or just another enigma with unfulfilled potential remained an open question.

Too often we put such talent on a pedestal. It's certainly understandable. Nothing makes us sit up more in our seats than pure ability and untapped potential. But we need to remember that talent, no matter how breathtaking and seemingly invincible, often struggles to come into its own.

In writing *High Heat*, I was struck by how difficult things are in this line of work. Nobody has it easy. Steve Dalkowski, Jay Franklin,

David Clyde, Herb Score, and "Sudden" Sam McDowell are just a few of the pitchers who had plenty of potential but never reached baseball's Hall of Fame in Cooperstown, New York. For every Randy Johnson, every Goose Gossage, there are plenty of others who never made it, whose talent became an albatross—a gift that in the end they perhaps would have gladly given away, if they could.

At its core, baseball is a game of balls or strikes, safe or out. The lines are clearly delineated. Yet when it comes to the epic fire-ballers, the game is arguably played at another level. Here things are often measured in shades of gray rather than black and white, and success or failure can come down to something less tangible, spoken of in terms such as blessing or curse.

Strasburg certainly wasn't alone is his struggle to do right by his gift. More experienced pitchers struggled to master what had been bestowed. In San Francisco, two-time Cy Young winner Tim Lincecum lost velocity, perhaps even faith, in his fastball for a time. But he certainly roared back in postseason play. In Denver, Ubaldo Jimenez dispelled the belief that Coors Field was nothing more than a launching pad for mile-high home runs. He fired the first no-hitter in Colorado Rockies' history and for a time even stirred echoes of 1968—the Year of the Pitcher—and the prospect of the first thirty-win season in the majors since Detroit's Denny McLain. Yet coming down the stretch, Jimenez, like so many fireballers before and after him, strived simply for consistency.

In a showcase of power arms, Jimenez squared off against Tampa Bay's David Price in the 2010 All-Star Game. Every time I saw Price pitch during the 2010 season, I was tempted to say that I knew him back when.

In researching *High Heat*, Price was the latest phenom, a season or so ahead of Strasburg and the new crop. Still, at the time, he was very much on the outside looking in. When I first interviewed Price, he was at Triple-A Durham, wondering if a move to the bullpen would hasten his final call-up to the majors. In 2010, though, the left-hander came into his own, establishing a club record for victories and perhaps providing a sense of confidence and solace for the young guns following in his wake.

From the starting rotation to the bullpen, guys who can throw hard are now in abundance throughout baseball. "It's hard to find a guy throwing only 85–86 miles per hour in most rotations," says ESPN analyst Aaron Boone. "More starters throw hard and more relievers seem to be in the mid-90s or higher."

When the dust settled, five no-hitters had been recorded in the 2010 regular season. (The modern-day record of seven was set in 1990 and tied in 1991.) The Phillies' Roy Halladay, a hard thrower in his own right, pitched just the second no-hitter in the postseason and tied Johnny Vander Meer (1938), Allie Reynolds (1951), Virgil "Fire" Trucks (1952), and Nolan Ryan (1973) as the only ones to throw a pair of no-no's in the same season.

"It's the time of the pitcher right now," says New York Yankees manager Joe Girardi.

Still, when it comes to the fastest of the fast, one must always give a nod to the past. After *High Heat* came out, I returned to New Britain, Connecticut, the home of Steve Dalkowski, the subject of what is perhaps the ultimate tale of what could have been. The amphitheater room at Central Connecticut State University was filled with young faces much more familiar with today's stars. But shortly before I began, a half dozen older men filed in, taking seats in the front row. I recognized several as Dalkowski's boyhood friends.

In a nod to them, I talked at length about the left-hander nicknamed "White Lightning." While I suspect the students didn't know much about Dalkowski or Nuke LaLoosh, his cinematic alter ego from *Bull Durham*, talk of this select brotherhood resonated with all.

The morning after it became official—Stephen Strasburg would require a ligament replacement operation, a.k.a. Tommy John surgery—I received an intriguing e-mail from a baseball insider.

"Did you catch this?" he asked, alluding to the attached story about how Aroldis Chapman, the promising left-hander from Cuba, had been clocked at 105 miles per hour the night before in a Triple-A game.

A few nights later, when Chapman hit 104 in winning his first game at the major-league level, I was struck once again by the threads that run through and bind the game together and how in looking back at the history of baseball, one can simply follow the epic fireballers. How the era of Walter Johnson and Smoky Joe Wood rolls into Bob Feller's heyday. How Sandy Koufax steps away from the game just as a young Nolan Ryan strives to gain a place in it. How "The Express," along with such hard-throwing peers as J. R. Richard and Bob Gibson, became the standard for a new generation to emulate.

Blessing or curse? That's the question baseball's hard throwers, the fastest of the fast, will always struggle with. And therefore, in a sense, there's a story to be told with every fastball. Triumph and tragedy, epic moments and colossal failures, can be often encapsulated in a single pitch.

Of course, the rest of us are more fortunate. For it seems that just as one fireballer fades from view, another one steps up to take his place. Then once again we can gaze upon the pitching mound with anticipation and enjoy one of the greatest parts of the game.

Acknowledgments and Sources

In this hectic world, nothing is finer than to slow down and shoot the breeze with a guy who really knows his baseball. That's what I've been doing with Phil Pote, the self-proclaimed "Ancient Mariner," since my days at *Baseball Weekly*, and my work always has been the better for it.

Greg Downs, another good friend, accompanied me on one of the first road trips for this book, the visit on a winter's afternoon to Green-Wood Cemetery. He saved the day by finding the grave site of James Creighton, the original fireballer, and then was kind enough to read several sections of this book, too. Thanks, Greg.

Jonathan Crowe, my editor at Da Capo Press, not only did a great job of directing this project but he went out of his way to listen. The day after seeing David Price in Durham, North Carolina, I suggested we scrap the chapter outline and go with sections based on the phases of a pitching delivery instead. He agreed and made sure the new organization worked. Renee Caputo and Margaret Ritchie were there to help me bring it home.

Chris Park believed in this project when few did and improved upon it significantly with her insight and encouragement. Thanks to Peter McGuigan and the good folks at Foundry Media, and Gary Brozek for once again paving the way.

This book wouldn't have happened without the help of Bill Francis, a top-notch researcher at the National Baseball Hall of Fame in Cooperstown, New York. Also, thanks to other guiding lights on the banks of Lake Otsego—Jeff Idelson, Jim Gates, Tim Wiles, Ted Spencer, Erik Strohl, Mary Quinn, Tom Shieber, John Odell, and Pat Kelly. Closer to home, Thomas Mann and David Kelly were there for me at the Library of Congress in Washington.

Paul Dickson, Dave Raglin, Tom Stanton, Barbara Mantegani, Frank Ceresi, and David Whitford kept me on the straight and narrow, while Sam Moore made sure I got in touch with many of the people I needed to talk with. Anne-Marie McNally and Jose Luis Villegas unearthed key photographs of several classic fireballers at the eleventh hour.

I am grateful for interviews and conversations with Jim Abbott, Bruce Adams, Mike Andrews, Bud Anzalone, Ralph Avila, Budd Bailey, Dusty Baker, Mike Berger, Scott Boras, Dick Bosman, Larry Bowa, Jim Bowden, Nellie Briles, Mike Brito, Kevin Brown, Pat Cain, Orlando Cepeda, Tom Chiappetta, Roger Clemens, Jerry Coleman, Leonard Coleman, Chris Colston, Billy Conigliaro, Billy Coward, Steve Dalkowski, Bob DiBiasio, Rob Ducey, Dave Duncan, Andy Etchebarren, Bob Feller, Phil Garner, Tim Gay, Pat Gillick, Peter Golenbock, John-William Greenbaum, Jack Hamilton,

Roland Hemond, Derek Holland, John Holway, Tom House, Frank Howard, Bill Huber, Monte Irvin, Reggie Jackson, Tommy John, Dick Johnson, Bill Koenig, Tony La Russa, Jim Leyland, Tim Lincecum, Mike Maddux, Howard Mansfield, Juan Marichal, Rob Matwick, Buck Martinez, Tim McCarver, Tim McQuay, Kevin Millwood, Orestes Minoso, Robb Nen, Rob Neyer, Jim Palmer, Jonathan Papelbon, Len Pare, Tony Pena, Troy Percival, Johnny Pesky, Boog Powell, David Price, Debbie Price, Jimmie Reese, Bill Rigney, Billy Ripken, Mike Rizzo, Frank Robinson, Nolan Ryan, Mike Scioscia, Mike Sowell, Hank Thomas, John Thorn, Syd Thrift, Jeff Torborg, Joe Torre, James Vilade, Billy Wagner, Earl Weaver, Don Welke, John Wetteland, Paul White, Pete Williams, Lisa Winston, Rick Wolff, and John Young.

Every fireballer seemingly has his own advocate, often his own Boswell at the ready to chronicle and even champion his accomplishments on the mound.

Walter Johnson has several esteemed wordsmiths in his corner. Shirley Povich's profile of the Big Train in *Sport*, January 1950, has few equals. In 1914, Johnson told his life story to that point to Billy Evans, a former player, umpire, and newspaper columnist. That interview can be found in the October 1914 issue of *St. Nicholas Magazine*. But sometimes it's good to talk with somebody who's still alive. Nobody carries the torch for Johnson like Hank Thomas, who is also his grandson. In *Walter Johnson: Baseball's Big Train*, Thomas makes several key moments of the Hall of Famer's career, especially the 1924 World Series, come alive. When Thomas and I would meet, I'd pepper him with questions about his grandfather to the point where Thomas would say, "Check out the book. It's all in there." Indeed, when it comes to the Big Train, it usually is.

The thick files on Johnson and Leroy "Satchel" Paige were the first two that I requested upon my initial visit to the research library in Cooperstown. They just seemed like logical places to start, as I didn't know much about Amos Rusie, Pud Galvin, or Lefty Grove at that point. Soon I discovered that Paige has several storytellers in his corner, too. *Maybe I'll Pitch Forever,* as told to David Lipman, moves as quickly as Satch's old "bee" ball and also offers a better understanding of a pitcher who many believe should have been the first to break the color barrier.

As part of my travels, I was one of several hundred who helped Bob Feller celebrate his 90th birthday in Washington. All I can say is that I hope I'm still as enthusiastic about life at that age as "Rapid Robert" is. Not only did Feller show me the footage of his famous motorcycle test, but he also detailed other attempts to clock his fastball, as well as his days barnstorming with Paige. Feller has two entertaining books to his credit: *Now Pitching, Bob Feller,* which he coauthored with Bill Gilbert, and *Bob Feller's Little Black Book of Baseball Wisdom,* which he did with Burton Rocks.

When it comes to Sandy Koufax, there's no better place to start than Jane Leavy's *A Lefty's Legacy*. Interviews with Norm Sherry helped me understand how and when Koufax turned the corner from troubled prospect to Hall of Fame hurler. Conversations with Jeff Torborg, another top-notch catcher and student of the game, fleshed out the rest of Koufax's story and led to Nolan Ryan. After all, Torborg caught them both in their prime.

Most athletes' autobiographies aren't much to write home about. But I was struck by how candid *Throwing Heat*, Ryan's autobiography with Harvey Frommer, was. This is where I learned how close Ryan came to walking away from the game in his early years—all because he was so frustrated by his inability to do right by this gift of a great fastball. That became the starting point for an extended interview we had in Arlington, Texas. I thank "the Express" not only for his time but for his thoughtful answers. A special nod to Rob Matwick, Dale Petroskey, and John Blake for again getting me in the door. In Durham, North Carolina, Matt DeMargel made sure I caught up with the people I needed to see, especially David Price. Thanks to Dick Bosman, Milton Jamail, and Rick Vaughn with the Tampa Bay Rays. And, of course, when it came to one of baseball's newest pitching phenoms, nobody knows him like his mother, Debbie Price.

Perhaps it takes one star-crossed pitcher to understand another. I've followed Pat Jordan's writing for some time, starting with his memoir, *A False Spring*. Time and again, Jordan can be found writing about Steve Dalkowski. His profiles for *Sports Illustrated* (October 12, 1970) and *Inside Sports* (July 1982) remain classics.

No doubt that Dalkowski has proven that a person can go home again. In New Britain, Connecticut, he was reunited with his sister, Pat Cain, as well as his old coach, Bill Huber. Thanks to all of them for their time and a nod to Ken Lipshez at *The (New Britain) Herald* and Mat Olkin. It's always good to catch up with my friend Mary Collins in the Hartford area. Special thanks to John-William Greenbaum, the scholar of all things Dalkowksi.

There may be few experiences as humbling as throwing your best fastball for the folks at the American Sports Medicine Institute in Birmingham, Alabama. But if one really wants to understand the dynamics behind a well-thrown ball, the trip needs to be made. Thanks to Glenn Fleisig and his crack staff for being such great hosts.

And, finally, a thank-you to David Everett and my students in the Johns Hopkins University writing program.

Bibliography

Books

Collins, Mary. *American Idle: A Journey Through Our Sedentary Culture*. Capitol Books, 2009.

Conigliaro, Tony. *Seeing It Through*. Macmillan, 1970.

Deford, Frank. *The Old Ball Game: How John McGraw, Christy Mathewson, and the New York Giants Created Modern Baseball*. Atlantic Monthly Press, 2005.

Dickson, Paul. *The New Dickson Baseball Dictionary*, 3rd ed. W. W. Norton, 2009.

Dierker, Larry. *My Team: Choosing My Dream Team from My Forty Years in Baseball*. Simon & Schuster, 2007.

Einstein, Charles. *Fireside Book of Baseball*. Simon & Schuster, 1968.

Eisenberg, John. *From 33rd Street to Camden Yards: An Oral History of the Baltimore Orioles*. Contemporary Books, 2001.

Enders, Eric. *Baseball's Greatest Games*. Major League Baseball Insiders Club, 2008.

Engh, Fred. *Why Johnny Hates Sports*. Square One, 2002.

Felber, Bill. *The Book on the Book: A Landmark Inquiry into Which Strategies in the Modern Game Actually Work*. Thomas Dune Books, 2005.

Feller, Bob, with Bill Gilbert. *Now Pitching, Bob Feller*. Kensington, 1990.

Feller, Bob, with Burton Rocks. *Bob Feller's Little Black Book of Baseball Wisdom*. Contemporary Books, 2001.

Gleick, James. *Faster: The Acceleration of Just About Everything*. Vintage Books, 1999.

Groff, Lauren. *The Monsters of Templeton*. Hyperion, 2008.

Gutman, Dan. *Banana Bats and Ding-Dong Balls*. Macmillan, 1995.

Hogan, Lawrence D. *Shades of Glory: The Negro Leagues and the Story of African-American Baseball*. National Baseball Hall of Fame and Museum, 2006.

James, Bill. *The New Bill James Historical Baseball Abstract*. Free Press, 2001.

James, Bill, and Rob Neyer. *The Neyer/James Guide to Pitchers*. Fireside, 2004.

Johnson, Dick, and Glenn Stout. *Ted Williams: A Portrait in Words and Pictures*. Walker, 1991.

Jordan, Pat. *A False Spring*. Dodd Mead, 1975.

_____. *Sports Illustrated Pitching: The Key to Excellence*. Sports Illustrated, 1989.

_____. *The Suitors of Spring*. Warren Paperback Library, 1974.

Kinsella, W. P. *Shoeless Joe*. Ballantine Books, 1982.

Koufax, Sandy, and Ed Linn. *Koufax*. Viking, 1966.

Leavy, Jane. *Sandy Koufax: A Lefty's Legacy.* HarperCollins, 2002.

Light, Jonathan Fraser. *The Cultural Encyclopedia of Baseball.* McFarland, 2005.

MacCambridge, Michael. *The Franchise: A History of Sports Illustrated Magazine.* Hyperion, 1997.

Madden, Bill. *My 25 Years Covering Baseball's Heroes, Scoundrels, Triumphs and Tragedies.* Sports Publishing, 2004.

Mazzone, Leo. *Tales from the Mound.* Sports Publishing, 2006.

Nash, Peter. *Baseball Legends of Brooklyn's Green-Wood Cemetery.* Arcadia, 2003.

Newcombe, Jack. *The Fireballers: Baseball's Fastest Pitchers.* Putnam, 1964.

Paige, Leroy (Satchel), as told to David Lipman. *Maybe I'll Pitch Forever.* Bison Books, 1993.

Pearlman, Jeff. *The Rocket That Fell to Earth: Roger Clemens and the Rage for Baseball Immortality.* HarperCollins, 2009.

Price, S. L. *Heart of the Game: Life, Death, and Mercy in Minor League America.* HarperCollins, 2009.

Ritter, Lawrence S. *The Glory of Their Times: The Story of the Early Days of Baseball Told by the Men Who Played It.* Vintage Books, 1985.

Ryan, Nolan, and Harvey Frommer. *Throwing Heat: The Autobiography of Nolan Ryan.* Doubleday, 1988.

Scheinin, Richard. *Field of Screams: The Dark Underside of America's National Pastime.* W. W. Norton, 1994.

Shelton, Ron. *Bull Durham: The Script,* 1988.

Sowell, Mike. *The Pitch That Killed: Carl Mays, Ray Chapman and the Pennant Race of 1920.* Macmillan, 1989.

Stang, Mark, and Phil Wood. *Nationals on Parade: 70 Years of Washington Nationals Photos.* Orange Frazer Press, 2005.

Stout, Glenn, and Richard A. Johnson. *Red Sox Century: The Definitive History of Baseball's Most Storied Franchise.* Houghton Mifflin, 2004.

Thomas, Henry W. *Walter Johnson: Baseball's Big Train.* Bison Books, 1995.

Thorn, John, and John Holway. *The Pitcher: The Ultimate Compendium of Pitcher Lore, Featuring Flakes and Fruitcakes, Wildmen and Control Artists, Strategies, Deliveries, Statistics and More.* Prentice Hall Press, 1987.

Trucks, Virgil, as told to Ronnie Joyner and Bill Bozman. *Throwing Heat: The Life and Times of Virgil "Fire" Trucks.* Pepperpot, 2004.

Vowell, Sarah. *Assassination Vacation.* Simon & Schuster, 2005.

Ward, Geoffrey C., and Ken Burns. *Baseball: An Illustrated History.* Knopf, 1994.

Wolff, Rick. *The Baseball Encyclopedia.* Macmillan, 1993.

———. *Coaching Kids for Dummies.* For Dummies, 2000.

Newspapers/Magazines/Internet Reports

Ain, Morty. "(Durham Bulls) Promotions Director," *ESPN: The Magazine,* July 27, 2009.

Allen, Maury. "Lefty Grove at 70," *Boston Herald-American,* July 15, 1981.

Arangure, Jorge. "Anyone Need a Lefty Who Throws 100 MPH?" *ESPN: The Magazine,* August 24, 2009.

Aron, Jaime. "J. R. Richard Is Trying Not to Be Bitter," Associated Press, *Philadelphia Inquirer,* July 23, 1995.

Berler, Ron. "Arms-Control Breakdown," *New York Times Magazine,* August 9, 2009.

Boswell, Thomas. "Armed, but Dangerous," *Washington Post,* May 12, 2009.

———. "Strasburg Is the Pick, If the Price Is Right," *Washington Post,* June 9, 2009.

Bradlow, Eric, Shane Jensen, Justin Wolfers, and Adi Wyner. "Report Backing Clemens Chooses Its Facts Carefully," *New York Times*, February 10, 2008.

Broeg, Bob. "Grove's Badges: Hot Temper, Blazing Fast Ball," *Sporting News*, July 12, 1969.

_____. "Lefty Grove: Cantankerous Pitcher Star," *St. Louis Post-Dispatch*, May 25, 1975.

Brown, Frank. "Richard Suffered Stroke," *(New York) Daily News*, August 1, 1980.

Buys, Donna. "Baseball's Most Heroic Comeback," *Family Weekly*, February 26, 1978.

Carmichael, John. "Baseball Intent Tough Issue," *Baseball Digest*, August 1958.

Chass, Murray. "Wohlers Coming Back After a Disastrous Year," *New York Times*, March 9, 1999.

Chastain, Bill. "Price Optioned to Triple-A Durham," MLB.com, March 25, 2009.

_____. "Price Thrilled to Join Rays," MLB.com, September 13, 2008.

Condon, David. "Jim Galvin," *Chicago Tribune*, July 27, 1965.

Conlin, Bill. "Organizing a Revolt Against the Pitching Count," *Philadelphia Daily News*, May 29, 2009.

Crowe, Jerry. "Tommy John Gave His Name to Surgery That Saved His Game," *Los Angeles Times*, September 22, 2008.

Daley, Arthur. "Sports of the Times: Walter Johnson," *New York Times*, September 17, 1951.

"Dalkowski Again Hurls No-Hitter as New Britain Tops Southington," staff report, *New Britain Herald*, July 12, 1956.

"Dalkowski Allows One Hit," staff report, *New Britain Herald*, June 1, 1956.

"Dalkowski Allows One Hit but Loses Legion Game to Bristol," staff report, *New Britain Herald*, July 15, 1956.

"Dalkowski Allows One Hit, Walks 13," staff report, *New Britain Herald*, May 23, 1957.

"Dalkowski Barely Misses His Third No-Hit Game," staff report, *New Britain Herald*, May 17, 1957.

"Dalkowski Fans 20 and Walks 13," staff report, *New Britain Herald*, May 26, 1956.

"Dalkowski Hurls No-Hitter Again," staff report, *New Britain Herald*, April 19, 1957.

"Dalkowski Hurls No-Hitter as Legion Nine Defeats Bristol," staff report, *New Britain Herald*, July 2, 1956.

"Dalkowski Strikes Out 20 for Second Successive Time," staff report, *New Britain Herald*, May 16, 1956.

"Dalkowski Strikes Out 26 Batters as Legion Nine Beats Farmington," staff report, *New Britain Herald*, June 28, 1956.

Deford, Frank. "Rapid Robert Can Still Bring It," *Sports Illustrated*, August 8, 2005.

Deitsch, Richard. "Catching Up with . . . J. R. Richard," *Sports Illustrated*, March 23, 1998.

Dodd, Mike. "Overcoming Fear Usual Aftermath of Pitch to Head," *USA Today*, March 18, 1997.

Dodd, Mike, and Tim Wendel. "Prominent Beanings," *Sports Weekly*, August 13, 1997.

Donovan, Richard. "Satch Beards the House of David," *Collier's*, June 6, 1953.

Dozer, Richard. "Ryan Challenges Feller Speed Limit," *Chicago Tribune*, September 8, 1974.

Dufresne, Chris. "The Patients of Jobe," *Los Angeles Times*, August 24, 1998.

Durso, Joseph. "J. R. Richard," *New York Times*, August 3, 1980.

Edwards, Harry P. "Lefty Grove," press release, American League Service Bureau, December 30, 1928.

Eisenberg, John. "The Lost Phenom," *Baltimore Sun*, February 16, 2003.

Farhi, Paul. "The History of Chemistry in Baseball: Elixirs, Potions Came Long Before Steroids," *Washington Post,* May 25, 2009.

Farlekas, Chris. "Wood Recalls Glory Days with Bosox, Tribe," *(Middletown, N.Y.) Times-Herald,* September 6, 1967.

Fisher, Bart. "Dalkowski to Finally Throw a Pitch in Baltimore," *New Britain Herald,* August 11, 2003.

Fitzgerald, Ray. "Old Mose: He Had It," *Boston Sunday Globe,* May 25, 1975.

Gallo, Greg. "Flaky Fireballer Turned Hermit Ends His Silence," *National Star,* July 13, 1974.

Green, Paul. "Joe Wood," *Sports Collectors Digest,* August 30, 1985.

Gurnick, Ken. "Tommy John Loses Bid for the Hall," MLB.com, January 12, 2009.

Gustkey, Earl. "Baseball's Comet," *Los Angeles Times,* August 3, 1985.

Harlan, Chico. "New Ace May Be in Play for Nats," *Washington Post,* February 8, 2009.

_____. "With No-Hitter, Strasburg Tops Even Himself," *Washington Post,* May 10, 2009.

Herrick, Steve. "3 1/3 Innings in '09 Debut," MLB.com, May 26, 2009.

Herskowitz, Mickey. "Former Richard Still Charming Astros Fans," *Houston Chronicle,* July 10, 2004.

_____. "J.R. Still a Fan After Life Throws Him a Curve," *Houston Chronicle,* July 31, 2002.

Heyman, Jon. "Projected No. 1 Pick Strasburg's $50 Million Figure and Much More," SI.com, March 30, 2009.

Hyman, Mark. "Pitcher's Scare Leaves a Nagging Mark," *New York Times,* April 26, 2009.

Jacobson, Steve. "D-A-L-K-O-W-S-K-I," *(St. Louis) Globe-Democrat,* April 14–15, 1979.

Jenkins, Lee. "Stephen Strasburg Is Ready to Bring It," *Sports Illustrated,* March 30, 2009.

_____. "Young, Gifted and Black," *Sports Illustrated,* August 4, 2008.

John, Tommy. "Give Him 3 Fast Ones, Tommy," *Guideposts,* May 1979.

Johnson, Dan. "Bullet Joe: A Son's Memories," *Kansan,* November 11, 1999.

Johnson, Rick. "Amos Rusie: The World's Greatest Pitcher," *Indianapolis Star Magazine,* October 21, 1973.

Johnson, Walter. "The Meanest Thing in Baseball," *Baseball Magazine,* September 1918.

Johnston, Joey. "Wake-Up Call," *Tampa Tribune,* May 19, 2009.

Jones, Chris. "Jonathan Papelbon Grinds His Teeth," *Esquire,* April 2009.

Jordan, Pat. "The Wild and the Innocent," *Sporting News,* June 5, 1996.

Keown, Tim. "Just Go with It," *ESPN: The Magazine,* March 9, 2009.

Keri, Jonah. "Forty Years Later, Gibson's 1.12 ERA Remains Magic Number," ESPN.com, February 25, 2008.

_____. "Interview with Dr. Frank Jobe," ESPN.com, September 13, 2002.

Klapisch, Bob. "Giants' Lincecum Freak of Nature," *Bergen Record,* March 19, 2009.

Koppett, Leonard. "How About Triple Crown for Hurlers?" *Sporting News,* November 18, 1978.

_____. "Oriole, Dodger and Met Pitchers Under Gun," *New York Times,* June 22, 1975.

Kugel, Seth. "You Can Come and Go. They're Staying Awhile," *New York Times,* November 30, 2008.

Lane, F. C. "One Hundred and Twenty-two Feet a Second!" *Baseball Magazine,* December 1912.

"Lefty Grove Taught Himself How to Pitch," special dispatch, *Boston (Sunday) Globe,* October 19, 1924.

"Listen to the Silence of J.R.," staff report, Cox News Services, January 1980.

Longman, Jere. "Steroid-Assisted Fastballs? Pitchers Face New Spotlight," *New York Times,* May 18, 2005.

Lyon, Bill. "Tommy John Gives Thanks for the Bad Things," *Philadelphia Inquirer,* February 18, 1978.

Madden, Bill. "Safe at Home," *(New York) Daily News,* May 17, 1998.

McCreary, Joedy. "More Crash Davis Sequel Stuff to Inhale," Associated Press, *Los Angeles Daily News* blog, April 30, 2008.

McEntegart, Pete. "The Wild One," *Sports Illustrated,* June 30, 2003.

McGuire, John M. "Satchel Paige," *St. Louis Post-Dispatch,* February 15, 1981.

Merry, Don. "Baseball's Fastest Pitchers," *Street & Smith's Baseball,* 1975.

Miller, Dick. "Angels Turn Ryan Speed into MPH Contest," *Sporting News,* September 7, 1974.

"New Britain High Nine Winds Up Season by Beating Bulkeley 8–7," staff report, *New Britain Herald,* June 1, 1957.

"New Britain's Dalkowski Does It Again," staff report, *New Britain Herald,* April 25, 1957.

Nigro, Ken. "Steve Dalkowski: DTs Dead but Legend Lives," *Sporting News,* June 30, 1979.

Olney, Buster. "David Price," *ESPN: The Magazine,* March 27, 2009.

O'Neil, John "Buck." "Unforgettable Satchel Paige," *Reader's Digest,* April 1984.

Overfield, Joe. "'Gentle Jeems' Jim Galvin: Buffalo's First Superstar," *Bisongram,* February/March 1993.

Pepe, Phil. "Everybody Talked Satch but Jackie Was 1st," *(New York) Daily News,* February 12, 1971.

_____. "The Satchel Paige Legend," *(New York) Daily News,* February 11, 1971.

Plimpton, George. "The Curious Case of Sidd Finch," *Sports Illustrated,* April 1, 1985.

Posnanski, Joe. "The Best Pitcher in Baseball," *Sports Illustrated,* May 4, 2009.

_____. "Talkin' Pitch Counts and Nolan Ryan's Crusade, with Bill James," SI.com, June 15, 2009.

_____. "Talkin' Randy Johnson: 300 Wins and History, with Bill James," SI.com, May 20, 2009.

Povich, Shirley. "This Morning . . . Walter Johnson," *Washington Post,* May 6, 1936.

Price, S. L. "Hit in the Head," *Sports Illustrated,* April 20, 2009.

Rancel, Tommy. "David Price Pitches His Way Out of Rays' Rotation?" DRaysBay Web site, June 23, 2009.

Ripp, Bart. "Echoes of 'Thunderbolt,'" *(Tacoma) News Tribune,* October 15, 1990.

Roberts, Selena, and David Epstein. "Alex Rodriguez Tested Positive for Steroids in 2003," SI.com, February 7, 2009.

Rosenheck, Dan. "Backing Up an Agent's Pitch," *New York Times,* June 14, 2009.

Sakamoto, Bob. "Fate Threw These Two Pitchers a Curve," *Chicago Tribune,* April 9, 1989.

Saunders, Ken. "Speaking of Sports," *New Britain Herald,* June 6, 1957.

Schulz, John. "Recalling 'Lefty' Grove . . . No Better Left-hander," *Washington Star,* May 23, 1975.

Schwarz, Alan. "An Old Baseball April Fools' Hoax," *New York Times,* April 1, 2005.

_____. "Radar Love," *Baseball America,* November 25–December 8, 1996.

_____. "Sure Thing? No Such Thing for Pitching," *New York Times,* June 7, 2009.

Serna, Javier. "Bulls' Price Working on Consistency, Changeup," *(Raleigh) News Observer,* April 16, 2009.

Shelton, Ron. "Hard-Throwing Dalkowski Led to 'Bull Durham,'" *Los Angeles Times,* July 19, 2009.

Smith, Red. "The Terrible Tempered Mr. Grove," *New York Times*, May 26, 1975.

Socca, Tom. "The Yankees Make a Myth of Joba Chamberlain," *New York Observer*, May 5, 2008.

Stark, Jayson. "Tommy John Surgery: Cutting Edge to Commonplace," ESPN.com, August 13, 2003.

Steadman, John. "On Hilly Streets of Lonaconing, Native Son 'Lefty' Is Still a Giant," *Baltimore Sun*, September 22, 1996.

"Steve Dalkowski No-Hit Streak Ended," staff report, *New Britain Herald*, May 1, 1957.

Svrluga, Barry. "At Last, Bound for Glory," *Washington Post*, August 1, 2007.

Taaffe, William. "Gone . . . and Forgotten?" *Sports Illustrated*, October 26, 1987.

Telgemeier, Denis. "Lefty Grove: One of a Kind," *Oakland Athletics Official Magazine*, 1986.

Thompson, Teri, Nathaniel Vinton, Michael O'Keeffe, and Christian Red. "Fall from Grace," *Sports Illustrated*, April 27, 2009.

Tompkin, Marc. "Price in the Zone, Rays Out of Luck," *St. Petersburg Times*, June 17, 2009.

_____. "Price Makes a Leap," *St. Petersburg Times*, August 5, 2009.

Treder, Steve. "Delving Into the Dalkowski Depths," *Hardball Times*, May 29, 2007.

Tully, Mike. "Flame Throwers," *Play Ball!* Magazine, 1996.

Verducci, Tom. "The Freak," *Sports Illustrated*, July 7, 2008.

_____. "Randy Johnson Will Grind Your Bones to Make His Bread," *Sports Illustrated*, May 25, 2009.

_____. "What's Girardi to Do with A-Rod?" SI.com, June 19, 2009.

_____. "With Vastly Improved Defense and Pitching Depth, Rangers Are for Real," SI.com, May 20, 2009.

Weber, Bruce. "Wildly Out of Control: Is It Pitcher's Motion, or Emotion?" *New York Times*, August 23, 1998.

Wentworth, John. "Speaking of Sports," *New Britain Herald*, April 25, 1957.

"The Wildest Pitcher," staff report, *Time*, July 18, 1960.

Wilson, Bernie. "Stephen Strasburg," Associated Press, February 22, 2009.

Wulf, Steve. "They're Up in Arms over Beanballs," *Sports Illustrated*, July 14, 1980.

Index